D1446462

PROMISING

PROMISING

William Vitek

Temple University Press
PHILADELPHIA

Temple University Press, Philadelphia 19122
Copyright © 1993 by Temple University. All rights reserved
Published 1993
Printed in the United States of America

The paper used in this publication meets the minimum
requirements of American National Standard for Information
Sciences—Permanence of Paper for Printed Library Materials,
ANSI Z39.48-1984 ⊚

Library of Congress Cataloging-in-Publication Data
Vitek, William, 1957–
    Promising / William Vitek.
        p.   cm.
    Includes bibliographical references and index.
    ISBN 1-56639-052-4 (hard)
    1. Promises. I. Title.
BJ1500.P7V58   1993
170—dc20   92-29439

Excerpts from John Searle, *Speech Acts: An Essay in the Philosophy of Language* (Cambridge: Cambridge University Press, 1969), are used by permission of Cambridge University Press.

Excerpts from Julius Kovesi, *Moral Notions* (London: Routledge & Kegan Paul, 1967), are used by permission of International Thompson Organization, Inc.

Excerpts from George Eliot, *The Mill on the Floss*, ed. Gordon S. Haight (Oxford: Oxford University Press, 1986), are used by permission of Oxford University Press.

To my teachers, beginning with my parents.

Delightful task! to rear the tender thought,
To teach the young idea how to shoot.
JAMES THOMSON
"The Seasons: Spring"

Contents

CONTENTS

Acknowledgments

This project began long ago with a desire to break free and to give some sense to my prephilosophical views. I was raised in a home where wistful intentions were cast as promises and broken promises cast as lies. Years later I realized that my dad is, by disposition, a Kantian, whereas I am an Aristotelian. He sees moral rules as imperatives, and I see them as rules of thumb. He sees promises as closing doors to alternatives, and I see them as possible impediments to unseen but desirable futures. His life is ordered, mine complex (where "ordered" and "complex" function normatively). Where he assigns blame, I see tragedy. Both of us are on firm philosophical ground, though our ways of thinking could not be farther apart. I thank my father for his unintentional but primal push.

Special thanks go to Virginia Held, who first encouraged me to pursue this topic, and to Annette Baier and Doug Lackey for invaluable help along the way. I owe warm and heartfelt thanks to my friends and mentors David M. Rosenthal and Bernard (Stefan) Baumrin. Their influence on my teaching, research techniques, and ways of thinking has been inspirational and long-lasting.

My Clarkson University colleagues John Serio and Jan Wojcik supplied persistent encouragement. I thank them for their intentional push. Thanks also go to my dean, Owen Brady, for release time in which to revise the manuscript; to my editor Jane Cullen for expert advice; to an anonymous reviewer for insightful and helpful comments; to Joanna Mullins for her diligent copyediting; to Laura Pluta and Don Purcell for help

ACKNOWLEDGMENTS

with the page proofs; and to Joan Vidal for guidance during the production stage.

I thank Herb McArthur for our long and fruitful correspondence and for his helpful comments on earlier drafts.

My children, Andrew and Elizabeth, are the inspiration for many of the examples found in the book. I am grateful for their unsolicited love and enthusiasm.

And I am grateful to my wife, Maria, relentless editor and terrific mate, there at the beginning of this project on a beach in Westport, Connecticut, in 1982 with Mike DeCata and an old shoe, and here with me at its conclusion in Potsdam, New York, in 1993. Because of her, it has been a wholly delightful decade.

PROMISING

The Paradox of Promise: Some Introductory Remarks

To breed an animal *with the right to make promises*—is not this the paradoxical task that nature has set itself in the case of man? is it not the real problem regarding man?
FRIEDRICH NIETZSCHE, *On the Genealogy of Morals*

The Paradox

Friedrich Nietzsche's prose cuts clear to the center and identifies the fundamental paradox of promising: human beings can intend a future they see only vaguely. In promising, we engage our wills in the process of getting the future to turn out as we planned. But it is precisely our relative blindness about the future that requires us to predict it boldly and then to guide our lives' activities—and the lives of others—toward it. Hence, the promise demands assertiveness, commitment, and certainty at precisely the point where we are least able to give it. It is not surprising, then, that promises are attended with pomp and circumstance: the oath, the marriage ceremony, the signing of a contract.[1] Perhaps not fully trusting our abilities, we often require promises to be made in public or to God. Ceremonies and public expressions of intent serve to inspire, cajole, and threaten the promisor.

Despite such precautions, broken promises are found everywhere in history and literature. Indeed, who has not broken a promise, however mundane? Who has not felt the will weakened by unforeseen contingencies or has spoken words in politeness only to have them misinterpreted as a sincere expression of intention? The paradox is real and often felt. In an act of promising we seek to steady an otherwise uncertain future into which we blindly hurl ourselves. Can anything be at once more necessary and more foolish? There is hubris: in promising, I boldly assert that the future will turn out as I say. There is danger: a broken promise can lead to financial penalty or the loss of one's standing in the community. Why would anyone but the most desperate accept a promise or risk making one? Yet there are times when one cannot imagine not making a promise, despite its dangers.

Not long ago my friend Steve asked me for a philosophical perspective on a moral problem he was having.[2]

A year before, Steve had lost both his mother and sister to cancer within three months of each other. He had lost his father to cancer ten years earlier. His sister, Moya, had an eight-year-old son, Johnny, whom she raised by herself. Johnny's father disappeared long ago. On her deathbed Moya asked Steve if he would care for Johnny and take him into his family. Steve said yes, believing that he was the only living relative who was both willing and able to care for the boy. Two months after Moya's death, Steve's wife, Helen, gave birth to their own daughter, whom they named Moya. The next year proved difficult for everyone. They moved across country, where Steve had taken a new job. The stress of mourning took its toll on everyone, especially on Steve and Johnny. Helen was adjusting simultaneously to motherhood and stepmotherhood. Johnny was your average rambunctious eight-year-old boy, with the added rage brought on by the loss of his mother and grandmother, by displacement, and by being forced to live with relatives who, at their best, were no substitute for his mother. He was loud, wild, disobedient, and uncooperative. He would listen only to Steve. Helen, a petite Indonesian woman, was not accustomed to such behavior from a young boy and soon found daily life unbearable. After a year of patience and family therapy, Helen announced that either Johnny would have to leave or that she and the baby would return permanently to Indonesia. Steve assured me that her threat was no bluff.

We have here in a single moment a brother's promise to Moya; an uncle's commitment to Johnny; a husband's vow to Helen; and a father's love for baby Moya. Promising is a fundamental human experience. Our lives are filled with promises, not all of them consistent or easily discharged. Promising shows us at once our talents and our frailty. Our very existence as social, self-conscious, creative, and productive human beings depends, in large part, on the promise in all its myriad forms. David Hume said it best when he described humans as an "unnatural conjunction of infirmity and necessity." Our needs and wants greatly exceed our natural capacities, and so we must invent artifices to supplant our defects. One of these defects is our inability to conceive the future with any clarity or detail. The convention of promise seeks to remedy this problem by allowing otherwise disinterested parties to cooperate with one another in the future.

Promising is paradoxical in another way: it is simultaneously an inherently communal or social act and the single most forceful expression of the self. The promise is both symbol and structure of the symbiotic, interdependent relationship between the self and community. The promise both creates and is created by the self-in-community.[3]

The Literature

The importance that promise plays in our lives is reflected in its frequent use in literature and philosophy. Many of the great books have as their theme an oath, a marriage, a promise to marry, a covenant between a God and his people. The promise has long fascinated philosophers as well. It is found in the writings of, among others, Aristotle, Cicero, Thomas Aquinas, Hugo Grotius, Samuel Pufendorf, Benedict Spinoza, Thomas Hobbes, John Locke, David Hume, William Paley, Jeremy Bentham, Immanuel Kant, G.W.F. Hegel, and Friedrich Nietzsche. It serves as a social contract, the paradigm of obligation, a foundation to contract, a favorite moral example—who has not heard of the deathbed promise, the promise to a thief, and the promise for lunch interrupted by a stricken passerby—a linguistic act, and an intentional act of the mind. It is no coincidence that the majority of philosophical writings on promise occur in the modern period, beginning with Hobbes;[4] nor is it difficult to understand why promising is given so much attention in the modern philosophical tradition.[5] To the extent that moral philosophy since Hobbes has been concerned with constructing nontheistic foundations of ethics, it has often used the promise to derive and explain the original social contract or the contractual relations among members of civic communities. Contracts of any sort naturally lead one back to an initial promise.[6] Modern moral philosophy has also been more than a little interested in obligations and duties. Hume uses the promise to demonstrate his claim that obligations of justice are artificial, and Kant posits the obligation of a promise as a categorical duty. Promise is the paradigm of obligation, and it is the modern moral philosopher's stone. Contemporary philosophical theories as well focus largely on promissory obligation, and despite the range and depth of their work, contemporary theorists cut the paradox of promise down to a mere puzzle: namely, how do promises create obligations? This is an interesting and important puzzle, but we ought to expect more from a theory of promise than mere puzzle-mongering.

I identify five representative contemporary approaches to promise in terms of the single feature each employs to answer the central question about promissory obligation. I label these theories (1) institutional, (2) expectational, (3) evidentiary, (4) intuitionist, and (5) intentional. Institutional accounts are characterized primarily by their use of constitutive rules. Constitutive rules define how promises are made, how they create obligations, and, in some instances, how obligations are defeated. In essence, constitutive rules define the institution, game, or social contract of promise. The rule-governed approach is used by, among others, John Austin, H.L.A. Hart, John Searle, and John Rawls. I take the work of Searle and Rawls as representative of the institutional approach to promise.[7] The expectational approach explains promise in terms of creating and raising expectations and is represented in the work of Henry Sidgwick and Jan Narveson. The evidentiary approach sees promise in terms of the detrimental reliance it creates in the promisee. The writings of P. S. Atiyah are used to outline this position. The intuitionist approach explains promise in terms of its intuitive clarity and is used by H. A. Prichard and W. D. Ross. The intentional approach is employed by Michael Robins, and it explains promise in terms of the intention of the promiser.

Two points should be kept in mind. First, this is a representative sampling of the contemporary literature. Though the above taxonomy covers a wide range of literature, it should not be taken as complete or exhaustive. Second, in addition to what is said about promise, many of these accounts are embedded in larger theoretical projects. Though it is not always easy to isolate accounts of promise from their larger parent theories, I do not, for the most part, discuss theories of language, mind, ethics, or law. I do not believe that this excision methodology weakens the theories, or turns them into straw men. Because this study focuses on conceptual treatments of promise, it is important to focus on the contemporary accounts listed above as approaches to promise and not as theories of ethics, language, mind, or law. Even if none of these accounts is capable of functioning as a theory of promise, each is invaluable in its role as a source of data and a guidepost.

In the first half of this study, I argue that there are three fundamental problems with contemporary accounts of promise. First, surprisingly enough, none of them claims to be a theory of promise.[8] Despite the great deal of philosophical ink that has been spilled in attempting to fathom the mystery of promissory obligation—a mystery Hume facetiously compares to the Catholic mystery of transubstantiation—an examination of this literature reveals that accounts of promise are usually found within larger parent theories of language, ethics, law, or mind. John Austin and John Searle employ promise as the central case in their respective theories of language. W. D. Ross, H. A. Prichard, Henry Sidgwick, Jan Narveson, and John Rawls, among others, use promise as the central example in their moral treatises. H.L.A. Hart and P. S. Atiyah give promise a jurisprudential perspective, and Michael Robins makes use of promising to address issues in the philosophy of mind. Described one way, promise elucidates a theory of language or mind; described another, promise validates a moral theory. In short, there are theories of ethics, language, and mind but no theories of promise. It would be disingenuous, then, to criticize any of these approaches only in terms of incompleteness as an account of promise, since none of them makes this claim. These approaches, however, are open to other sorts of criticism. They suffer from a number of internal inconsistencies and fail to square their theoretical explanations adequately with the data of promise.

These problems lead to my second concern. In seeking to solve a puzzle rather than to describe and explain a paradoxical human activity, contemporary approaches have under-described promise. In reducing promise to a speech act or to the raising of expectations, contemporary approaches to promise squeeze a fundamental and complex human experience into theories that are already too tightly drawn. The result is to "lace up in formulas" a complex human practice.[9] In focusing entirely on the question of obligation, the practice of promise emerges as unproblematic and unfettered with life's surprises. Its complexities are labeled "extraneous conditions." The paradox is eliminated in favor of a clean and precise account of doing our duty—an account better suited for the pulpit than the academy.

All of the approaches evaluated in this study underdescribe promise in this way: the great puzzle to be solved about promise is how one's words or actions can create an obligation where none existed before. By focusing on this one problem, these accounts fail to consider or underemphasize other important features of promise. For example: How do promises cease to be obligatory? How are disagreements resolved concerning the contents and conditions of a promise, or concerning the validity of the conditions that will nullify a promise? How does one make a promise? How does one explain the variations that exist between cultures and generations regarding the practice of promise? What are the effects of the double-tensed—present and future—nature of promise? How does the relationship between promisor and promisee affect a promise? Why is promising such a seemingly important part of our lives? When these questions and questions like them are ignored or discussed cursorily, the resulting accounts of promise suffer from underdescription.

Underdescription likewise occurs when contemporary accounts cast promise in terms of a single identifying feature: for example, a performative speech act, raised expectations, intentions, or the creation of reliance. The most dramatic example of this underdescription occurs in the approach of H. A. Prichard and W. D. Ross. They believe that it is intuitively clear that a promise creates an obligation, and that all attempts at further explanation are unnecessary. But even if their view captures the intuitive clarity of promissory obligation, one can still inquire about additional aspects of the social practice of promise. All of the contemporary accounts of promise discussed below focus on solving the puzzle of how promises create obligations, and each of their answers focuses on a single aspect of promising.

Contemporary theories underdescribe promise in another way when they ignore the data of the social sciences, of history and literature, and of our personal experiences in favor of linguistic analysis and rational—as opposed to empirical—arguments. The analytic method, in my view, reflects more the influence of Immanuel Kant than of David Hume. Hume was a student of history and literature and he traveled frequently. He believed that the study of history and our own experiences help shape and inform our philosophical judgments. Kant, by contrast, had a large collection of travel atlases in his home, but he never left his native Konigsberg. Philosophically he was content to rely on the machinations of reason to do his theoretical work. After nearly a century of a kind of Kantian isolationism and recent charges of irrelevance, philosophers have begun to consult and incorporate the works of historians, literary theorists, social and natural scientists, and writers of fiction. This book is part of the ongoing renaissance of an applied philosophy wherein theory and practice converge.

Each of the contemporary accounts of promise discussed below ignores in various ways the data of promise. John Searle presents an idealized account of promise and argues away any discrepancies between his idealization and everyday conceptions by ignoring or refuting those conceptions. One would think that where there are discrepancies it should be the idealization that is changed or ignored, not the data from which the idealization supposedly originates. W. D. Ross claims that his intuitions about promise coincide with the "common person" of Great Britain, but this claim is made without having asked many people about their intuitions.[10] P. S. Atiyah argues that unilateral promises (promises not in fulfillment of a previous obligation, not given in return for any benefits, and not yet relied on in any way) produce little or no obligation for the promisor, and he cites legal cases as evidence of this view. But promises occur outside of the courtroom, and we need to take seriously what people outside the law believe about unilateral promises. There is a wide range of historical, sociological, anthropological, and psychological data that can be used in developing a theory of promise, and it is unclear how such a theory can be successful if it ignores these data or is unable to account for them.

A third problem with contemporary accounts of promise is that they are not always clear or coherent. John Searle, for example, claims that promising is a performative speech act that takes place within an institution wholly defined by constitutive rules. These rules create institutional facts, one of which is that when Smith utters the proposition "I, Smith, hereby promise to pay you, Jones, five dollars," Smith creates for himself an obligation to pay Jones five dollars. But it is less than clear how rules of any kind could create institutions *de novo* (for the first time). Constitutive rules may define the names of chess pieces and how they are moved, but such rules seem less able to define the cooperative and competitive spirit that goes into playing games such as chess. The same may be said of the institution of promising. The rules of promise that Searle lists seem to presuppose a great deal of human behavior

9

that makes promising possible, and it is not clear how constitutive rules alone would define or create this behavior. John Rawls holds a similar view about promising. He claims that the rules of promise are constitutive and public, but he admits that these rules are not codified and that they are learned within the context of one's moral training. But how can promising be an institution, the way baseball and chess are games, if its rules are not codified or learned in precisely the same way? What are the rules of promise that we all supposedly learn in precisely the same way? How would we explain the almost certain differences we would find if we were to generate and compare lists of rules drawn from a homogeneous community?

These are serious problems. It is not simply a matter of filling out one or another existing approach with empirical content or of making small changes. Contemporary accounts of promise *qua* accounts of promise are unsatisfactory in terms of providing a theory of promise. The fundamental goal of this study is to restore and accommodate, in theoretical terms, the paradoxical nature of promise, to see it not merely as a speech act or an expression of obligation—a mere puzzle—but as a fundamental human activity. Such a theory requires both a methodology that treats promise as the central phenomenon to be explained and a framework able to capture the richness and complexity of promise. I provide both below. I posit the outlines of a theory of social practice that is not itself part of a larger theoretical framework, and I demonstrate how a social practice account of promise succeeds where other approaches do not. The book, then, fails or succeeds on two fronts. It is possible to reject its specific account of promise as a social practice while otherwise accepting the underlying philosophical methodology used to delineate promising or any other complex human practice.

The Paradox of Promise

Questions of Method

It is not easy to make sense of the paradox of promise in theoretical terms, though it is important that we try. Even if philosophers have not always taken up this challenge, their over-
whelming interest in promise suggests that it is a fundamental
human activity, interesting in its own right and for what it
can tell us about other human practices. Despite my dissat-
isfaction with the methods of modern and contemporary
promise theorists, their numerous works suggest an interest
in promise that correlates with the importance of the subject
matter. Inquiry into its complexities are likely to reveal the
nature of the internal conditions that make promising possible: memory, a conception of the future, and language, for example. A theory of promise will be able to elucidate the many
uses to which promises are put: the everyday promises of
common life—contracts, vows, and informal promises ("meet
you at six")—as well as the promises that underlie communication, relationships, and human activity generally.

A theory of promise can also provide a look at the many
traditions of promise that exist in various times and places.
Nietzsche, for example, tells us that the soul of an Egyptian
debtor found no peace and that a Roman creditor could disfigure the debtor's body more or less as he deemed appropriate.
Hume suggests that the failure to keep a promise leads one to
never being trusted again. Even modern American bankruptcy
law is not that harsh; it attempts to give the creditor some
recourse to repayment while protecting the debtor from losing
everything. Since 1978, debtors in America have had the op-
tion of voluntarily filing for bankruptcy, thereby protecting
their assets from creditors. American culture with its high di-
vorce rates, governmental and industrial deception, and frequency of perjuries has, generally speaking, not taken an ex-

tremely stringent view regarding promise. There is value in understanding the history of promise, and even if it cannot fully explain these differences, a theory of promise may still be able to account for them.

A theory of promise is important also for what it can do for philosophical theory. The paradox of promise challenges philosophical theory to go beyond specialized analysis and to confront an important and complex social practice. Such theorizing must rely on alternative methods and hence must ask different questions and accept different answers. Application of such methods to a theory of promise, if successful, bodes well for similar philosophical theorizing about other human practices and may, once again, bring philosophy into the mainstream of intellectual life.[11]

Regarding a choice of method, I am interested in a theoretical account of promise and not in using promise as an example or test case for a theory of something else. A theory of promise should see promising as a widely divergent yet coherent and recognizable social practice, and not merely as a vehicle for creating obligations or for signaling intentions. A theory of promise will have a texture that is open to addressing numerous questions and that can accommodate a wide range of promise behaviors across time and place. At its best it will exhibit descriptive accuracy, explanatory power, and, perhaps, predictive power.

These goals are not unfamiliar to the social scientist, but they are likely to frighten analytical moral philosophers who—trained in the traditions of Plato, René Descartes, and Immanuel Kant—are not accustomed to dirtying themselves and their theoretical enterprise by working with data. But my philosophical roots go back to Aristotle and Hume, theorists who seek to describe and explain human practices and the role they play in facilitating human happiness.[12] Both philosophers construct theories of human action and motivation that are "only as precise as the subject matter allows" and that are informed by a "cautious observation of human life."[13] Both rely heavily on the data of history, literature, and their own observations of contemporary life. Their theories are firmly grounded in human experience, what Martha Nussbaum describes as the "priority of the particular."[14] Aristotle and Hume likewise make good use of rival accounts either in terms of their capacity to provide the data in need of explanation—Aristotle's reference to the rival accounts of what the good is—or as explanations of these data, which serve as insights to be incorporated or as mistakes to be avoided.

For both Aristotle and Hume, the data are primary and prior to the theory that accounts for them. Put another way, any theoretical account of human action should be sandwiched between experiences. A theory is generated to explain and describe an aspect of human experience and is further tested against this experience. To accomplish this requires that we do not strip away complexity to accommodate a theoretical structure, or delimit the data of promise so as to say something theoretically meaningful about it but end up with a theoretical account that ceases to describe the data. We ought to resist settling on a theory that is unable to do any work. In constructing a theory of promise along these lines, one wants least of all to follow Searle's lead in constructing *ceteris paribus* (other things being equal) conditions and then doing away with them when they threaten the logical clarity of our theory. What makes theories of human action so different from other sorts of theories is precisely the absence of conditions where "other things are equal." It is because other things are not equal that human action is filled with uncertainty, choice, tragedy, and complexity.

I make no apologies for engaging in some old-fashioned philosophy and using for data my own observations and experiences, as well as the observations and experiences found in history and literature. Although I occasionally make reference to the data of the social sciences, it is not, I believe, necessary to make reference only to these data. What is important is that a theory of promise be able to accommodate these data, whatever their source. Unfortunately, there is no one place one can go to gather these data. Though philosophers often discuss promising, they rarely appeal to its data; and though social scientists provide the data of practices and institutions, they rarely discuss promising. There do exist in the philosophical literature some references to the data of promise. These data are unambiguous in demonstrating that the practice of promise has undergone change and varies within homogeneous cultures. I have already made reference to Nietzsche's account of some of the more gruesome history of promise in its contractual guise.[15] Atiyah charts much of the change in the contractual aspects of promise in his book *The Rise and Fall of Freedom of Contract*.[16] And it is interesting to note that both Sidgwick[17] and Ross[18] appeal to the data of promise. The apparent differences in their data would indicate that the data are in fact different, and this is just what a social practice account of promise predicts. These differences crop up in the recent literature as well. Narveson[19] uses data that are different from data used by C. K. Grant.[20]

The data of promising are also revealed in the writings of philosophers who provide treatments of promise without necessarily referring to its data. We can note the differences between the treatments of promise provided by Cicero, Hobbes, Hume, and Kant. Though they all share certain views about promising, their individual treatments vary in detail. Cicero discusses promises that ought not to be kept;[21] Hobbes discusses forgiveness;[22] Hume claims that a man who breaks a promise will never be trusted again;[23] and Kant uses promising as an example of an absolute duty.[24] These differences, I assert, are indicative of the differences among their respective cultures and in the practice of promise as it existed in these cultures.

The consideration of excusing conditions and the use of practical reasoning in resolving conflicts of duty are also found in the works of Cicero, Aquinas, Hobbes, Adam Smith, and Sidgwick. The use of casuist methods for resolving conflicts and disagreements is occasionally found in the philosophical literature on promising and reflects the complexity of the practice of promise. An appreciation for this complexity is seen most vividly in works of fiction, however. In George Eliot's *The Mill on the Floss*, for example, Maggie struggles with a promise of fidelity she made in her youth to a bright but deformed young man. She instead elopes with another young man, only to return before they are married. Eliot captures the difficulties of a person caught in a community of practitioners whose interpretations of practice roles she cannot accept: Maggie's rebellion and violation of accepted interpretations cause her to be ostracized from the community. Eliot's criticism of the philosophy of her day is relevant to our discussion here. She says, "The great problem of the shifting relation between passion and duty is clear to no man who can apprehend it. . . . The casuists have become a byword of reproach; but their perverted spirit of minute discrimination has the shadow of truth to which eyes and hearts are too often fatally sealed—the truth, that moral judgments must remain false and hollow, unless they are checked and enlightened by a perpetual reference to the special circumstances that mark the individual lot."[25] Eliot's words serve as a reminder to all of us who theorize about social practices.

The importance of the social conditions of practices is appreciated by a number of authors whose work is relevant to this study. In his book *Whose Justice? Which Rationality?* Alasdair MacIntyre traces the practices of justice and practical rationality through four distinct social periods.[26] Pierre Bourdieu's *Outline of a Theory of Practice* makes a similar appeal to the social conditions of practices.[27] And the most thorough discussion of the practice of promise is found in Peter J. Wilson's *Man, The Promising Primate: The Conditions of Human Evolution.*

Good use likewise is made of the contemporary theories of promise presented and evaluated in Chapters Two and Three. These accounts serve a double duty: first, taken together, they highlight aspects of promise that are important to consider in constructing a theory; and second, in identifying their weaknesses we can seek to avoid them. Taken separately, none of these accounts functions as a theory of promise, but together they suggest a shape that a theory of promise must take.

There is, finally, the data gathered in one's own experience. I am confident that my experiences, as well as the various experiences of fellow promisors, constitute a rich data base from which to draw.

Wanted: A Theory of Promise

Having presented in outline form what sort of theory we are looking for and the type of data to be described and explained by it, I turn now to the details of a theory of promise. I have described promise as a paradox, a complex human practice that requires us to excel at what we are hardly able to do at all: namely, to will or conform a future state of affairs to an earlier communicative expression or intention of it. In many cases this requires only that we do what we promised we would do, but there are times when contingencies and surprises interfere with our ability to keep a promise or otherwise weaken our resolve. A theory of promise, then, ought to be able to capture this complexity.

At first glance, such a theory should address the following characteristics of promise. First, promise is a human activity with a history. This history suggests that the practice of promise originated at a specific period of time, either because of certain human needs or because humans developed the capacity to make promises. What is it about human beings that makes promising possible? How, why, and when did the activity begin; how is it maintained; and how does it undergo change? For any theoretical account of a human practice, these are important questions.

Second, and in conjunction with questions about origins, a theory of promise should address how individuals come to learn to promise. This pedagogical feature of practices is valuable not only because it can contribute to the task of educating our young but also because it serves as a critical test against which rival theoretical accounts can be judged. It is not unimportant, for example, that in stressing moral rules and rationality, modern moral theories often exclude any discussion of children, of how children come to be socialized, or of moral education generally. Contemporary accounts of promise fail to explain how children learn to make, keep, and break promises. Any parent knows that teaching children about promising does not begin with a rule book or lessons in how promises raise expectations or express intentions. Such lessons certainly do not begin with contracts. The success of any social practice depends upon its being transmitted from one generation to the next, and a theory of social practice ought to account for this feature.

Third, and along the same lines, a theory of promise should

be able to explain how practitioners interpret the practice of promise and how promisors make decisions in specific cases. It is hard to imagine Steve not agreeing to Moya's request, but it is another matter entirely to decide whether such a promise should be kept. Here is another example that impinges on a promisor's health and well-being:

Louise, who lives in New York City, has a younger brother, Russ, who lives in upstate New York and who has been wanting to visit her for a weekend in Manhattan for some time. In addition to his regular job, Russ works as a bartender on weekends, and it is very difficult for him to get time off. At last, he knows a month in advance that he has off the last weekend in January. He tells Louise that he is free then and would like to come for a visit. Louise knows that her brother is excited about coming and that this is the last weekend he will have off for a long time. She also knows that Russ does not know anyone else in Manhattan and would not visit if his sister were not living there. She tells him the weekend he has chosen is fine.

Meanwhile, Louise's law firm is passing around a weekend sign-up sheet for the Vermont country home it owns. At the beginning of the year a weekend sign-up sheet is passed around the office according to seniority. Because Louise is new there, the good winter weekends are usually all taken before she gets the list. This year, however, the last weekend in January is still open. Both Louise and her husband are very excited about getting out of the city, seeing some white snow for a change, and having an entire weekend to ski and hike. They also believe that a weekend in Vermont will help relieve some of the tension both of them have been feeling lately. Louise then remembers that this ski weekend is the same weekend that Russ planned to visit. While she would not mind seeing her brother, she would much prefer spending the weekend in Vermont, especially since the house is not available again until early April, Vermont's infamous "mud season." Louise has the sign-up sheet for the weekend and must decide quickly what to do.

How should Louise make her decision? What sorts of issues are relevant in making it? It would be naive to think that a promise closes off all decisions about future actions. After all, Russ might suddenly get a better offer for that weekend and cancel at the last minute. Such contingencies are possible any time we make promises. How are these hard cases resolved? It is rarely a matter of applying general rules to a specific case; it more often requires the use of practical reasoning: intuition, judgment, the weighing of one possible state of affairs against another, working through emotions, and, sometimes, making a choice that no one will like. The contemporary accounts evaluated in Chapters Two and Three have nowhere attempted to address the question of practical reasoning as it applies to promise:

The following example raises similar issues of how practitioners evaluate and make judgments about one another:

> A banker promises Clark, a financially strapped dairy farmer, that the paperwork for his refinancing will be completed by a certain date. Clark then promises his creditors payment by this date. The banker is then promoted and transferred before completing the work. The date passes, and the creditors inflict harsh financial penalties on Clark, even though they know the refinancing is pending.

Despite what Hume said, it is not always the case that a person who breaks a promise is never trusted again. The banker is now in another town; he did not sign a contract to the effect that the paperwork would be completed. He simply gave his word. How should we evaluate or judge this banker? Did Clark misinterpret comforting words for a promise? Should the creditors understand that the loan is forthcoming and extend the date? In any community of practitioners of promise, it is important to be able to distinguish between a promise that misfires and an intentionally false promise; between those members who are fully familiar with the community's practice of promise and those who are new to it. Such evaluation and judgment require on one occasion an understanding of a person's competence in the practice of promise and on another occasion the character of the promisor or promisee.

There are also more obvious aspects that a theory of promise should address. Hume is noted for having discovered that promising is a speech act that, as Annette Baier says, alters the moral situation. A number of contemporary approaches to promise have put a lot of weight on the linguistic characteristic of promise as an explanation of promissory obligation. But there are ways to make a promise other than uttering "I promise." It is easy to imagine promises being made that make use of informal language or a nod of the head, a wink of the eye, a handshake, or a warm embrace. Promises are made possible by acts of interpersonal communication, but such communication is widely and wonderfully varied. An open-textured theory of promise will not limit its discussion to only linguistic promises.

Promising is likewise a relational activity, insofar as it requires a promisor and promisee.[28] Promising would be made much easier if such acts of communication were clearly articulated and clearly understood, but the relational aspect of promise only complicates an already complicated practice. Promisors are often vague in stating their intentions; potential promisees mishear or misinterpret words and gestures; parties to a promise often take different attitudes toward it. For example, I loan you money on the condition that you promise to pay me back. I do not expect you to pay me back, but I do hope that by asking for an expressed promise I will make you more responsible. You take the promise seriously— even to the extreme—and engage in various kinds of activities, some criminal, in order to keep your promise.[29] One is reminded of Hyacinth Robinson in Henry James's *The Princess Casamassima*: unable to bring himself to kill a man and thus to keep his oath to the secret society to which he belongs, he kills himself even as members of the society are trying to reach him in order to relieve him of this task. Such misunderstandings are sometimes comic, sometimes tragic. But it is not possible to understand the practice of promise without seeing it as a relational activity.

Promising is also what Michael Robins calls a "double-tensed indexical." This is another way of saying that a promise is an expression of an intention in the present to be somewhere, to do something, or to be someone (a faithful spouse, for example) in the future. Even the etymology of "promise"—from the Latin *pro* (forth) and *mittere* (to send)—suggests a casting into the future. But most of us have experienced a promise wherein what we send forth does not arrive or is sent but not accepted because of a miscommunication, a change of heart, unforeseen events, or a loss of interest in the promise itself. A promise is thought to function as an impediment to breaking or otherwise altering one's commitment to the future; but because promising is double-tensed and we are relatively future-blind, there is always the possibility that a promise will misfire or altogether miss its target, especially when the duration is long or when events change suddenly or dramatically. The double-tensed indexical feature of promise causes no end of trouble for both promise theorists and practitioners.

There is, finally, the most frequently addressed issue of how promises create obligations. Whatever else a promise is or does, it changes the moral situation such that the promisor—and sometimes the promisee—feels committed to honor the promise. It is, perhaps, dangerous to refer to an obligation to keep a promise as a feeling, since it is not incorrect to say that if a person makes a promise, that person is obliged to keep it whether he or she feels obliged or not. I accept this danger because I believe that an account of promise must do more than analyze how certain words create obligations; it must be able to account for what it means to make a promise as well as to feel the obligation it creates. Neither mere words nor the analysis of mere words or concepts will fully explain this feature of promising. Promissory obligation is created and influenced not only by words but by how the parties to a promise understand these words, their interests in seeing the promise carried out, their abilities to discern conflicts, the tug between long-term and short-term interests, and, generally, the whole fabric of life in which the parties to a promise find themselves.

The philosophical literature takes a pretty hard line about promissory obligation. Most analyses begin by claiming that promises are obligatory and then go on to account for how promises manage to accomplish this feat. We have already seen what types of practices, inducements, and threats are used to impress upon people the seriousness of their promissory obligations. Hume suggests that a broken promise leads to the penalty of never being trusted again; and Kant's analysis suggests that any maxim used to justify a broken promise cannot be universalized, since to do so would make impossible not only all acts of promising but all cooperative acts, including communication itself. This view of promising brings to mind the image of a grappling hook. One end is attached to the promisor, the other end to the future action promised. The promisor then pulls himself—and is pulled by—this future action. Since the hook is well secured, one can only escape a promise by tearing oneself loose, a painful and, no doubt, messy affair. The image is a violent one, but it reflects a rather violent view of promise. It is a view, as Nietzsche suggests, that sees promising as a kind of dare: promise if you can or dare and prove yourself a person of your word; but if you fail, you shall fail miserably.

There is another, less stringent view of promise that I call promise as pathfinder. It recognizes that life is complex. Here a promise is seen as a strong intention, a best guess, an expression of sincere hope, a promising moment. This view sees a promise as a rough approximation of the future. It sketches out the promisor's best intentions and desires, though both the promisor and promisee recognize the future's contingencies and that intentions and desires change. Proponents of this view recognize that promising is an important practice but also that life sometimes intrudes, making a promise difficult or impossible to carry out.

These two positions reflect a deep division between dispositions. Promise as grappling hook sees promising as an act that freezes the future and that requires the promisor to insure a future. The promisor commits herself to a future and conforms the rest of her life to line up with the promise. Should events change, proponents of this view are likely to see the promise as nearly nonnegotiable: the promise is the one piece of the future that cannot or ought not to change. The promise stakes out the future, and we are then required to walk the line between our present selves and the future described by the promise. By contrast, promise as pathfinder is a casting into the future and a matter of uncertainty. It would be foolish and dangerous to close the future off to deliberation and choice. These two perspectives differ also in their philosophical styles: the grappling hook view sees experience as conforming to rules, while the pathfinder view sees rules as conforming to experience.

Both of these positions are reflected nicely in the characters of Tom and Maggie, brother and sister, in Eliot's *The Mill on the Floss*.[30] Tom "was a lad of honour" (p. 38) and had "more than the usual share of boy's justice in him—the justice that desires to hurt culprits as much as they deserve to be hurt, and is troubled with no doubts concerning the exact amount of their deserts" (p. 53). "'I'll do just the same again.' That was his usual mode of viewing his past actions; whereas Maggie was always wishing she had done something different" (p. 53). Tom said of her that she had "'no judgment and self-command. . . . At one time you take pleasure in a sort of perverse self-denial, and at another you have not resolution to resist a thing that you know to be wrong'" (pp. 392–93). Maggie was impulsive: she gave herself a haircut, pushed her cousin Lucy into the mud because Tom was showing her too much attention at Maggie's expense, and ran off with the gypsies. She was a free spirit and a bit of a rebel, but she was equally forgiving of the rebelliousness of others. Tom was restrained, judgmental, a man of his word. He neither forgot nor forgave. Maggie thought of Tom as "narrow and unjust, that he was below feeling those mental needs which were often the source of the wrong-doing or absurdity that made her life a planless riddle to him" (p. 393). "Maggie rushed to her deeds with passionate impulse, and then saw not only their consequences, but what would have happened if they had not been done, with all the detail and exaggerated circumstance of an active imagination" (p. 65). Tom "was much more willful and inflexible than Maggie. . . . But if Tom did make a mistake . . . he espoused it, and stood by it: he 'didn't mind.' If he broke a lash of his father's gig-whip by lashing the gate, he couldn't help it—the whip shouldn't have got caught in the gate. If Tom Tulliver whipped a gate, he was convinced, not that the whipping of gates by all boys was a justifiable act, but that he, Tom Tulliver, was justified in whipping that particular gate, and he wasn't going to be sorry" (p. 65). Tom was one whose mind was "strongly marked by the positive and negative qualities that create severity—strength of will, conscious rectitude of purpose, narrowness of imagination and intellect, great power of self-control, and a disposition to exert control over others—prejudices come as the natural food of tendencies which can get no sustenance out of that complex, fragmentary, doubt-provoking knowledge which we call truth" (p. 456).

There are four promises in *The Mill on the Floss* that I sketch briefly here and return to throughout the book:

The first occurs when Maggie is quite young. While visiting Tom at school, she puts her arms around the neck of Tom's schoolmate, the hunchbacked Philip Wakem, and kisses him. She says, " 'I shall always remember you, and kiss you when I see you again if it's ever so long' " (p. 184). When, years later, they met again, "she remembered to kiss him, but, as a young lady who had been at a boarding school, she knew now that such a greeting was out of the question, and Philip would not expect it. This promise was void, like so many other sweet, illusory promises of our childhood; void as promises made in Eden before the seasons were divided, and when the starry blossoms grew side by side with the ripening peach—impossible to be fulfilled when the golden gates had been passed" (p. 186).

The second is an oathlike promise that Tom makes to his father after Philip Wakem's father, a lawyer, causes Tom's father to lose his lawsuit with Pivart, the fellow upriver who is using river water for irrigation, thereby jeopardizing the operation of the Tulliver mill, which has been in operation—and in the Tulliver family—"a hundred year and better." In losing, Tulliver is forced into bankruptcy. At his father's request, Tom writes in the family Bible, " 'You'll remember what Wakem's done to your father and you'll make him and his feel it, if ever the day comes. And sign your name Thomas Tulliver.' 'Oh no, father, dear father!' said Maggie, almost choked with fear. 'You shouldn't make Tom write that.' 'Be quiet, Maggie!' said Tom. 'I *shall* write it' " (p. 267).

In the third instance of promising, many years later, Maggie meets Philip Wakem in the Reds Deep, a wooded area she frequents. Philip is very much in love with her and comes there hoping to see her. She reluctantly agrees to meet him there occasionally to discuss books and other intellectual topics. But this is no ordinary friendship, for Philip Wakem is the son of the enemy, and the implied victim of Tom's promise to his father. Soon after, Philip and Maggie speak directly of love, and Maggie says the following: "'I think I could hardly love anyone better: there is nothing but what I love you for. . . . I am telling you the truth. It is all new and strange to me; but I don't think I could love any one better than I love you. I should like always to live with you—to make you happy. . . . Yes, Philip: I should like never to part: I should like to make your life very happy'" (pp. 334–37). As we discover later, these words are taken by Maggie as a promise of engagement. Maggie kisses Philip twice during this scene, and after the second kiss Eliot observes: "She had a moment of real happiness then—a moment of belief that, if there were sacrifices in this love, it was all the richer and more satisfying" (p. 337).

The fourth instance of promising occurs when Tom finds out that Maggie is seeing Philip and that they professed their mutual love. Tom forces Maggie to make an agonizing choice: either to swear on the family Bible that she will never have another meeting or speak another word in private with Philip Wakem or to have Tom tell their father of Maggie's relationship with Wakem, causing "'him the blow of knowing that you are a disobedient, deceitful daughter, who throws away her own respectability by clandestine meetings with the son of a man that has helped to ruin her father. Choose!'" (p. 342). After some harsh words on both sides, Maggie promises only not to meet Philip or to write to him again without Tom's knowledge.

The stricter view of promise—what I call the grappling hook view, reflected in the types of promises made and kept by the likes of Tom Tulliver—suggests itself as coercive. To hold this view is to identify a promise with a threat. But if, as in most philosophical accounts, coercion is a morally suspect practice, then any social practice that relies on coercion is likely to be morally suspect as well. It is not surprising, then, that most contemporary accounts of promise see promising as a defeasible practice, that is, a practice that admits of exceptions that defeat an obligation before it comes due. Unfortunately, these discussions of defeasibility rarely go beyond the claim that promissory obligations are defeasible or that they can be defeated by exceptions of the right kind. W. D. Ross describes promissory obligation as a *prima facie* obligation: an obligation that at first glance is obligatory. Searle claims that an institution of promise will have a rule claiming that promissory obligations are defeasible, but he does not tell us what might count as an exception of the right kind. Searle suggests that promises are obligatory *ceteris paribus*, but eventually does away with these conditions, calling them extraneous and not relevant to his analysis. In most contemporary accounts of promise, the emphasis is put on how promises create obligations, but these accounts contain scant discussion of how such obligations are undone. It is a little like learning how to drive a car but not how to stop it, how to load a gun but not how to unload it. Ross is clearly aware that our duties conflict, and Searle must know that in common life all conditions are rarely equal. It is my view in this book that the notion of defeasibility is as important as the question of how promises create obligations. One can compare the making and breaking of promises to the relative ease of having sex and the often difficult times that follow when a resulting pregnancy is unwanted. One cannot unmake the pregnancy but must negate what one has made. It is this negation that attends a broken promise. Even if it cannot be fully explicit, a theoretical account of promise should be able to address the defeasible nature of promise and the methods of adjudication that are involved in resolving hard cases.

To review, a theory of promise should be interested in a large range of issues: how promises create obligations and how such obligations are defeated; the relational and double-tensed features of promise; how promises are made; questions of evaluation and judgment; the role of practical reasoning in making and keeping promises; how the practice is learned by new members of the community; the purpose of the practice; and how such a practice arises, is maintained, and undergoes changes in time. It is tempting to see this list as a set of necessary and sufficient conditions.[31] Such a temptation ought to be vigorously resisted. This book does not traffic in necessary and sufficient conditions. I make no pretense of viewing certain characteristics of a social practice generally, or of promising specifically, as necessary or sufficient conditions. Necessary and sufficient conditions are better used in the axiomatic systems of logic and mathematics than in theorizing about the practices of common life. Necessary and sufficient conditions are part and parcel of the modern style of philosophy: divide and conquer, reduce to clear and distinct words or concepts, circumscribe and subdue the subject matter. Such methods do not lend themselves to the description and understanding of human behavior. Human actions, and the social practices in which such actions are embodied are often variable and unpredictable. In suggesting the characteristics above, I am not defining what a promise is or is not but describing those aspects of promise that a theory of promise should be able to describe and explain. I am describing promise as I understand it and as I have been led to believe that others understand it. It is not impossible to imagine other aspects of promise not considered here or to generate cases where some of these characteristics do not hold. Nevertheless, what I have described above represents a healthy number of characteristics that a theory of promise ought to be able to address. The method employed here is Aristotelian in that we begin by identifying what characteristics the practice of promise is said or thought to have and then construct a theoretical picture of these characteristics.

Promise as Practice

It is obvious from what has already been said that I believe promising is best understood as a social practice. The theory that I propose as a candidate for understanding the phenomenon of promise is a theory of social practice. I argue that a practice is any human activity that is described and recognized as conventional behavior, and undertaken by two or more persons in a homogeneous community. Practices originate as a result of human action rather than human design; they are not conceived or designed in advance but originate spontaneously within forms of life. Practices are characterized by roles. These roles outline or circumscribe a practice; they give practices their shape. Practices are created, maintained, and undergo change by the actions of a community of practitioners acting within practice roles. The actual shape of any given practice must wait upon the actions of its practitioners. One learns these roles not by learning rules but through the imitation of role models and subconscious participation in the practice. Practice rules—or rulelike formulations—serve instead a descriptive or strategic function in a practice. They are used to talk about a practice or to give advice about how to succeed in a practice.

Subconscious learning and imitation of role models are the primary modes of practice-role acquisition. The transmission of practices depends upon the interrelationships between practitioners. Practices cannot be learned easily outside of their indigenous communities or on one's own within a community. Potential practitioners can interpret the practice roles each in his or her own way, though the range of interpretations is limited by tradition and the forms of life within which the practice functions. Taken collectively, these interpretations give a practice its particular shape. Practices have histories and local flavor. As interpretations of roles vary, so, too, do practices. They undergo change and revision, and they pass in and out of existence.

A theory of practice covers a wide range of human activities. Examples of practices include dating, telling jokes, making tea (for example, in Britain), booing at sporting events, walking on busy streets, standing in elevators, tipping in restaurants, standing in lines, and promising. One may be put off by seeing promising in a list with rather more mundane examples of conventional behavior, but I do not distinguish between moral and nonmoral practices. I take a wide view of the moral life. All human action is morally charged to the degree that it originates in free, responsible beings and takes place in a social or community setting.[32] This is not to say that every human action has moral content, only that it might and that we cannot always determine this content in advance. My predawn choice of clothing may be harmless until it triggers a tragic memory in a friend. The act of waste disposal, for so long an indifferent toss into the trash, now becomes a moral moment: Should I take the plastic window off the envelope, remove the label from the jar, or throw them both away wholesale, quickly, while my environmentally aware daughter is not looking? Many of the world's great tragedies—both literary and real—occur with sudden, violent, unexpected discharges of extreme moral force. The sheep-herder saves the boy Oedipus; an engineer OK's a space shut-tle launch in subfreezing temperatures; a school superinten-dent opts to keep the schools open and looses a busload of children to an icy road. In sports, the "wave" is relatively harmless, but the "chop" of the Atlanta Braves baseball team draws anger from Native Americans who are tired of being honored by cowboy shenanigans and racist nicknames. On the other hand, philosophers have accustomed us to thinking of promises only as serious, heavy moments, invested with solemnity and ritual.[33] But we are just as capable of playing with promise: using it to jest, with irony, or to make a point.[34] Not all promises weigh us down or drag us unwillingly to the future. Promising is a morally charged practice in the same way that other human activities described as practices are morally charged: practicing them well or badly will affect our well-being and the well-being of others.

It is my contention that a theory of practice can account for the various characteristics of promise cited above. It does not focus on one or two features of promise but instead describes promise in terms of its many features. It is, I believe, a rela-tively coherent approach. Unlike the institutional approach of Searle and Rawls, for example, it does not make presupposi-tions for which it cannot account. Furthermore, it is able to explain not only how promises produce obligations but how promises cease to be obligatory and why and, generally, how practitioners in this social practice interact and affect the practice as a whole. Because it is a comprehensive theory of promise, it does not underdescribe promise; nor does the the-ory ignore the data. Indeed, a theory of practice cannot suc-ceed without these data. A practice-theoretical account of promise has coherence, explanatory power, and empirical content. Chapters Four and Five take up the outlines of a theory of practice and demonstrate that promise is best described and explained as a social practice.

And now for the bad news. There are at least two ways that a social practice-theoretical account of promise will disappoint readers. The first is my doing; the second, a function of the theory itself. Both have to do with the open-textured features of a theory of practice. One is likely to say that what follows below is not a full-fledged theory—indeed, not a theory at all—but more like common sense or a common person's description. I do not claim that the theory is complete in every detail or capable of answering every question. It is an outline of a theory of promise. It is a promise of a theory, not yet fully formed or arrived at. As such, it makes a case for a philosophical methodology that Hume called a "science of human nature," consisting in a "cautious observation of human life"; and that Aristotle described as a practical science wherein the "degree of clarity fits the subject matter," and "questions about actions and expediency, like questions about health, have no fixed and invariable answers."[35] Though it does not fully assimilate all of the possible data from the social sciences and from common life, it is a theory that can accommodate these data. It is, as it were, a conceptual treatment waiting for verification. The book is my attempt to break free from contemporary accounts of promise and the philosophical methodology contained therein, and to offer an alternative, wide-angled look at promising.

The methodology itself, however, apart from my incomplete treatment of it, is likely to disappoint readers who were raised on a fare of analytic philosophy and who expect logically crisp conceptual analysis and maybe even a symbolic formulation or two. The history of twentieth-century analytic philosophy has yet to be fully accounted for, but when it is we shall see its strengths and benefits. Its account of moral philosophy, however, despite its clarity, will not be one of them. Moral philosophers are returning to actual moral problems—and not the problems of moral language—and finding the complexity of these problems right where they left them. Having been away from these problems for a while, we should not expect too much from our theoretical accounts of them. But we should expect that our moral theories, to the extent that they reflect, capture, and characterize moral life, will be no more precise or less complex than the data for which they account. That is, we ought to become accustomed to a different set of theoretical standards and appreciate again the complexity that is out there in our personal lives, homes, schools, and cities. Instead of the usual lists of necessary and sufficient conditions, we should welcome statements such as this:

> Some will be disappointed by the imprecise nature of the criteria provided. This would be unjustified. The criteria are not meant to provide operational legal definitions. . . . It is not really surprising that they are all matters of degree, admitting of many variants and many nuances. One is tempted to say "that's life." It does not come in neatly parceled parts. While striving to identify the features that matter, we have to recognize that they come in many shapes, in many shades, and in many degrees rife with impurities in their concrete mixing.[36]

Analytic moral philosophy is rightfully noted for its clarity, but the price for this clarity is high. Moral language—unlike its rambunctious, life-like counterparts—would at least sit still during the analysis. It could be handled and manipulated better than the vagaries of life. The price for the clarity is to ignore the complexity. In this book the complexity is back without, I hope, a complete loss of clarity or meaning. We want to avoid language and concepts that make our positions about common life unintelligible without losing the very complexity that moral philosophy addresses. Hence it is sometimes better to remain silent or to speak in a general way than to find ourselves trapped by a language of mere words, to try to say what can only be shown or experienced. I take the complexity as it comes and try to speak clearly about it, and when words do not work, I attempt merely to show the reader.

The methodology employed in this study is clearly unconventional. It is not limited by traditional distinctions, nor is it concerned with propounding or defending a theory of language or a moral theory. It extracts accounts of promise from wider theoretical pursuits, evaluates them, and then uses them constructively as data—along with examples from literature and common life—to offer an alternative account that is cast as nothing more or less than a theory of promise. Based on the less-than-satisfactory results of contemporary accounts of promise, I believe that such an alternative methodology is justified and will prove fruitful.

Approaches to Promise: The Contemporary Landscape

I am sitting with a philosopher in the garden; he says again and again,
'I know that that's a tree,' pointing to a tree that is near us.
Someone else arrives and hears this, and I tell him: 'This fellow
isn't insane. We are only doing philosophy.'
LUDWIG WITTGENSTEIN, *On Certainty*

I t is a perfectly good piece of common sense to believe that promises are obligatory and that after having made a promise one should, all things being equal, keep it. But as Ludwig Wittgenstein notes with frustration, philosophers cannot keep themselves from questioning the ordinary person's good sense and from seeking grounds to justify the ordinary person's claims. Wittgenstein would, no doubt, despair of the abundance of contemporary philosophical literature devoted to promise and to the problems of justification that arise when a philosopher asks, "Why should we keep our promises?" It would be a mistake, though, to reject this contemporary literature outright because it asks—and attempts to answer—questions that the everyday person does not think are important to ask, or because Wittgenstein believes that the questions themselves are not understandable, since to ask them undermines the very language game in which the questions are framed. I agree with Wittgenstein that we can go too far with our philosophical analysis and that sometimes our language runs up against its own limits. But I nevertheless believe that what Wittgenstein calls "forms of life" are capable of being described and talked about, though not with the kind of rigor and precision that most philosophers believe their theories can attain. An outline and evaluation of the contemporary literature on promise are important both in terms of what the literature says about promise and in providing evidence of where, from my perspective, this literature—and the approaches to which it is wedded—goes wrong. Even if we ultimately end up with a theory of promise very different from the accounts of promise discussed in this chapter, what we gain from these theoretical accounts is invaluable.

The literature is categorized in terms of the descriptive taxonomy provided in Chapter One: institutional, expectational, evidentiary, intuitionist, and intentional. I take each approach in turn and outline its basic features and main adherents. Where relevant, I appeal to the various examples from Chapter One, and I occasionally digress from an otherwise dispassionate review of the literature to set up the discussion and evaluation undertaken in Chapter Three. I devote the greatest space to the institutional approach, because it has received the most attention in the literature and because it most resembles the theory of practice I outline in later chapters.

Promise as Institution

The institutional approach describes promise as an institution that is defined and guided by constitutive rules. These rules give the various aspects of the institution their meaning. Every aspect of promise is defined by these rules. John Rawls expresses it this way: "That promising [is a practice] is beyond question. . . . This is shown by the fact that the form of words 'I promise' is a performative utterance which presupposes the stage-setting of the practice and the properties defined by it. Saying the words 'I promise' will only be promising given the existence of the practice. . . . Those engaged in a practice recognize the rules as defining it."[1] For John Searle, the normative claim against the promisor follows not from any "brute fact" but from the institutional fact that the promisor, Jones, has promised to pay Smith five dollars. This institutional fact exists as the result of the constitutive rule that states: "A person who utters the words 'I promise to pay you, Smith, five dollars' under the right conditions, has *in fact* an obligation to pay Smith five dollars and ought to do so."

Representatives of this approach include John Rawls, John Searle, H.L.A. Hart, and J. L. Austin.[2] I focus on the work of Rawls and Searle. Regarding terminology, I shall be faithful to Rawls's use of the terms "practice" and "institution." In "Two Concepts of Rules," he uses "practice" to identify his approach, whereas in *A Theory of Justice* he uses "institution" to identify a nearly identical approach. In both cases I take him to be presenting an institutional approach to promise.

Rawls

PARAMETERS OF A PRACTICE

In "Two Concepts of Rules," Rawls uses "practice" as "a sort of technical term meaning any form of activity specified by a system of rules which defines offices, roles, moves, penalties, defenses, and so on, and which gives the activity its structure. As examples, one may think of games and rituals, trials and parliaments."[3] A practice is any form of activity specified by constitutive rules. The establishment of a practice is the specification of a new form of activity in accordance with constitutive rules which are themselves logically prior to particular cases. Rawls gives examples from the game of baseball. One cannot strike out, steal a base, or balk unless there are rules that define these activities. Prior to the rules that define balking, it would be impossible to balk. "Unless there is the practice the terms referring to actions specified by it lack a sense."[4]

Constitutive rules cannot be tampered with, altered, or changed in any way by individual practitioners. A baseball player, for example, cannot say to the umpire that, judging by the present situation, it would be best on the whole were he allowed to have four strikes instead of the usual three. As Rawls explains, the strikeout rule is not a description of striking out or a summary of all past strikeouts that can be changed on special occasions. The strikeout rule defines striking out. To strike out is simply to have three strikes. Any exceptions to the strikeout rule must be carefully defined by the rule itself. "An exception is rather a qualification or a further specification of the rule."[5] A good example of this is the case when three strikes do not fully constitute an out: when a catcher drops a called third strike, the out is recorded only if the batter is thrown out at first base. This exception is clearly spelled out in the baseball rule book.[6] Rawls contrasts constitutive rules with what he calls summary rules. Summary rules are characterized as summaries of past decisions; they differ from practice rules in that they are not logically prior to cases. Summary rules function more as aids or guides, what Rawls calls maxims or "rules of thumb." Further, summary rules are generalizations from experience "and something to be laid aside in extraordinary circumstances where there is no assurance that the generalization will hold. . . . Thus there goes with this conception the notion of a particular exception which renders a rule suspect on a particular occasion."[7]

An important feature of institutional rules is that they be public.[8] It is assumed that a participating member of an institution knows the rules and what they demand of her and of other members of the institution. Likewise, other members of the institution know the rules, follow them, and expect her to follow them. When we know the rules, we also know what limitations on conduct are expected from us and what actions are permitted. Knowledge of the rules, in short, gives meaning to the actions of an institution's practitioners and provides them with a clear sense of what is expected of them.[9] Public rules place on members of an institution both the requirement of following the rules and the expectation that other members of the institution will follow the rules as well. Knowing the rules of an institution is crucial for meaningful participation in that institution.

Public rules also prevent unspecified or illegitimate moves within an institution. Unless the rules of the institution of punishment, for example, are made clear, an innocent person could be made a suspect and punished in an effort to stop a string of heinous crimes for which there are no suspects. To prevent this outcome, the rules must be made explicit; and if there are to be exceptions to this rule, they must be clearly stated in the rules of the institution. "It is utterly crucial to know who is to decide such matters, and by what authority, for all of this must be written into the rules of the institution. Until one knows these things one doesn't know what the institution is whose justification is being challenged."[10]

Rawls implies in a number of places that because constitutive rules are public and define meaningful behavior, institutions are capable of being designed and chosen by members of a community. He claims, for example, that in saying an institution is a public system of rules, he means "that everyone engaged in it knows what he would know if these rules and his participation in the activity they define were the result of an agreement."[11] This characterization would seem to follow necessarily from his conception of a constitutive rule, for if a constitutive rule creates an action and if the rule is logically prior to the action, then the rule must originate from a rule-maker(s). And if the rule is made by people in advance, then the rule must be made with a particular interest in mind.

This view of institutions as designed is expressed in Rawls's discussion of the institution of punishment. A particular institution of punishment is set up after legislators write laws and assign penalties for their violation.[12] In the essay "Justice as Fairness," Rawls makes the following claims: (1) rational persons can trace out the likely consequences of adopting one practice over another; (2) the restrictions that might arise in a practice can be thought of as those a person would consider if he were designing a practice in which his enemy were to assign him his place; (3) free persons are engaged in a joint activity whereby they settle or acknowledge the rules that define a practice; and (4) participants in a practice come to accept its rules as fair, choose one practice over another, and debate the form of their common practices.[13]

It is not necessary to imagine that such designs and choices are actually formalized. Rawls says that we should not imagine that persons actually come together for the first time to discuss how they will set up their institutions.[14] Although it is unlikely that some institutions were designed or set up for the first time using constitutive rules, it is still possible to imagine that once they were in place—however they came about—the rules that defined them could be discussed, modified, chosen, and reaffirmed by its practitioners. Even if no community, tribe, or nation has ever come together to discuss its institutions in this way, it is nevertheless a logical feature of institutions that such a meeting could take place. As for how institutions could arise without constitutive rules, Rawls suggests only that some of them may be set up *de novo* (for the first time).

A final feature of practices is how they are taught to new or visiting members of the community:

> It is the mark of a practice that being taught how to engage in it involves being instructed in the rules which define it, and that appeal is made to those rules to correct the behavior of those

engaged in it. Those engaged in the practice recognize the rules as defining it. The rules cannot be taken as simply describing how those engaged in the practice in fact behave: it is not simply that they act as if they were obeying the rules. Thus it is essential to the notion of a practice that the rules are publicly known and understood as definitive; and it is essential also that the rules of a practice can be taught and can be acted upon to yield a coherent practice.[15]

One learns, for example, how to be a judge or an umpire by learning the rules that define these offices and roles. To perform well in these roles is to follow the rules; to perform poorly is to fail to follow the rules. We engage in practice roles by learning the rules that define them.

It is obvious that the rules are an important feature of institutions. It is also clear how important it is that the practicing members of institutions be rule-followers. Indeed, it sometimes seems as if practitioners are defined entirely in terms of their ability to follow rules. Because institutions are defined by constitutive rules, members of the community necessarily become rule-makers, rule-followers, rule-changers, rule-interpreters, and rule-breakers. According to this account, we act spontaneously within institutions only when the rules allow us to or when there are no specific rules prohibiting spontaneous or creative actions, and we make exceptions only when the rules permit. Further, one learns institutional roles by learning the rules. In later chapters I question whether such a conception of rules and institutions captures the actions of human beings within their myriad roles and practices.

PROMISE AS PRACTICE

Rawls states emphatically in "Two Concepts of Rules" that promising is a rule-constituted practice:

> That . . . promising [is a] practice [is] beyond question. This is shown by the fact that the form of words "I promise" is a perfor-

mative utterance which presupposes the stage-setting of the practice and the properties defined by it. Saying the words "I promise" will only be promising given the existence of the practice. It would be absurd to interpret the rules about promising in accordance with the summary conception. It is absurd to say, for example, that the rule that promises should be kept could have arisen from its being found in past cases to be best on the whole to keep one's promise; for unless there were already the understanding that one keeps one's promises as part of the practice itself there couldn't have been any cases of promising.[16]

Promising is made possible because the actions that make up a promise are defined by a public set of constitutive conventions. According to Rawls, promising is primarily a linguistic convention. One promises by uttering certain words, specifically, "I promise," in the appropriate circumstances. This performative utterance and the circumstances in which it occurs are both defined by constitutive rules. Constitutive rules likewise define the exceptions that defeat a promise. To deliberate about whether one should keep his promise "is to deliberate whether the various excuses, exceptions, and defences, which are understood by, and which constitute an important part of, the practice, apply to one's own case."[17]

Rawls is quick to point out how the practice of promising is different from other practices. First, whereas most institutions and practices are defined by a system of rules, the practice of promising appears to be governed by a single rule, which, by itself, specifies the parameters of a promise. In *A Theory of Justice*, he says that the rule of promise specifies the appropriate circumstances and excusing conditions. The rule states that (1) the promisor is fully conscious and in a rational frame of mind, (2) he knows the meaning of the operative rules (here Rawls uses the plural), (3) the words are spoken freely or voluntarily, and (4) the speaker must not be asleep or suffering delusions. "In general, the circumstances giving rise to a promise and the excusing conditions must be defined."[18] Second, unlike rules in other institutions and practices, the single rule defining the practice of promise is not codified. Third, one's conception of the nature and extent of this rule depends on one's moral training, and hence there will occur considerable variations in how people understand the practice of promising.

There is some confusion in these passages as to whether promising is defined by a rule or by rules and to what extent promising is similar to other practices. Rawls does say that there are many complications here that cannot be considered, but his meaning is still unclear. He might mean either that there are more conditions to be described than the four mentioned above or that there remain unanswered questions regarding how one is to conceive the rule(s) of the practice of promising. Alternatively, he might be claiming that there are certain complications in understanding the practice of promising as a rule-constituted institution in the same way that games and legal practices are examples of rule-constituted institutions. Despite these complications, Rawls maintains his position that promising is a rule-constituted institution, insofar as the principles of justice apply to it in the same way that they apply to other institutions.[19]

Further evidence that Rawls is concerned about the closeness of fit between promising and other rule-bound institutions is found in two of his footnotes. In the final footnote to "Two Concepts of Rules," he says:

> As I have already stated, it is not always easy to say where the [practice] conception [of rules] is appropriate. Nor do I care to discuss at this point the general sorts of cases to which it does apply except to say that one should not take it for granted that it applies to many so-called 'moral rules.' It is my feeling that

relatively few actions of the moral life are defined by practices and that the practice conception is more relevant to understanding legal and legal-like arguments than it is to the more complex sort of moral arguments.[20]

This footnote seems to indicate one of two possibilities: either Rawls sees promising as an example of a legal practice, or he believes that promising—as an action of the moral life—is not captured by practice rules. Assuming he accepts the first possibility, promising falls under the practice conception of rules only if it is considered a legal practice. Unfortunately, Rawls does not address this issue further.

In a second footnote, Rawls distinguishes his view in "Two Concepts of Rules" from other positions with which it has been identified:

> What I did argue was that, in the *logically special* case of practices (although actually quite a common case) where the rules have special features and are not moral rules at all but legal rules or rules of games and the like (except, perhaps, in the case of promises), there is a peculiar force to the distinction between justifying particular actions and justifying the system of rules themselves.[21]

It appears here that he is claiming that the practice of promising is not like games or legal practices. But if the case of promising is an exception, what sort of exception is it, and what peculiar features make it an exception? Again, Rawls is silent.

There is no confusion, however, regarding Rawls's views about promissory obligation. The obligation of a promise originates not from the institution itself but from the principle of fairness agreed upon in the original position. In this way promising is different from other institutions and games. The obligation to leave the field after being called out at second base, whether or not it is a moral requirements, is an obligation one has within the game. It is an obligation that follows from the constitutive rule of being called out, specific to the game of baseball. The institution of promising apparently does not work this way. Its constitutive rule(s) does not produce its obligation-creating nature. The rule(s) of the institution creates a situation where one is obligated, but the obligation itself is derived from a moral principle. For Rawls, this is the principle of fairness, a principle agreed to in the original position. "All obligations arise from the principle of fairness: a person is under an obligation to do his part as specified by the rules of an institution whenever he has voluntarily accepted the benefits of the scheme or has taken advantage of the opportunities it offers to advance his interests."[22] This account of promissory obligation conceives the practice of promising as quite different from other social institutions and games. It appears that the constitutive rules of promising constitute only in a partial, nonmoral way.

Despite the apparent clarity provided by Rawls's account of constitutive rules in explaining how institutions are defined, a number of questions can be raised. First, how exactly are institutions designed and constructed out of constitutive rules? Do the leaders of a community get together to discuss problems and ways to solve them, using as one of their solutions rule-constituted institutions, which they design and then announce to the community? If so, how do they get everyone to play by the rules? More important, how—at the level of social institutions—are the rules communicated to the community unless the members of the community are already aware of the existence of the actions described by the rules? How, for example, do you introduce the institution of punishment into a community where there is no conception of punishment? In such a situation the rules would be absolutely unintelligible to the community. But when the members of the community are already aware of what punishment is, then the rules of the institution—or whatever rules the community leaders think they are promulgating—are not constitutive. And if the rules are not constitutive, then it is unclear how a community of rational persons could ever partake in the process of choosing its institutions. The same can be said about promising. Unless such concepts as *future*, *promise*, and *obligation* are grasped by members of a community, at least in a primitive way, there is little chance that rules defining these concepts can be understood by members of the community. But if such rules are understood, then the actions or concepts they purportedly define must exist prior to the rules. The result is that the success of the institutional approach depends on presupposing the concepts and actions that the rules purportedly define. As an explanatory device, then, constitutive rules succeed only if they make certain presuppositions that, in turn, make such rules redundant and unnecessary. These questions will be taken up in greater detail in the next chapter.

Second, there is an obvious tension between *de novo* institutions and institutions governed by constitutive rules. If we can imagine certain institutions arising on their own, without the need for preconceived rules, then why not assume that all practices and institutions arise in this way? Why not assume that all or most of our social institutions arise *de novo*, and then go on to describe the features of this conception of our social practices? Moreover, how do we distinguish institutions that were created out of preconceived constitutive rules from those that arose *de novo*, and how can we be certain where the institution of promising fits in? If there are *de novo* institutions, how do we evaluate, alter, and adopt them in terms of constitutive rules—as Rawls maintains we do—if they arose without such rules? Because Rawls admits the existence of *de novo* institutions, he must be able to differentiate them from institutions that arise through the development of constitutive rules and argue why promising is an example of the latter and not the former. If promising is an example of a *de novo* institution, then it is unlikely that its rules are constitutive for the simple reason that constitutive rules define actions, and *de novo* institutions precede any rules that might define actions taking place within them. It does not appear that Rawls can have it both ways. If the institutions that we evaluate and choose are *de novo* institutions, then their rules are not constitutive. But if the rules are constitutive, then the institutions must have been designed.

Third, in recognizing certain differences between promising and other institutions, Rawls seems to hedge in describing promise as an institution. Some of these differences include the singularity of the rule defining promising versus the plurality of the rules defining other institutions (admittedly, Rawls is unclear about this); the uncodified rule(s) of promising versus the codified rules of legal institutions and games; the noncodification of the exceptions to a promise versus the codification of the exceptions to legal laws and game rules; and the additional principle of fairness arrived at in the initial position. Such differences would appear to preclude promising from the framework of a legal institution and of games and institutions generally. If Rawls were to deny this, he would have to show how these disanalogies can be accommodated within the institutional framework.

Finally, Rawls maintains that promising is a performative speech act. According to this view, one can promise only by using the words "I promise" or certain other well-defined words or phrases. Since Rawls does not mention any other alternatives, we should take him to mean that the words "I promise" are the only ones available to promisors. This view denies the possibility of using informal language or no (linguistic) language at all to make promises. Steve's promise to his sister, Moya, could have been made with informal language or even the squeeze of a hand or a nod of the head. The same is true of the promises made between Louise and Russ or Clark and his banker, and of Maggie's understanding that she was engaged to Philip even though no words were spoken in this regard. Rawls's view appears to contradict the experience of everyday promisors, who do make and keep promises made in these informal ways. Using certain well-defined words does facilitate the making of promises; but if everyday experience is any indication, these words do not constitute a necessary condition for making promises, if indeed there are such conditions.

To review, a practice or institution for Rawls is characterized by constitutive rules that define any form of activity taking place within it. These rules must be part of a public system of rules. Practice rules can be created, debated, and revised by a community of rational persons engaged in choosing their social institutions. Though some practices arise *de novo*, it is a logical feature of a practice that a meeting in which its rules are chosen could take place. Finally, one becomes conversant with a practice by learning its constitutive rules. These rules tell us everything we need to know to engage in the practice. Rawls believes that promising is a clear example of a practice so conceived, though he admits to certain disanalogies. I have suggested that there are some problems facing Rawls's development of the institutional approach to promise. Searle's version of the institutional approach avoids some of these problems but raises new ones in the process.

Searle

PARAMETERS OF AN INSTITUTION

As in Rawls's approach, the most important feature of Searle's conception of an institution is that it is defined by constitutive rules. "The activity of chess is constituted by action in accordance with . . . rules. Chess has no existence apart from these rules. . . . Constitutive rules constitute (and also regulate) forms of activity whose existence is logically dependent on the rules."[23] Constitutive rules are thus almost tautological in nature. They provide us with such definitions as those of "checkmate" or "touchdown." An example of such a rule would be "A touchdown is scored when a player has possession of the ball in the opponents' end zone while play is in progress"; or, more generally, "X counts as Y" or "X counts as Y in context C." On Searle's account, examples of rule-defined institutions include baseball, football, chess, marriage, promising, and money. "The institutions of marriage, money, and promising are like the institutions of baseball or chess in that they are systems of such constitutive rules or conventions."[24]

Searle likewise claims that without constitutive rules there is no institution and one's actions lack a sense.[25] He is careful to include in his conception of a rule-defined institution more than the rules defining the moves in a game. "I intend to include the rules that make clear the 'aim of the game'. . . . For example I think it is a matter of rule of competitive games that each side is committed to trying to win."[26] Hence the rules not only give meaning to one's actions in a game or institution but also define the motivations one is assumed to bring to the game: the motivation of wanting to win and to play fairly, for example. Constitutive rules define a wide range of activities and behavioral dispositions.

Searle contrasts constitutive rules with what he calls regulative rules. The latter rules regulate antecedent forms of behavior. The rules of polite behavior regulate eating, for example, but eating exists independently of these rules. Examples of regulative rules include "When cutting food, hold the knife in the right hand"; "Officers must wear ties at dinner"; or, more generally, "Do X," or "If Y do X."[27] Regulative rules regulate one's behavior within a practice or a nonruled convention. The practice exists whether or not any regulative rules exist. "In general, social behavior could be given the same specifications even if there were no rules of etiquette. But constitutive rules, such as for games, provide the basis for specifications of behavior which could not be given in the absence of the rule."[28]

Constitutive rules create facts that do not otherwise exist. These facts Searle calls "institutional facts," contrasting them with "brute facts." Brute facts are expressed by statements such as "Jones is six feet tall" and "Smith has brown hair." Institutional facts are expressed by statements such as "Smith made a promise" or "Jones has five dollars" or "Mays hit a home run." In the institutional approach, commitment, responsibility, and obligation are institutional facts, which derive their meaning from constitutive rules. It is an institutional fact, for example, that promises create obligations; and institutional facts are defined by the constitutive rules of the institution.

Searle's conception of constitutive rules is similar to Rawls's conception and therefore suffers from similar problems. If rule-defined institutions are logically dependent on constitutive rules, then these institutions cannot exist prior to the design and instantiation of their constitutive rules. But how could such institutions arise, if their members did not already understand what the rules were defining? Furthermore, if institutions are governed by constitutive rules, then it would seem to follow that a person could not participate in an institution unless he or she knew the rules. How is it, then, that people are apparently able to participate in an institution without being aware of its rules?

Searle answers this question with an example from phonetics to show how it is possible to discover certain rules of phonetics even though we have followed them all along without being aware of their existence:

> In my dialect, "linger" does not rhyme with "singer", nor "anger" with "hanger", though from the spelling it looks as though these pairs ought to rhyme. . . . If you get a list of examples like this, you will see that there is a rule: Wherever the word is formed from the verb the /g/ phoneme does not occur; where it is not so formed the /g/ is separately pronounced. Thus "sing" : "singer"; "hang" : "hanger"; "bring" : "bringer"; but "linger", "anger", "finger", "longer" do not come from any verbs "ling", "ang", "fing", and "long". Furthermore, I want to claim that this is a rule and not just a regularity, as can be seen both from the fact that we recognize departures as 'mispronunciations' and from the fact that the rule covers new cases, from its projective character. . . . Not all English dialects have this rule, and I do not claim there are no exceptions—nonetheless, it is a good rule. It seems obvious to me that it is a rule, and that it is one which we follow without necessarily knowing (in the sense of being able to formulate) that we do.[29]

Hence to explain an action, we sometimes have to suppose that it was done in accordance with a rule, even though a person is unable to state the rule and may not be conscious of the fact that he is acting in accordance with the rule. This would explain how someone could act in accordance with the rules of promise without being aware of them.

Despite the explanatory power of Searle's phonemic rule, we should notice that the fact that such a phonemic rule can be formalized and shown to work with new cases is not in itself proof that this rule necessarily is constitutive of the institution of language. It could be a descriptive rule of how native speakers pronounce certain words of the language. If Searle wants to maintain that this rule is a discoverable, constitutive rule of language—as he claims to have discovered— then we can inquire into this rule's initial origin. If it is a constitutive rule rather than a rule created to describe or explain English pronunciation, then it must have come from somewhere; presumably it was designed by some initial speakers of the language. There must be some procedure to demonstrate that the rule Searle has generated corresponds to a particular constitutive rule of language. More argument is needed to show that a formalized phonemic rule is a constitutive rule and not a descriptive or regulatory rule. This criticism applies as well to the rules of promise he generates.

Searle ignores the questions surrounding an institution's origins, however, and instead focuses on how someone like himself could extract the set of rules defining an institution:

> If we get such a set of [necessary and sufficient] conditions [for the act of promising to have been successfully and nondefectively performed] we can extract from them a set of rules for the use of the illocutionary force indicating device. The method here is analogous to discovering the rules of chess by asking oneself what are the necessary and sufficient conditions under which one can be said to have correctly moved a knight or castled or checkmated a player, etc. We are in the position of someone who has learned to play chess without ever having the rules formulated and who wants such a formulation. We learned how to play the game of illocutionary acts, but in general it was done without an explicit formulation of the rules, and the first step in getting such a formulation is to set out the conditions for the performance of a particular illocutionary act.[30]

According to Searle, it simply is not necessary to know anything about the origins of such rules. Careful observation of what it is we do when we play chess or promise—the set of necessary and sufficient conditions—will allow us to extract the rules from the institution.

PROMISE AS INSTITUTION

Searle believes that promising is a clear example of a linguistic institution. He chooses promising because "as illocutionary acts go, it is fairly formal and well articulated; like a mountain terrain, it exhibits its geographical features starkly."[31] In promising one invokes the constitutive rules of the institution, whereby one commits oneself to a future act by using the speech act "I hereby promise" in the appropriate conditions. In the same way that the rules of chess create certain institutional facts about how to move the knight or how to checkmate, the rules of promise create the institutional fact of obligation. The definition of promising is a tautology, stating that promises produce obligations. This tautology generates an obligation only if certain institutional facts—which are defined by constitutive rules—hold. Asking how promises produce obligations is like asking how a touchdown creates six points: the only way to answer the latter question is to point to the rule that defines a touchdown as creating six points.

Searle also thinks that questions about the institution of promising ought to be kept separate from questions asked within the framework of the institution. He leaves the external question aside, choosing instead to answer the internal question of how individual promises obligate. He does this by referring to the rule-defined institution of promise. Searle states explicitly that his conception of promising is a simple and idealized case. He defends this method of constructing an idealized model by saying that it is analogous "to the sort of theory construction that goes on in most sciences, e.g., the construction of economic models, or accounts of the solar system which treat planets as points. Without abstraction and idealization there is no systematization."[32] He directs his analysis toward the concept of promising and suggests that even though counterexamples can be produced that do not fit the analysis, such examples do not refute the analysis but instead require an explanation of how and why they differ from the "paradigm" cases of making promises.[33] Searle limits his discussion to what he calls "full-blown categorical promises."

We now come to Searle's idealized conception of promising, as expressed in his list of the necessary and sufficient conditions of successful promising, and the constitutive rules he generates from these conditions. We are less interested in these conditions and rules *per se* than in how these rules and conditions reflect upon his conception of the institution of promising. In *Speech Acts*, Searle sets out the necessary and sufficient conditions in the following way:

> Given that a speaker S utters a sentence T in the presence of a hearer H, then, in the literal utterance of T, S sincerely and non-defectively promises that *p* to H if and only if the following conditions 1–9 obtain:
>
> 1. Normal input and output conditions obtain; e.g.,
>   a. speaker and hearer both know how to speak the language
>   b. both are conscious of what they are doing
>   c. they have no physical impediments to communication
>   d. they are not acting in a play or telling jokes
> 2. S expresses the proposition that *p* in the utterance of T.
> 3. In expressing that *p*, S predicates a future act A of S. (In a promise an act must be predicated of the speaker and it cannot be a past act.)
> 4. H would prefer S's doing A to his not doing A, and S believes H would prefer his doing A to his not doing A. (This distinguishes promises from threats, warnings, and invitations.)

5. It is not obvious to both S and H that S will do A in the normal course of events.
6. S intends to do A.
7. S intends that the utterance of T will place him under an obligation to do A.
8. S intends (i–I) to produce in H the knowledge (K) that the utterance of T is to count as placing S under an obligation to do A. S intends to produce K by means of the recognition of i–I, and he intends i–I to be recognized in virtue of (by means of) H's knowledge of the meaning of T.
9. The semantical rules of dialect spoken by S and H are such that T is correctly and sincerely uttered if and only if conditions 1–8 obtain.[34]

Searle claims that from an analysis of the necessary and sufficient conditions of the successful performance of a promise, one will be able to extract the underlying, constitutive rules of the institution. These rules are

1. *Pr* is to be uttered only in the context of a sentence (or larger stretch of discourse) T, the utterance of which predicates some future act A of the speaker S.
2. *Pr* is to be uttered only if the hearer H would prefer S's doing A to his not doing A, and S believes H would prefer S's doing A to his not doing A.
3. *Pr* is to be uttered only if it is not obvious to both S and H that S will do A in the normal course of events.
4. *Pr* is to be uttered only if S intends to do A.
5. The utterance of *Pr* counts as the undertaking of an obligation to do A.[35]

In "How to Derive 'Ought' from 'Is'" Searle injects a *ceteris paribus* rider covering situations that would release a promisor from an obligation, and cases where the obligation has been removed by the promisee or is overridden by a prior obligation. He admits that there is no established procedure for objectively deciding such cases in advance. In *Speech Acts*, however, he does away with the *ceteris paribus* rider altogether. He does this, he says, as a way to sidestep a large body of criticism that focused on the *ceteris paribus* clause. But he also believes that the exclusion of defeasibility conditions to promising in no way seriously affects the logical analysis of the institution of promising as an idealized case.

Regarding the list of necessary and sufficient conditions, Searle remarks that the list will no doubt be incomplete because the boundaries of the concept of promising are a bit loose. But despite this looseness and the difficulty involved in deciding hard cases, "one thing is clear . . . the conditions under which a man who utters 'I hereby promise' can correctly be said to have made a promise are straightforwardly empirical conditions."[36]

Searle believes that the analogy between the rules of promising and the rules of games holds up remarkably well: "If we ask ourselves under what conditions a player could be said to move a knight correctly, we would find preparatory conditions such as that it must be his turn to move, as well as the essential condition stating the actual positions the knight can move to. There are even sincerity conditions for competitive games, such as that one does not cheat or attempt to 'throw' the game."[37]

Despite Searle's optimism in this regard, there are some problems with the analogies between the institution of promise and the games of chess or baseball. First, he compares a person who extracts the rules of promising from a set of necessary and sufficient conditions to the person who has learned to play chess without ever having the rules formulated and who wants such a formulation. How does a person learn the game of chess without ever having formulated the rules? Such a person cannot play chess or even observe a game of chess with the intention of extracting some of its rules, unless she already knows—and can formulate—some of its rules: for example, the rule that chess is a competitive game. But if she already knows chess is a competitive game, then she already knows—and can formulate—one of the constitutive rules of chess. This implies that she cannot formulate game rules from her participation in or observation of a game of chess unless she knows beforehand some of the game's rules. Suppose further that the person who attempts to formulate her own rules comes up with rules somewhat different from the constitutive rules of chess. Is she still playing chess? It would seem that if the rules of chess are constitutive, then they define the game, and a person plays chess only when she plays by these rules and not some others, however close those others resemble the constitutive rules of chess. In this situation, any rules that one comes up with on one's own, even if they work reasonably well, are unlikely to be identical to the constitutive rules of chess. In comparing social institutions to games, Searle wants to have it both ways: he wants the rules of conventional behavior to define the behavior taking place within the convention, but he also wants conventional behavior to be able to occur without the practitioners knowing any explicit rules. It would seem either that one must know consciously the rules of an institution in order to participate in it or that one's participation in a social institution does not require the conscious or unconscious possession of any constitutive rules.

A second problem concerns the important differences between phonemic rules and the rules of the game of baseball, for example. You cannot play baseball without having at least a rudimentary understanding of the rules if, as in Rawls's and Searle's accounts, the rules define a version of the game; nor can you be said to be playing baseball if you somehow managed to internalize the rules but were unable to indicate—by formulating them—which rules you were following. But you can speak phonemically without knowing phonemic rules and without being able to formulate them. Further, as Searle admits, there are exceptions to phonemic rules. In a game such as baseball, frequently occurring exceptions are generally well defined by the rules. If Searle is right about the function of constitutive rules, actions that are not defined by rules lack a sense. Hence behavior described as an exception to the rules, unless it was itself defined by a rule, would be meaningless. But as I argue in Chapter Three, many aspects of grammar described as exceptions to phonemic rules are perfectly meaningful, even though no rules define these exceptions. Though referred to as exceptions, phonemic exceptions are not created or defined by constitutive rules. Searle would, no doubt, diminish these differences between institutions and games; but if more than a few nontrivial differences exist between the rules of institutions and game rules, then we are justified in calling into question the parallels between the institution of language or that of promising and the game of baseball or of chess.

Third, one can likewise question Searle's method of idealization. He compares his idealization of promising to the type of theory construction used in science and economics. But models in economics and science are abstracted from empirical data, and those who are involved in model construction are familiar with these data. Further, if these data change significantly, so will the model. What are the empirical data of promising, and is Searle familiar with them? Does he use these data to inform his idealized model of promising, or is his idealization of promising derived from an already abstract and idealized notion of promising? There appears to be a significant difference between what Searle claims to be doing and what other theoreticians are doing in other disciplines.

He seems to be doing just the opposite of what they do: he is using his idealization of promise as the standard against which the data of promise are to be evaluated, rather than using the data to judge the validity of the idealization. In Searle's analysis, it is not clear that any of the promises mentioned in Chapter One are "full-blown categorical promises." We should not fault him for failing to provide a theory of promise, since this is not his intention; but neither should we seek to mimic his idealization methodology when attempting to describe the practice of promise.

A fourth question arises regarding Searle's depiction of defeasibility conditions as "extraneous factors." Though defeasibility conditions have to do with conditions occurring outside a promise, they nonetheless appear to be an essential part of the concept of promise. Defeasibility conditions in many ways give the institution of promise its peculiar shape. They are part of what makes promising so interesting and so complex. If you exclude defeasibility conditions from a discussion of promise, then there is a sense in which you are no longer talking about promise. What makes Steve's promise to his sister so complex and morally difficult for him—and philosophically interesting to the philosopher—are precisely the types of conditions that would defeat his promise. It is irrelevant to Maggie that her engagement to Philip was made informally with the words "Yes, Philip: I should like never to part: I should like to make your life very happy." For Maggie, it is ludicrous to suggest that her commitment to Philip is defeated because of a linguistic loophole.

A fifth, similar problem arises with Searle's list of necessary and sufficient conditions constituting a successful promise. Searle admits that the concept of promising is a bit loose and that defeasibility conditions may undermine or cause additions to the list of conditions. If the boundaries of the concept of promising are loose, what are the parties to a particular promise to do if exceptions arise that are not covered by the rules? Both Searle and Rawls make explicit mention of the ruleless exceptions to promises, noting their impreciseness and their effects on the looseness of the institution of promising; but neither discusses why the exceptions are imprecise and not defined by rules nor expresses any concern that this inability to be precise about exceptions seriously undermines his respective position. If promising is an institution, then its various aspects must be defined sharply by rules. If the rules about exceptions are incomplete or imprecise, then these rules are not constitutive, and there is good reason to fault the institutional approach for this contradiction. Refusing to discuss *ceteris paribus* conditions altogether, as Searle does, avoids the appearance of contradiction, but it does so at the cost of failing to talk about promise altogether.

To review, Searle believes that promising is characterized as a performative speech act, governed by constitutive rules. The rules define institutional facts, one of which is that a person who makes a promise under the right conditions creates an institutional obligation for himself. Unlike Rawls, Searle ignores questions about origins and about external questions generally. But he does provide an explanation of how language and promising could be rule-governed institutions without members of these institutions being consciously aware of the constitutive rules that govern them. In addition, Searle generates a list of necessary and sufficient conditions from which he abstracts the rules of promising. He actually gives us a list of rules that, he believes, govern the institution of promising. Finally, he admits that his conception of promising is an idealized one.

Rawls and Searle provide similar accounts of an institution, and both claim that promising is an example of an institution.

The institutional approach is a powerful and elegant tool in explaining how certain types of language function and in describing rule-governed institutions. But whatever the virtues of the institutional approach as it applies to various topics in theories of language or ethics, I have sketched a number of arguments that question the validity of using this approach in providing a theory of promise. In Chapter Three I develop these arguments in greater detail.

We turn now to four alternative approaches to promise. The expectational approach concentrates on how promises create and raise expectations in the promisee; the evidentiary approach, on how a promise gives evidence to a preexisting obligation, which arises only when the promisor benefits from his obligation or the promisee relies on the obligation to his detriment; the intuitional approach, on the intuitive clarity of promissory obligation; and the intentional approach, on the promisor's willing of an obligation. These approaches are mostly unconcerned about how the practice of promise arises or how it is taught to new members of the community. In this respect, then, they are full-blown alternatives neither to the institutional approach nor to the theory of practice to be outlined in later chapters. They are, nevertheless, indicative of contemporary approaches to promise and valuable as sources of insight and data, even if they ultimately fail as theories of promise.

Promise as Raised Expectations

The view that promising derives its obligatory force from the expectations that a promise raises in the promisee has a long history.[38] At least part of what Louise feels in the example in Chapter One is that her brother, Russ, is excited about visiting her and that to break her promise is to dash her brother's expectations and hence to cause him harm. When Maggie is strongly tempted by her love for Stephen, she cannot forget, even for an instant, the pain she will cause Philip. When Stephen tells Maggie that she is not absolutely pledged to Philip, she exclaims, " 'You don't believe that—it is not your real feeling. . . . You feel as I do, that the real tie lies in the feelings and expectations we have raised in other minds. Else all pledges might be broken, when there was no outward penalty. There would be no such thing as faithfulness.' "[39] Whatever else we do when we break a promise, it is apparent that we often do harm to the promisee when her expectations are not met. Henry Sidgwick and Jan Narveson are two contemporary proponents of this view of promise.[40]

Henry Sidgwick's discussion of promise is in book 3 of his *Methods of Ethics*.[41] The essential feature of promising (what Sidgwick calls the "Duty of Good Faith") is the conformity not to what we say but to the expectations we have intentionally raised in others. Sidgwick recognizes the difficulty of differentiating between promises and other sorts of situations where we raise another's expectations but are not thereby obligated. He says that *common sense* tells us that we are responsible for the expectation we have raised, if the expectation was natural and one that most people would form under the circumstances. The obligation of a promise is "perfectly constituted when it is understood by both parties in the same sense. And by the term 'promise' we include not words only, but all signs and even tacit understandings not expressly signified in any way, if such clearly form a part of the engagement."[42]

Sidgwick recognizes that this approach to promise gives the power of annulment solely to the promisee. If the promisee's expectations are not raised because he has no interest in the promise, or if circumstances occurring in the interim alter his expectation level, then the promise is no longer binding. Additional problems may arise if the promisee is dead or otherwise unavailable to release the promisor; or if the promise has raised expectations in the promisee that the promisor will commit immoral acts; or if the promise was obtained by force. Sidgwick says that common sense is uncertain on these points. But even in cases where there is little doubt, questions still remain:

> Even if a promise has been made quite freely and fairly, circumstances may alter so much before the time comes to fulfill it, that the effects of keeping it may be quite other than those which were foreseen when it was made. In such a case probably all would agree that the promisee ought to release the promiser. But if he declines to do this, it seems difficult to decide how far the latter is bound. Some would say that he is in all cases: while others would consider that a considerable alteration of circumstances removed the obligation—perhaps adding that all engagements must be understood to be taken subject to the general understanding that they are only binding if material circumstances remain substantially the same. But such a principle very much impairs the theoretical definiteness of the duty.[43]

A promise may indeed raise a person's expectations; but if circumstances arise after the promise is made that make the keeping of the promise difficult, immoral, or impossible, it is no longer clear how strong this obligation is, regardless of how high it has raised the promisee's expectations. Sidgwick imagines a situation in which a promisor cannot get in touch with the promisee to discuss the fact that, between the times when the promise was made and when it is to be performed, conditions have changed to such an extent as to call into question the obligatory nature of the promise. One solution would have the promisor do what he sincerely thought would have been the intention of the promisee. "But the obligation thus becomes very vague: since it is difficult to tell from a man's wishes under one set of circumstances what he would have desired under circumstances varying from these in a complex manner: and practically this view of obligation leads to a great divergence of opinion."[44]

Sidgwick also addresses the question of what to do when a person unintentionally raises another's expectations. He asks the reader to form the conception of an average person, to consider what expectations this person would form under the circumstances, and to infer from this what beliefs and expectations people generally have in similar circumstances. In this thought experiment we are to refer to the customary uses of language and the customary tacit understandings between people who stand in relationship to each other as promisor and promisee. If a person has deviated from this common standard without giving either notice or reason for his deviation, then he should suffer any loss that may result from the misunderstanding. This criterion is generally applicable. "But if custom is ambiguous or shifting it cannot be applied; and the just claims of the parties become a problem, the solution of which is very difficult, if not strictly indeterminate."[45] Sidgwick admits that promissory expectations can be created in a person without the use of specific words, though he points out that the use of informal language may occasionally cause problems in that it may result in the unintentional raising of expectations. In short, he assumes that the common understanding of what a promise entails—when it creates an obligation, and the conditions under which it is defeated—is incomplete, variant, and diffuse.

Jan Narveson is also a proponent of the expectational approach. According to Narveson, we have a *prima facie* obligation to keep a promise because the promisee has an interest in the performance of it and we have led him or her to expect this performance. If I break a promise, it is more serious than if I had not promised, because the promisee's expectation is disappointed. Narveson asks the reader to consider how people actually behave in promising. If, for example, you make a promise to meet someone for dinner, and this promise has the effect of raising the promisee's expectations quite high and he goes out of his way to be there, then you'd better have a good excuse if you fail to show up. If you and he get together often, however, and it is understood that either of you will occasionally not make it—or if the promisee does not much care whether you show up or not—then the reason you give for not showing up will not matter much. "It all depends, and quite transparently depends, on the amount of trouble the promisee goes to, and the degree of his expectation created by the promise. These are plain facts with which anybody is familiar from daily life, as well as from novels, movies, and history books."[46]

Narveson reiterates this view in the essay "Promising, Expecting, and Utility." Each promise comes with its own context and special circumstances, what Narveson calls the *weight* of a particular promise, "against which we are to weigh the onerousness to us, or the reduction of benefit to the promisee, of doing the promised thing."[47] Sometimes a promise should not be kept because of a conflict of obligations in which another duty is stronger than the promise. When this occurs, the promisor should not keep his or her promise. There are promises that are wrong to keep from the start (a promise to kill your neighbor's dog, for example), but these promises should be distinguished from those that cannot or should not be kept because of unforeseeable circumstances or the emergence of contrary obligations. Narveson offers the following generalization: "Promises are by no means regarded as sacred and unbreakable, but rather are thought of as having

(1) a certain moral *'weight'*, varying from case to case but present whenever the promise is tolerably normal, which (2) may be exceeded by other factors, some natural, some moral, and some simply matters of self-interest. The question is, how do we measure the said *'weight?'* "[48]

Narveson considers the "logically" normal case of promising. Such a logically normal case implies that both promisee and promisor are acting voluntarily; both know the circumstances and are acting rationally. Both believe, at the time of the promise, that what is promised is more desirable than any alternative. The situation may change between the time the promise was made and the time it is to be carried out, but promising, as opposed to a mere contemplation without commitment, allows few avenues of escape from the obligation incurred. The difference between mere contemplation and promising is that in a promise one is led to expect that the promisor will do the promised thing. "And in defaulting, I disappoint this expectation, a disappointment which is additional to the loss of the promised benefit, whatever it may have been."[49] The *prima facie* obligation of a promise, then, is to be grounded upon the expectations raised in the promisee.

Narveson denies that this approach is circular. The promisee's expectation that I will do what I promised does not depend on his thinking that I am under an obligation but, rather, stems from the simple fact that I told him that I would do it (whatever it is I promised to do): "To promise, or say that I will do something, in the context in which this is taken as having the force of a promise, is to say that I will make the point of doing it, that I am setting myself to doing it, and hence to 'assure you' that I will do it. This being the sense of the words, you need no further reason for expecting performance: in the situation, this is exactly the reaction that is so to say, linguistically appropriate."[50]

There is a further problem about what should count as reasonable expectations. Narveson refers to H. A. Prichard's example of someone who has his expectations raised by overhearing a conversation. For Narveson, this is a clear case of not having promised, since the expectations were not intentionally raised. He reiterates that it is important at the outset of a promise or a perceived promise to be clear that one has promised or that one has heard a promise, what conditions attach, and so forth. If I overhear a conversation in which my expectations are raised, I should make certain that the speaker intends his or her remarks to be taken as a sincere expression of intention and as an expression of intention to me.

For Narveson, then, promising is used in both formal and informal modes to intentionally express a speaker's future intentions and to allow the hearer to form expectations and to act "along the way" in accordance with these expectations. If either the speaker speaks unintentionally or the hearer forms no expectations, then no promise is made. As with all communication, there is always a chance for misunderstanding, so it is crucial that the parties to a potential promise make their intentions and dispositions known. As with all promises, there may arise conditions in keeping a promise that would be worse than the frustration of expectations, and for this reason the promise should not be kept.

The raised expectations approach to promise is not without its positive features. It takes seriously the problems caused by the circumstances and contingencies that intervene between when a promise is made (t_i) and when it is discharged (t_j). Promises help us to form reasonable expectations about the future, but it is unreasonable to assume that the expectations of promising are any different from other sorts of expectations in that they may be disappointed by circumstances out of the promisor's control. This approach to promise likewise accommodates the many ways—both verbal and nonverbal—in which promises are made, from the most formal "I promise" to informal expressions of intention. Many of the examples of promises in Chapter One were of the informal sort, but they did raise expectations, and if such expectations are disappointed, then some harm is done in not keeping a promise. The expectational approach expands what is to count as a promise and closes off to the promisor an illicit line of retreat that relies on his not having used a specific form of words. As Narveson suggests, this view of promise better accounts for how promising is used by everyday people. Finally, in focusing on raised expectations, this approach captures an important emotion often attached to the obligation of a promise. We look out a window and see a man standing in the rain, looking expectantly down the road at each car that goes by. He does this for an hour and then walks away. We imagine that he was waiting for someone whom he expected to meet. Whomever it was he expected to see in one of those cars did not come. We feel bad for him, and our own stomachs twinge in the memory of similar wet afternoons in our own lives; or we remember a promise or two we have broken. What we feel in either case, I suggest, is not some abstract obligation tugging at us to keep our promises or the charge of inconsistency in breaking a constitutive rule but the pain caused by taking someone at their word, acting on these words, and being left in the rain, momentarily forgotten or lowered in someone's eyes. Perhaps there is more to this feeling than the disappointment of expectations, but raised expectations do increase the pain we feel when we are disappointed. To the extent that a promise raises expectations, it is *prima facie* wrong to break it.

There are, however, serious problems with this approach; I shall only outline them here.[51] The first problem is concerned with differentiating between raised expectations that create promissory obligations and those that do not. How does this approach distinguish between those expectations that do and those that do not create promissory obligations? We can see immediately that the answer to this question forces the expectation theorist into a dilemma. If one says, as Sidgwick and Narveson do, that it is important to establish at the outset that one is or is not speaking with the intention of creating an expectation in another or that one does or does not expect the speaker to do as he said he would, then informal promising would appear to drop out of the picture. Clarity about one's intention to create expectations in another is best expressed in formal ways. But if a successful promise occurs only when the promisor expresses himself in a formal way, then it is no longer clear that raised expectations in the promisee create the obligation. If clarity of intent is achieved by using a formalized utterance, then promising becomes dependent on—at least in part—a speech act, and this is something the expectational approach wants to deny.

A second problem concerns the emphasis put on the promisee's raised expectations. It is always possible that a promisee has formed unreasonable expectations. Perhaps Clark was so eager to secure his loan that he took friendly words as a promise when no such promise was intended. Would it have been reasonable for Philip to expect Maggie to marry him, when no formal expression of engagement was expressed? In short, the expectational approach relies on a conception of promissory obligation that seemingly gives the promisee the sole power to relieve a promisor of his or her obligation and hence ignores the relational features of promising.

Third, even if this approach accounts for conditions or exceptions that can defeat a promissory obligation, it provides no method to explain how this is done. It makes ample room

CHAPTER TWO

for the defeasible nature of promise, but it offers no methodology to explain how the tensions between exceptions and expectations are resolved. These problems are fully detailed in Chapter Three.

Promise as Evidence of a Previous Obligation

The evidentiary approach to promise has been given a strong voice by P. S. Atiyah. His contribution to the promise literature is noteworthy for a number of reasons. First, he is generally critical of how philosophers have understood promise. Atiyah believes that part of the problem with traditional approaches to promise is that the vocabulary and techniques used therein are less rich and less flexible than those of the law. There is no moral language that can convey the notion of a promise that is binding but that does not carry any sanctions if it is breached. There is, he claims, a great danger that "morality will overshoot the mark in encouraging too great a degree of respect for the rule that promises should be kept."[52] Second, and in keeping with his own advice, Atiyah makes great use of the history of promising, using sources drawn primarily from the law. Third, Atiyah argues that promises serve an evidentiary role rather than a substantive one. According to this approach, a promise does not produce an obligation but is merely evidence of what one already has (or will have) an obligation to do. The obligation of which it is evidence, as with a contract, exists only when it produces either benefit for the person creating the obligation or detrimental reliance on the part of the person accepting the obligation. If no benefit is received or if there is no detrimental reliance, then the moral grounds for enforcing the obligation become quite weak.

Atiyah divides the literature on promising into two categories: the internal point of view and the external point of view. He places his own position in the latter camp. Writers in the first group think that the object of moral inquiry is to assist those who seek guidance as to the "right thing to do." They tend to begin by asking such questions as, What ought I to do? Why should I keep my promises? "Those who take this position appear to think that the primary functions of rules about promising are, first, to instruct people how to make promises, and secondly, to give them guidance as to why and when they are obliged to observe promises."[53] Writers in the second group are more concerned with why people in general should observe moral rules and why it is socially necessary that moral rules should exist and be respected. They begin by assuming the social context of promising. "The externalist's position is likely to be similar to the lawyer's who in the last analysis is concerned with behavior, but who is therefore concerned with intentions insofar as they bear on behavior."[54] Atiyah believes that it is not possible to give a coherent explanation of why promises should be morally binding unless one first posits a social context in which the obligations arise.

The evidentiary approach relies on the parallels Atiyah sees between the legal context of promising and its moral context. He places promissory obligation within the broader context of moral obligation and analyzes the relationship between promising and the receipt of benefits and the causing of harm or injury, insofar as each of these create obligations. He suggests that promise is reducible to a species of consent and that consent is a broader and more basic source of obligation. He traces this notion of promising as consent to *Leviathan*, where Thomas Hobbes argues that a promise is an expression of consent not to interfere with others in their enjoyment of their natural rights. Atiyah also cites H.L.A. Hart's argument in "Are There Any Natural Rights?" as suggesting a similar idea. A promise for Hart is a surrender of the promisor's freedom in certain respects. "By thus surrendering his freedom he [the promisor] legitimates the conduct of the promisee in now having the right to demand something from the promisor."[55]

An important feature of the concept of consent is that it is a revocable concept. Revocability attaches to consent because, in general, consent has to do with binding oneself to a future act. It is because of the double-tensed nature of consent that the consenter, in some cases, is allowed to revoke his initial consent. Atiyah points out that there are many cases where we allow revocation of a consent to act in the future or prohibit such consents outright. A patient who consents to an operation is allowed to change his mind. A tenant protected under the British Rent Acts can surrender her tenancy for payment if agreed, but she cannot bind herself to the future even for payment. An accused person can plead guilty to a crime, but he cannot bind himself to plead guilty by any sort of agreement or contract. In determining when consent is revocable, it is necessary to conduct a balancing exercise from the external point of view. It is not simply the consenter's intentions that determine the obligation he or she has incurred. Instead, it is necessary to examine the rendering of benefits and acts of reliance as sources of obligation.

If promising is a species of consent and all consent is *prima facie* revocable, then promises are *prima facie* revocable. Now, the puzzle about promising is to understand how this is possible, since a promise is usually understood as a way the promisor binds herself *not* to revoke her consent. Here Atiyah reminds us that a promise is by no means always binding, either in law or in morality: "We thus find that, whether a consent is or is not expressed in a form which amounts to a promise, its revocability is a matter to be settled by external factors: a decision by the social group (or the judges appointed by the group) is necessary before one can say whether the consent is irrevocable. The expressed willingness of the party to treat his consent as irrevocable is neither a necessary nor sufficient condition for the social group to hold the consent to be irrevocable."[56] If a promise is considered irrevocable by a promisor or a promisee but judged revocable by the social group, it is the social group that has the last word. What is important here is that there are conditions that defeat a promise and that allow the promisor to revoke what was promised.

There are many ways of expressing consent, and one way is to make an admission. If I owe you ten dollars and I admit that I have this debt, then I admit that I have an obligation to you and that you have a claim on me. The crucial point of Atiyah's argument comes when he claims that the common justification for treating a promise as obligatory is that the promise is evidence of or an admission of some other obligation already owed by the promisor. In making an explicit promise, a promisor concedes or admits the "existence and extent" of a preexisting obligation. For Atiyah, this is the paradigm of an explicit promise. The sources of promissory obligation are either that one person has done good or rendered some benefit to another or that one person has done harm to another. Although these sources of obligation can arise without any consent or express promise, Atiyah claims that they often coexist with explicit promises.

Atiyah offers examples to support his case, beginning first with examples where the source of obligation is neither benefit nor reliance. If one party (the defendant) is guilty of fault or negligence, he is legally liable to pay compensation to the other person (the plaintiff). Often this liability is expressed in a promise to pay compensation, but, as Atiyah points out, the promise overlaps or coincides with the prior duty to make compensation. The purpose of the promise in this case is to clear up any uncertainty regarding the prior obligation. In cases of this nature, it is mistaken to view the promise as creating a wholly new obligation. Atiyah argues that, similarly, a promise to tell the truth in a courtroom adds emphasis and ritual to an existing obligation and makes it more difficult for the promisor to deny that he had the prior obligation. Such a promise is essentially still evidentiary in character.

The evidentiary nature of promising can also be seen in cases where no prior obligation exists. Assume that I offer to give you eighty thousand dollars, and you agree to give me your house. It would seem that our joint offers constituted a promise that bound us to our word. Atiyah argues that such an agreement can be broken down into the consent to the terms of the proposed exchange and the binding commitment to consummate the exchange. In terms of consenting to the terms of the proposed exchange, a promise is still nothing more than an expression of each party's willingness to exchange on the terms proposed. In cases where a person relies on another's promise, it is the reliance itself and not the promise that creates the obligation. Atiyah claims that all promises have an assertion content. Whether or not a promisee is justified in relying on a promisor's assertion is a judgment made by the social group, but in rendering its decision, the social group will pay close attention to how the intention or assertion was made. It is here that explicit promises serve as evidentiary or clarificatory.

Because of the evidentiary nature of promising, neither mutual executory promises nor unilateral gratuitous promises are binding. This is because neither of them generally creates benefit or reliance. Atiyah suggests that breaking a social engagement is rarely considered a grievous offense, provided that due warning is given so that no reliance will take place. Likewise, if I promise to pay you one hundred dollars for your cow, and you show up with the cow and I tell you that I have changed my mind, I have no obligation to pay you the money as long as I do not also try to take the cow. Atiyah's interpretation is that I only promised to give you the money upon receipt of the cow; I never promised to accept the cow. My promise does not oblige me to accept the cow, and so I have not broken my promise.[57] One cannot say that mutual promises are obligation-creating acts since the question we are trying to answer is why we should create a moral system that would recognize such obligation-creating acts. Atiyah argues that the usual reasons for making bare mutual promises obligatory—that they are an important way of allocating risk, that they create expectations, that such a principle is necessary for the maintenance of our way of life, and that they are mutually beneficial—all fall to various counterarguments and fail to cover a wide range of cases. "The right conclusion is not to continue the somewhat desperate search for more satisfactory reasons for upholding the binding nature of mutual executory promises. The right conclusion is to recognize that we are prone to think of mutual executory promises as having a more binding character than is in truth warranted by the reasons."[58]

Atiyah draws a similar conclusion about unilateral gratuitous promises. These sorts of promises have the weakest claim on the creation of obligation, because the promisor draws no benefit from them and, in general, they produce only expectation in the promisee. But expectation without reliance is a weak source of obligation, and reliance upon a unilateral gratuitous promise is unlikely to create much of an obligation because the promisor has given no reason why he should do what he has promised.

To review, the evidentiary approach states that promissory obligation is grounded in the promisor's benefit and the promisee's detrimental reliance. The function of a promise is to act as an admission of or as evidence of an already existing obligation. A promise is an admission by the promisor to the promisee that she already is under an obligation or, that she may come to be under an obligation. Such promises are obligatory only if they create benefit for the promisor or detrimental reliance on the part of the promisee. Promises that have neither benefit nor reliance attached to them—mutual executory and unilateral gratuitous promises—create little or no obligation on the part of the promisor.

Atiyah's evidentiary approach has broken new ground. Unlike other approaches, it is informed with historical evidence of how promising has been understood. The evidentiary approach is also better able to explain why some raised expectations create obligations and others do not. To create an obligation, an expectation must be a legitimate one and must be relied on. Hence even an expectation that is relied on may not create an obligation if the promisee formed an expectation that was illegitimate. Perhaps the greatest strength of the evidentiary approach is its ability to handle the revocable nature of promising. Not only does Atiyah claim that the concept of promising—as a species of consent—is a revocable concept, but he also tries to provide a mechanism for evaluating defeating conditions and for resolving disagreements. For Atiyah, promising takes place in a social context, and the disagreements and uncertainties surrounding promises are to be resolved in a social context as well. He suggests that just as there are legislators and judges who make decisions about what the law is to be, who has broken the law, and to what extent, so too there are (or ought to be) moral legislators and judges who decide on the details of the practice of promising, as well as whether particular promises are morally binding. He gives us no indication of how this would work in the moral sphere, but he believes such a process is necessary.

But for all of the attractiveness of this approach as a methodology for treating promise, the form and content of the evidentiary approach are flawed. The first problem stems primarily from the identification of promise with contract. Even if a contractual notion of promise explains how some of our promises create obligations, it does not appear to explain how all of our promises do so. Using Atiyah's criteria, none of the examples cited in Chapter One would count as promises. What would we think of Steve if he rejected his promise to Moya since it did not and could not create any reliance on her part? Clark did rely on the banker's promise, but no consideration was provided and there was no previous obligation between them that the promise evidenced. It is not a particularly effective argument to deny the validity of promises that do not fit the contractual mold. If we take the data of promise as primary, then we see that there are promises that do appear to create obligations but do not fit the contractual mode of promising, and these types of promises need to be explained as well. Surely there exist promises unlike anything found in the law. There are likewise a number of important disanalogies between contract law and the practice of promise, and I detail them in Chapter Three.

A second drawback is that this approach relies exclusively upon what Atiyah calls the external viewpoint. The external viewpoint, he says, focuses on behavior and on intentions insofar as they bear on behavior. Although an external account may be able to explain how some promises create obligations, such an account will not be exhaustive. This is because it does not consider the promisor's intentions. The external viewpoint asserts that only intentions that are expressed, to the degree that they create benefit or reliance, create obligations. It is hard to know what to say from the external viewpoint about a person who informally intends to make an appointment for lunch with a friend, and who thinks she has done so in such a way as to create a detrimental reliance in her friend, but who fails to do so. The person shows up at noon for lunch, but the friend does not. It seems somewhat hollow to refer to the absence of a detrimental reliance in demonstrating to this person that no promise was made. The promise has clearly misfired, but this is hardly conclusive evidence that no promise was made. When external behavior does not correspond to a person's internal states, we should not always conclude that the internal states are mistaken. We may not want to rely on intentions alone when deciding when a promise is made, but neither ought we to ignore intentions when they contradict the external evidence.

Like the approaches before it, the evidentiary approach to promise gets a mixed review. Atiyah gives us a rich and detailed account of promise. He has made a serious attempt to develop a theory that is informed by the actions of historical and contemporary promisors. But I show in Chapter Three what goes wrong when a slice of common life, the legalistic slice, is used exclusively to develop an account of promise. The evidentiary approach replaces the relational aspects of promise with adversarial and judicial ones. It recognizes that promises are made between persons, but it prefers that conflict resolution be done by third parties. The practice of promise is, I believe, much richer than its legalistic version.

Promise as Intuitively Clear

The fundamental assumption of moral intuitionism is that we have the power to see clearly what actions are right in themselves and reasonable. The view presented in this section holds that the proposition "promises are obligatory" is to be understood either as an analytic proposition or as a synthetic a priori proposition. It holds further that one can see intuitively that promises are obligatory. There is no need to demonstrate that—or how—promises produce obligations. One need only to examine the concept *promise* to see that promises create obligations and that one ought to keep one's promises. I concentrate on the writings of H. A. Prichard and W. D. Ross.[59]

In the essay "Does Moral Philosophy Rest on a Mistake?" H. A. Prichard argues that all historical attempts to trace moral obligation to a teleological ethical theory fail. Prichard argues that obligation is a *sui generis* concept and is not reducible to or explainable in terms of any other concept. To consider whether or not we have an obligation does not require a utilitarian calculation or an appeal to moral rules. One need only to ask oneself if an obligation exists to do such and such an action and the answer will be forthcoming. In a number of places Prichard compares what one does in ethics to what one does in mathematics or to the theory of knowledge generally. Prichard believes the question "Is what we hitherto thought knowledge really knowledge?" an illegitimate one. We shall stop asking that question only when we realize the inevitable immediacy of knowledge. Further, if we somehow come to genuinely doubt that $7 \times 4 = 28$, the only remedy is to do the sum again. "Or, to put the matter generally, if we do come to doubt whether it is true that A is B, as we once thought, the remedy lies not in any process of reflection but in such a reconsideration of the nature of A and B as leads to the knowledge that A is B."[60]

Prichard suggests a similar remedy when considering moral knowledge. We want to have it proved to us that all of our obligations are really our obligations. He claims that it is a mistake to suppose that it is possible to prove what can only be apprehended directly by an act of moral thinking. It is not possible to prove that we have a particular obligation, but it is also unnecessary, as long as we carry the process of self-reflection to the point where we realize the self-evidence of our obligations. Similarly, our doubts about whether we should pay our debts are allayed when, in essence, we do the moral "calculation" over again. In the essay "The Obligation to Keep a Promise," Prichard argues that an obligation is a fact of the kind that is impossible to create or to bring into existence. That I am bound to do some action seems no more a fact that I create than is the fact that the square of three is odd. Promissory obligation is not created by the rules of an institution or in raising expectations or by the intentions of the promisor. The question "How are we to explain the obligation of a promise, an obligation that seems very much the type we create or change?" remains open and unanswered. But, more important, it is a question that is unanswerable and "illegitimate."

W. D. Ross shares with Prichard the view that intuition alone is needed to see that promises produce obligations, but unlike Prichard and other intuitionists before him, Ross recognizes that promissory obligations can conflict with obligations of other sorts.[61] He offers as a solution to this problem his notion of a *prima facie* duty. Ross suggests that "*prima facie* duty" be used to refer to "the characteristic (quite distinct from that of being a duty proper) which an act has, in virtue of being of a certain kind (e.g. the keeping of a promise), of being an act which would be a duty proper if it were not at the same time of another kind which is morally significant. Whether an act is a duty proper or actual duty depends on *all* the morally significant kinds it is an instance of."[62] He adds that a *prima facie* duty is not itself a duty but something related in a special way to duty. Further, a *prima facie* duty is not simply something that appears to be a duty at first sight, which may turn out to be illusory. A *prima facie* duty is "an objective fact involved in the nature of the situation, or more strictly in an element of its nature, though not, as duty proper does, arising from its *whole* nature."[63]

Keeping promises is a *prima facie* duty for Ross. He believes that the "plain man" fulfills a promise because he thinks he ought to do so, not because he thinks doing so will produce the best consequences overall. The plain person thinks much more about the past than the future and acts in a certain way simply because she has promised to do so. Of course, there will be cases when the duty to act benevolently will overcome the duty to meet a friend for a "trivial purpose." What we (most people) really think, he says, is "that normally promise-keeping, for example, should come before benevolence, but that when and only when the good to be produced by the act is very great and the promise comparatively trivial, the act of benevolence becomes our duty."[64] Ross reminds us that we have many types of relationships with many different people, and each of these relationships is the foundation of a *prima facie* duty.

How do we know that the keeping of promises is a *prima facie* duty? Ross's answer is a clear example of the intuitional approach:

> I should make it plain at this stage that I am *assuming* the correctness of some of our main convictions as to *prima facie* duties, or, more strictly, am claiming that we *know* them to be true. To me it seems as self-evident as anything could be, that to make a promise, for instance, is to create a moral claim on us in someone else. Many readers will perhaps say that they do *not* know this to be true. If so, I certainly cannot prove it to them; I can only ask them to reflect again, in the hope that they will ultimately agree that they also know it to be true. The main moral convictions of the plain man seem to me to be, not opin-

ions which it is for philosophy to prove or disprove, but knowledge from the start; and in my own case I seem to find little difficulty in distinguishing these essential convictions from other moral convictions which I also have, which are merely fallible opinions based on an imperfect study of the working for good or evil of certain institutions or types of action.[65]

Like Prichard before him, Ross suggests that we put aside our subtle analyses of promise and just look. If we do, we will see that promises are obligatory. It is not important or perhaps even possible to explain or understand promising. What is important is that a person act in accordance with the duties incurred by promises and, when conflicts arise, try to see clearly what path one must take.

Ross's view of promise is well illustrated in his example of the person who has promised a friend that he will return a book he has borrowed and decides to return the book by mail. Ross believes that the person's duty is to fulfill his promise, and he fulfills his promise only when the book is securely in his friend's hands. If the book is lost by an airline or rail worker or is stolen by a dishonest postal service employee, he is required to send another copy of the book. If the book comes to the hand of his friend, he has done his duty, even if it was carelessly dispatched. If it does not reach his friend, he has not done his duty, regardless of how carefully he has dispatched the book.

Prichard and Ross make a very strong case for doing away with the analysis of obligation in terms of other concepts. Whatever else promises are and however they arise, they are obligatory. As Ross says, "What, exactly, a promise is, is not so easy to determine, but we are surely agreed that it constitutes a serious limitation to our freedom of action."[66] All that is left to do—and what it is that Ross and Prichard do—is to expose the flaws in the arguments and theories that try to say more.

There are some obvious strengths to this nonexplanatory approach to promise. By relying on intuitions alone, it avoids having to construct a theory of promise. It stops the analysis one step earlier than most other accounts and blocks any and all attempts to go further by demonstrating that such attempts are incoherent or conflict with one's intuitions. Another positive feature of this approach is that it recognizes the need to introduce a way of handling conflicts of obligation. Ross's account describes the decision procedure as a careful rendering of the specific situation, followed by an intuitively correct decision. As Ross says, what a person forms in this situation is never more than a considered opinion. Finally, there is something powerful about an argument that asks us to imagine ourselves as the promisors in such and such a situation, or which asks us to see for ourselves that promises are obligatory. We nod in agreement that the proposition "promises are obligatory" is analytic and as obvious as statements in nonmathematical languages can get. We are also likely to agree with Ross when he says that we rarely appeal to rules or engage in complex calculations when deciding if we have a duty to keep a promise. Steve did not wrack his mind considering whether his promise to Moya was obligatory. Louise felt the intuitive force of her promise to her brother, Russ. It is a good bet that our intuitions will mesh in these cases, because most of us have been raised to believe that promises are *prima facie* obligatory. And, as Ross or Prichard might say, we are raised to believe this because, in fact, promises do create obligations.

One is tempted, then, to rest content with the intuitional approach, because it refuses to answer the "philosophical" question of how promises create obligations. Wittgenstein would, no doubt, be pleased. Nevertheless, we can ask more of philosophical theory than to acknowledge the intuitive clarity of promise and be done with it. Even if we cannot get to the root of promissory obligation—"It's turtles all the way down"[67]—we can still seek to explain and describe the social practice of promise.

But even as a nonapproach, the intuitional account is not without problems and weaknesses. First, it can be criticized for the seriousness and solemnity that it attaches to promise. This criticism has been made in a general way by P. S. Atiyah, who chides philosophers for ignoring the empirical data found in law. A second argument against this approach is that intuitions about promising are not always shared in common. Intuitionists have a strong case as long as they are correct about our shared intuitions regarding promising, but if there is a clash of intuitions, it would seem necessary to explain it. It is this fact that our intuitions about the nature of promise do not form a single position, that has inspired so many philosophers to work in this area. A third problem with the intuitional approach is its method for resolving conflicts of duty. I do not think we can hold the view that whenever there is a conflict of duty, the promisor should consult his intuitions in deciding what to do. This method simply ignores the relational aspect of promising. Finally, this account makes little mention of how promises are defeated. Although the concept of *prima facie* duties allows for the possibility of conflicts of duty, it is otherwise uninformative about the exceptions to promises. There may be legitimate exceptions to a promise that are not also duties, though these exceptions might likewise interfere with one's duty to keep a promise.

I address these criticisms in greater detail in Chapter Three, but we can already see that close attention to the practice of promise is not ruled out just because it is considered unnecessary or impossible to explain the source of promissory obligation. Even if we understand with intuitive clarity what promises entail, we still need to know how promises are made, how they are broken, and, in general, how to navigate in this social activity. The activity of promising is worthy of study not only because it accords with our intuitions but also because it is used and abused, misunderstood, difficult to apply, and full of possibilities and interpretations. Unfortunately, the intuitional approach tells us almost nothing about these important details.

Promise as Intention

The intentional approach to promise has been out of philosophical fashion since David Hume showed it to be indefensible.[68] This is a rather curious state of affairs, considering Hume's cursory critique. Perhaps the reluctance of philosophers to explain promise in terms of intentions had to do with the lack of conceptual tools needed to say anything meaningful about what goes on inside people's heads. What was needed to resurrect this approach was a theory of intentionality rich enough to handle the conceptual issues surrounding the willing of voluntary obligations. Michael Robins uses action theory to develop just such a sophisticated intentional theory of promise.

Robins argues that promissory obligation is unintelligible without presupposing a more primitive concept of commitment. He claims that the traditional approaches to promising succeed only by "smuggling in a yet unexplained, non-social sense of commitment which comes dangerously close to 'willing an obligation'."[69] Commitment, he argues, is embedded in the very possibility of intending. This normative concept of commitment is to be distinguished from and defended against a causal theory of action. It is a normative concept because it is used to explain a person's being mistaken in her action in a way that cannot be explained by reference to a mistaken intention or belief. He argues further that at the level of *basic action*, it is a principle that one should honor one's nonmistaken intentions—a principle that rules out changing one's intentions or choosing not to abide by them.

Upon the foundation of basic action Robins builds an *architectonic*, "whereby each ascending floor represents a different kind of intention or action which is governed, correspondingly, by a distinctive 'mandate' that was reconstituted out of the one governing the lower floor."[70] On the second floor are nonbasic actions; on the third floor, a special kind of intention associated with vows and other private decisions; and on the fourth floor, promises, which Robins describes as distinctively social acts. A promise is a social act that creates not only an obligation but also a right of another to whom the obligation is owed. Promises transfer to another the exclusionary mandate created by a vow. When the transfer is effected, the promisee holds an exclusionary mandate over the promisor. Robins's view does not allow any social act to create a binding sense of obligation unless the possibility of obligation is embedded in nonsocial intentional action.

Intentional Basic Actions

Robins claims that when a person acts intentionally he exercises a causal power, but the causal power does not run from the intention to the bodily movements. Instead, the intention is noncausally related to a volition, which later executes that intention. Intention and volition are related to commitment, which is a three-place operator ranging over an intention, a volition, and an agent. Robins posits a normative theory of commitment. It recognizes that intending, like commitment, is doubly temporally indexed. This means that both intention and commitment refer to the time at which we are intending or committing ourselves (t_i) and to the later time we are to honor our intentions and commitments (t_j). He considers an example of a person who intends today to wake up early tomorrow. He suggests that the point of a person intending today to wake up early tomorrow is to settle for both today and tomorrow that one will have a reason tomorrow to wake up early. If this is correct, then one will have a reason tomorrow whether or not one still intends tomorrow to rise early. There may be good reasons for why one should change one's mind tomorrow, but Robins asserts that one may not change one's mind tomorrow simply by disregarding or ignoring the reason that one intends today. There is an important asymmetry between forming intentions and changing them. Though one can form intentions arbitrarily, one may not change them at will unless it can be shown that the intention is mistaken.

Robins turns next to an account of volitions. A volition is distinguished from an intention in that a volition plays some executorial role with respect to what was intended and is contemporaneous with the movements it causes or controls. He relies upon philosophical argument and scientific evidence to show that volitions are causally related to actions. Making reference to this scientific evidence, he claims that a volition is not any act of will but one that occurs under the guise of a "response image." A response image is a representation of sensory feedback that provides a mental conception of a certain act and that defines this act. Unlike event causation, which assumes that the first event is a sufficient condition for the other, agent causation assumes that the agent always has the power to change his mind.

Nonbasic Actions

Just as he argues that intentional basic action succeeds only if one posits a normative concept of commitment, Robins claims that the same normative concept applies to nonbasic

actions, "actions which occur . . . when we successfully intend our basic action to achieve a significance beyond the
bounds of our own body, to achieve that significance by embracing portions of the world as well."[71] Nonbasic actions are
significantly different from basic actions and do not merely
reduce to them. For one thing, intentional nonbasic action depends as much on us as it does upon the world. For intentional nonbasic action we need the cooperation of the world,
to perform or contribute as required. Relying upon Alvin
Goldman's theory of level generation and supplementing it
with what he calls *adverbial requirements*, Robins shows
how nonbasic actions commit us to new mandates beyond
those involved in basic action. These mandates amount to
further constraints on the way we are to move our bodies.

Vows

Robins uses vows to bridge the gap between intentions and
promises. He suggests three reasons why vows can be seen as
serving this function. First, vows intuitively create a stronger
commitment than a mere intention. Second, vows need not
be essentially social acts. The nature of a vow is that of self-
imposed commitment. Third, vows need not be communicated in language and in this way appear to be prior to language and convention.

Robins then derives deciding from intending and vowing
from deciding. A decision is an intention that was arrived at
by some process of deliberation between alternatives. Hence a
decision is a kind of intention, but not all intentions need be
decisions. What makes a decision a "decision" is the intention at t_i not to reconsider (or to place limits on reconsidering)
it at t_j. The distinctive marks of a decision are that it is a
second-order intention and an exclusionary intention that

grows out of and is justified by deliberation. Robins suggests that a vow is an exclusionary intention that is not, like a decision, necessarily a product of deliberation. A vow that is not a decision is the forming of an exclusionary intention without deliberation even in the minimal sense. "All that need be before one's mind in an act of vowing is the *concept* of an alternative, for that, after all, is what one in the act of vowing intends to exclude."[72]

Finally, it can be seen that vows are related to nonbasic acts in that a commitment does not approach the strength of a vow until its scope has involved a nonbasic act. We do not vow unless the action vowed is considered a nonbasic action.

Promises

Unlike vowing, promising is a social act, but its commitment is traced to the personal or inner act of commitment that creates an exclusionary intention not to change one's first-order intention. What makes promising an inherently social act is that, unlike vowing, the promisee is seen as playing a crucial role in the act of promising. A promise confers a special right on the promisee, a right that entails that the promisee is the beneficiary of the promise, as well as that the promisee has the power to waive the promise. Robins explains how an exclusionary intention on the part of the promisor can commit him not only to the content of the promise but also to the promisee, and at the same time it can create a waivable right for the promisee to demand the promise from the promisor. He claims that "A [the promisor] wants to communicate to B [the promisee] not merely his unilateral commitment to φ [the promise], but somehow involve B in that very commitment's taking effect."[73] The promisee's involvement in a promise reflects his acceptance of the commitment, and his acceptance is at least one condition on which the commitment is in effect. Based on their (promisor and promisee) common knowledge that A can make vows, A might say to B, in promising, that "I, A, intend, exclusionarily at t_i (that you, B, will hold the exclusionary requirement for me to ϕ at t_j, conditional upon your continuing assent)."[74] This formulation, Robins asserts, contains all of the elements to represent in logical form both the common origin and difference between vows and promises. In short, promising is vowing plus conditional transferring.

Promises differ from vows in another important way. Whereas there is only a requirement to honor one's vows and intentions, there is an obligation to keep one's promises. The distinction between a requirement and a moral obligation is not simply verbal. A failure to do what is required affects the individual who vows or intends, whereas a failure of moral obligation affects another person and fails to recognize his or her autonomy. A person who does not keep his vows or who cheats at solitaire is likely to be viewed as weak-willed rather than as morally deficient or viewed with amusement rather than scorn. This is not the case with persons who do not keep their moral obligations.

Robins claims that his account of promise has the advantage of showing the transition from vows to promises—from private acts to social ones—without presupposing any antecedent convention, practice, institution, or rule of promise. In addition, Robins believes his account is able to handle insincere or unintentional promises, promises that Atiyah and others claim undermine an intentional approach to promise. He argues that Atiyah and others confuse the concept of an exclusionary intention with having that intention. Promises, to be sure, cannot be obligatory without the concept of an exclusionary intention being communicated or being present;

but this does not also imply that the promisor has that intention. "Even though the promise can take effect without the speaker having the appropriate intention, it is still the concept of that intention that is so semantically represented and by means of which we come to understand what promising is in the first place."[75] Hence insincere promises are quite compatible with this account.

Finally, this theory is evolutionary in that it shows how human beings have developed into social and moral beings. Promising stems from the evolutionary development of internal states and is a necessary feature of our evolutionary and moral development. Without it, according to Robins, there could be no conventions, games, or even language.

In the hands of Michael Robins, the intentional approach has many strong points. In analyzing intention, volition, and commitment, he has incorporated into a theory of promise other branches of philosophy, as well as the tools of science. He has greatly informed our understanding of promising with the latest results from action theory and cognitive psychology and once again made the intentional approach to promise a viable theoretical alternative. The reemergence of a healthy and sophisticated intentional theory will enliven the dialogue among promise theorists and will enrich future theories of promise. This account is also important because it shows how promise arises out of a state of nature that is evolutionary in character. For Robins, promising is not simply a matter of what we say but a matter of what we do. To explain this feature of promising requires that we look at our social development from an evolutionary point of view. He recognizes that promising is a peculiarly human practice and that to explain it, we need to know what it is that allows humans to engage in it.

Despite the richness of this approach, however, it fails to

provide an adequate theory of promise. The intentional approach suffers most from underdescription. Just as the evidentiary approach focuses primarily on benefit and reliance, both of which are determined by behavior, the intentional approach focuses extensively on what goes on inside of the promisor, the ascertainment of which is not always determined by her behavior. On another issue, Robins rightly points out that promising has an irreducible double-tensed indexical temporal reference, that is, promises take place in the present (t_i) and in the future (t_j). As I demonstrate in the next chapter, he recognizes this feature without fully appreciating it. One can also question the degree to which the promisee exercises power in determining whether a particular promise remains in effect. One is reminded of Nietzsche's example of the creditor who could disfigure a debtor's body "more or less" as he deemed appropriate for rendering what was owed to him. The intentional approach is a clear example of the promise-as-grappling-hook view discussed in Chapter One.

This completes the outline of five contemporary approaches to promise. I have suggested in a cursory way their problems and limitations. As a general conclusion, it can be stated that although each approach captures one or another aspect of promising, each fails to capture promise in its complex entirety. Each approach underdescribes promise by seeing it exclusively in terms of one feature or another and by focusing almost entirely on how promises create obligations. Promises create obligations, but they also create situations when such obligations are defeated, and this feature must be explained as well. The defeasible quality of promise is not an additional problem to be solved. There are not two questions to answer here but one: namely, how does the practice of promise function in our form of life? If we pose the question in this way, we can see that it is not enough to explain how promises create obligations. Each approach also makes claims that appear to conflict with one's perceptions of the data of promise.

The short answer to why all of these approaches are lacking in this way is that promising is a complex moral practice, perhaps more complex than most promise theorists believe. To make matters worse, the present range of methodologies employed by promise theorists is too narrow to deal with this complexity. Each approach focuses on one particular aspect of promise; but are we to believe that promising is so easily captured by its intuitive clarity, its similarities to contract, or its ability to raise expectations? Is there really nothing more to promise than a rule-governed institution, which creates obligations the way touchdowns create six points? If we are to have any success in capturing the practice of promise, we will need to expand the range of concepts we use. It will not be a matter of mere tinkering with the above approaches, an addition here or a deletion there. What is required is an entirely different approach.

In addition to the paucity of explanatory devices, there seems to be very little interest in checking one's theory against the data of promise or in incorporating fields of study outside of the traditional philosophical bounds. We are told in a general way by Searle and Rawls how institutions work, but there is no attempt to show or interest in showing that the institutional approach is corroborated in anthropological or sociological studies. Both intentional and expectational theorists could begin to take advantage of the data of the psychological sciences, and yet, with the exception of Robins, none to date has done so. Intuitionist and evidentiary theorists claim to have empirical evidence to support their accounts, but the intuitionists tell us only that the common person agrees with them, and Atiyah concentrates only on the evidence provided by law. If we take seriously the notion that theories of promise should be informed by what promisors and promisees think and do, then we ought to attempt to gather such evidence or at least be able to incorporate such evidence into our theoretical accounts. We should expect both greater and finer detail from our theories of promise.

In the remaining chapters I offer detailed criticisms of each of these approaches, as well as an alternative account of my own, which I call a theory of practice.

Laced Up in Formulas: Contemporary Approaches Considered

Amidst all this bustle 'tis not reason, which carries the prize, but eloquence. . . . This victory is not gained by the men at arms, who manage the pike and sword; but by the trumpeters, drummers, and musicians of the army.
DAVID HUME, *A Treatise of Human Nature*

When we do philosophy we are like savages, primitive people, who hear the expressions of civilized men, put a false interpretation on them, and then draw the queerest conclusions from it.
LUDWIG WITTGENSTEIN, *Philosophical Investigations*

Collectively, the material cited in Chapter Two represents some of the best work in contemporary philosophy. The authors are well known and their contributions are much discussed in the literature. It is perhaps presumptuous to take them to task for failing to generate a theory of promise when they never intended to formulate such a theory to begin with. It would certainly be presumptuous if I were to offer an alternative approach along the lines of what we have just seen. Instead, I intend to offer an alternative method: to ask and address not only how promises create obligations but also how the practice of promise functions in our form of life. The latter is significantly different from asking how words create obligations. But getting to the point of actually offering an alternative approach to promise requires first a consideration and evaluation of the five contemporary approaches outlined in Chapter Two.

The purpose of this critical chapter is to point out the ways in which these contemporary approaches—as indicative of a specific philosophical method—fail in their efforts to describe promise as a social practice. While it is true that none of the authors cited above claimed to be offering a theory of promise, it is more importantly true that none of their approaches could ever stand as a theory of promise. This is because each approach underdescribes the social practice of promise and lacks coherency as a theoretical model. To put the matter in structural terms, the five contemporary approaches examined herein are simply unable to support the load that promise as a social practice would put on them. To use George Eliot's language, these approaches are laced up in formulas and incapable of conceptualizing a human practice such as promise. The complexity of human interaction is replaced in these approaches by the complexity of philosophical jargon. If we are impressed by these linguistic performances, it is because we have forgotten the task that philosophy sets itself in seeking to explain and describe human behavior. Although each approach offers a detailed and impressive account of a facet of promise, none can function as a theory of promise on its own. The intent of my evaluation, then, is not to demonstrate the validity of one approach over another but to show that the whole lot of them represent a philosophical method that we are better off doing without, at least in terms of outlining a theory of promise. I am not concerned with picayune objections, as someone who is sympathetic with an approach but unhappy with some of its details might be. I am arguing for wholesale rejection.

Paving the Road with Good Intentions

I suggested in Chapter One that a theory of promise would approach promise with an open texture, interested in how the practice arose and why; how practitioners come to learn to promise; and how they evaluate and judge other members of the practice. Such a theory would see promise as a relational and double-tensed practice that creates obligations, some of which function as grappling hooks and others of which function as pathfinders. It is not, I argued, a matter of defining promise by using a set of necessary and sufficient conditions but, instead, a matter of describing and explaining a complex social practice. It is disappointing that none of the approaches outlined herein comes close to satisfying this conception of a theory of promise. Each of them focuses on one or another aspect of promise: its rules, its intuitive clarity, its function, the promisor's intention, or the promisee's expectations. But none of them attempts to answer the larger questions. A successful approach to promise requires a wide range of techniques and methodologies. If we focus too much on the behavioral features of promise, as does P. S. Atiyah, we are likely to ignore the promisor's intentions, and this seems mistaken. But if we focus on the internal states of the promisor, as does Michael Robins, we are likely to ignore the external, behavioral features of promise, which can greatly influence the success or failure of communicating intentions; and this seems equally mistaken.

The intentional approach, for example, offers a naturalistic and evolutionary explanation of how we move from nonsocial acts of intending to the inherently social act of making promises, but it does so by assuming, first, a state of nature wherein humans are solitary and, second, that one cannot make promises without first learning to intend and to vow. We should not, I suggest, think of promise as a product of evolution, as if we began as solitary animals—like Homer's Cyclops—and evolved into social creatures who make promises. We are no more solitary creatures than we are creatures who reproduce asexually. We emerge helpless from the womb, but we are already part of a social group and already capable of engaging in social acts: suckling at a human breast and recognizing our parents' voices, for example. We emerge, as it were, poised to promise: fully capable and open to the possibility. Robins's linear architectonic is not supported by the facts of our earthly existence. I do not mean to imply that newborns are capable of making promises, but I do believe that they are already, and in important ways, social creatures, themselves the offspring of promises and vows. Although Robins's account is neat and tidy and proceeds in logical steps, there is no reason to think that the social lives of human beings are in any way accurately modeled by such an approach. I have never met a solitary human being about to move from vowing to promising, and I doubt that I will meet such a being anytime soon. A theory of promise is not helped any by fictional or constructed accounts of the human condition or by relying on explanations that, though elegant, belie our everyday experiences and our careful observations. The infinite regress that stalks any account of promissory obligation may be missing from Robins's account, but so is the complexity of our social lives.

The intentional approach likewise tells us little about conditions that defeat a promise, about how one goes about learning a promise, or about how we evaluate and judge other members of the practice of promise. If promising has a double-tensed indexical temporal reference, then it is important to recognize that external conditions may arise between t_i and t_j and how such conditions may change the conditions or even the possibility of the original promise. Because promising occurs both in the present and in the future, an adequate theory must say something about the conditions that defeat a promise. Robins points out that a promise takes away from the promisor the freedom to change his mind and hence rules out one type of defeating condition, though the promisee is free to waive the promisor's obligation. These remarks still hardly begin to address the nature of defeasibility as it relates to promise. Is Steve relieved of his promise to his sister because she is no longer alive to exercise her exclusionary right over him? Does Clark's banker have an out because he can justifiably say that he did not have an exclusionary intention not to change his first-order intention to complete the paperwork by a certain date? I am inclined to think that Clark's banker is a bit of a cad even if he did not make a formal promise to Clark, and that Steve is an honorable fellow even if he chooses to break his promise to his sister and nephew. Neither the intentional approach nor any of the other approaches above is even remotely helpful in highlighting decision criteria that could be used in evaluating a particular performance of a promise or in judging a person's character.

By contrast, the intentional approach makes perfect sense both of Tom's promise to his father, to make Wakem and his family pay for what Wakem has done to Tom's father by forcing him into bankruptcy, and of Maggie's promise to Tom, not to meet with Philip or to write to him again without her brother's knowledge. Both promises can be seen as the transfer of an exclusionary mandate already created by a vow, with the promisee holding the exclusionary mandate over the promisor. The intentional approach is a clear example of the grappling hook view of promise. The promisor transfers an exclusionary mandate to the promisee, who holds it for as long as he assents to it. Tom is the sort of fellow who sees promising as a way to commit oneself forever. He believes that by having Maggie swear on a Bible never to see Philip again, he will effect the complete and final dissolution of their betrothal. Such promises and the intentional approach itself ignore the ways in which human desires and the surprises of life intrude and make a mockery of our best intentions. There are rare occasions when the fear of the loss of honor associated with breaking a promise holds us to our word, but there are a great many more occasions when there are good reasons to break a promise, even without the promisee's permission, and there are even occasions when it would be a mistake to honor a promise. The grappling hook approach to promise succeeds only by cutting off the possibilities and potentialities of our wonderfully uncertain human lives. By freezing our future, it denies our human capacity to make practical judgments and to be responsible to others for our choices and decisions. It secures our future but destroys our freedom.

Along these same lines, the intentional approach to promise gives the promisee the greater say in determining when a promise is made or broken. But why should a promisee have any stronger claim or certainty to a future that for all of us remains unclear and uncertain? Why should a promisee be given a right to a future that is more certain than the future is generally? The same may be said of the expectations of promisees. It seems artificial to try to make the future more reliable by making it conform to the promisee's right to expect a certain future. Like the rest of us, the promisee must be prepared for a future that is not to her liking. She may blame the promisor for failing to keep the promise, and she may be correct in doing so, but she clearly has no right to a certain future. It is pure foolishness on the part of a promisee to think that mere words and commitment from a promisor give her a right to the future or can guarantee a future to her liking.

To take an example, you may intend to get up early tomorrow and go for a bike ride while the sun rises. This intended future, as with all futures, is precarious: you may change your mind in the early hours of the morning; it may be raining furiously; or your child may awaken an hour earlier than he usually does. In each case you do not go for the bike ride because events have altered the future/present. In the first case you change your mind, so your intentions change. In the second case nature intrudes, making the ride difficult or impossible to take. But your child's crying seems different. He always sleeps until seven, and your intention to take a bike ride is dependent upon your expectation that he will sleep until seven today. Why is he crying and ruining your ride? He appears to be breaking an implicit promise he has made to you. His crying upsets you more than your change of intention or the rain, and yet each cancels the ride. You may become more frustrated with this version of the alteration of the future, but in many ways it is identical to the first two. The future—and your actions in it—is altered in many ways: you alter it, events alter it, and other people alter it.

Like the bike rider, a promisee may change his mind and waive the promisor's obligation; the weather or other natural events may interfere with the performance of the promise; or the promisor may decide not to honor the promise any longer. Unlike your child, the promisor has consciously decided to break her promise, but from the promisee's perspective little else has changed. In each case the promisee's future has changed. In the first instance, he has changed it; in the latter two instances, it has been changed for him. We might say that this is often how life is and that it would be better if it were not this way; but this does not change our tender grip on the future or necessarily warrant an account of promise that holds us down against the current.

Another way in which this approach gives the promisee too much power is that it gives her the sole power to waive a promise. Is there no reciprocal obligation—however weak— that a promisee incurs when she accepts a promise? Most accounts of promising focus on the obligation incurred by the promisor but fail to discuss the degree to which the promisee incurs an obligation by accepting a unilateral promise. The social practice of promise is a relational practice, and the expectations and obligations of a promise are, in many cases, bidirectional. Imagine if, after much thought, Louise and her spouse decide to pass up their Vermont trip so that Russ can visit. Suppose also that Russ is made aware of his sister's decision to forgo a trip to Vermont. Do we really want to say that the promise is in effect only as long as Russ continues to assent to it? Russ, it is clear, has not made a promise, but it does appear that there is some moral weight on him—by virtue of his relationship to his sister—to make the visit, even if something else comes up. It would be a poor excuse if Russ said that the reason he did not show up on the stated weekend was that he had decided to waive Louise's promise. Even if the promisee announces this waiver ahead of time, it is not clear that he is always morally correct in doing so. A successful account of promise would see the commitment incurred by a promise as extending to both promisor and promisee, even with unilateral promises. To do otherwise leads to counterintuitive and possibly immoral results.

The intentional approach to promise construes the obligation of a promise as conferring upon the promisee a right to a particular future, and such a right is clearly impossible to provide. At most a promise allows him to expect a certain future. Promise does have a double-tensed indexical temporal reference, and between t_i and t_j innumerable circumstances can arise that make the promise impossible, immoral, or simply inconvenient to perform. If a right is the strongest moral claim one can possess, it seems too strong to say that one has a right to a particular future by the mere fact that one is a promisee. At most, I believe, the promisee ought to share this power with the promisor. The so-called right to the future that a promisee gains by a promise involves the promisor's future as well. To allow the promisee sole power in deciding to waive this right would seem to take away the promisor's autonomy in a way that is coercive. The promisee may, after all, be unreasonable. The promisee has some power in choosing to waive or not to waive a promise but not the sole power.

To sum up, the intentional approach fails as a theory of promise because it focuses exclusively on the will of the promisor and on the right of the promisee, without thereby explaining how the will becomes unbound or how the will of the promisor and the right of the promisee interact. It ignores the behavioral and observational conditions of promise and fails to see promising as a relational affair between two or more persons. A promise is not a bare expression of a will or a strict transference of a right. It is a relationship between promisor and promisee. The nature of this relationship—as well as the conditions of a specific promise—greatly affect how promissory obligations are created and defeated.

Intuitive Clarity and the Eye of the Beholder

The intuitional approach is clearly not a theory of promise but more like an invitation to stop theorizing. It suggests that we rely on our intuitions in guiding us through the moral life. But the question remains whether our intuitions are sufficient in getting us to see that promises generally are obligatory, that a particular promise is obligatory, or that one duty trumps another. There are at least two ways in which our intuitions can differ regarding promising. The first concerns the ordering of *prima facie* duties. As W. D. Ross maintains, some duties are clearly more important than others. Perhaps all of us share the intuition that the duty to tell the truth is more important than the duty of gratitude and therefore higher on the list of duties. It is easy to agree that there are more important duties and less important duties and to order these duties at both extremes, but the task becomes more difficult when we try to fill in the middle. To take Ross's example, how do we order the duties of benevolence and the fidelity to promising? My intuitions tell me that, in general, the duty of benevolence is greater than the duty to keep promises. I believe that many promises—though not all—are immediately defeated by the duty of the promisor to perform a good act: helping someone in need, for example. This is not how Ross sees it. He tells us that, normally, promise keeping should come before benevolence. But our different intuitions about the ranking of these duties are a perfectly legitimate case of a disagreement at the level of values. There is no reason to think that every person is in agreement regarding the ranking of moral duties or even that moral duties can be ranked. Ross downplays possible clashes of intuitions and the difficulty in resolving them. He tells us only that his intuition gives him this ranking and that the average person shares this intuition. There is no recognition that two relatively rational and moral persons might disagree about how to rank these two duties. Ross does tell us that if a person does not see that promises are obligatory, there is nothing he could do to convince that person, and he is probably right about this. But here the problem is different. Both Ross and I believe that keeping promises and acts of benevolence are duties; the disagreement comes in knowing how to rank them.

It would seem incumbent upon intuitionists either to refuse to rank our duties or to provide a method by which such a ranking could be established and conflicts resolved. The intuitional approach appears unable to do either without undermining its position. If it allows for the possibility of disagreement and provides a method for resolving such disagreements, then the knowledge of our duties is no longer intuitive. If it no longer considers the ranking of duties important, it will be unable to account for how conflicts of duty are resolved. The issue, I believe, is not really where such duties should go on a list or how this list should be arrived at, but rather how, each time we are faced with a conflict of duty, such an ordering is to be made. Ross wants to make the list out in advance, and he depends on our shared intuitions to do so. I would argue that he cannot count on large numbers of people to share his intuitions and that, in any case, a ranking of duties cannot be made out in advance of situations where such duties are required.

Intuitions may likewise clash at the level of individual promises. Even if all the members of a community share the intuition that promises are obligatory, intuitions are likely to differ over what this obligation entails. One community member might understand promissory obligation to be very serious indeed. He might have been taught that broken promises lead to ruin and despair. Another community member might have the intuition that the obligations of promises are, in general, pretty weak. She considers the frequent breaking of promises by religious leaders, politicians, businesspeople, lawyers, physicians, spouses, and so forth to be a fact of modern life. She believes that one cannot make it to the top unless one is prepared to break promises consistently; that truth telling, playing fairly, and promise keeping are for losers. How would Ross resolve this clash of intuitions? It is not a matter of indifference that people learn about promising and obligation in different ways. Our intuitions about promise are shaped by the community and time period in which we live. Even Ross's England was not so homogeneous as to lead one to conclude that everyone who is English understands the duty of fidelity to promises in the same way. Intuitionists give us no way of resolving these conflicts of intuitions other than to point to the high road of their own intuitions.

Conflicts of duty are likewise a problem for intuitionists. Steve clearly has a conflict of duty. He has made a promise to his sister and nephew as well as a promise to his wife. It appears that he must either give up his wife and daughter or send his nephew away, thereby breaking his promise to his sister. No mere review of his intuitions is likely to generate a solution here. Cases such as these put our intuitions into serious gridlock. But it is not just the seriousness of this conflict that causes problems here. Even relatively simple promises can create unintended conflicts whose solutions are not easily gained by a moment's reflection on one's intuitions. It also should not always be a matter of the promisor consulting her intuitions. A promisor's decision to keep or to break a promise may adversely affect the promisee, and it would seem appropriate that the promisee not merely be informed that the promisor has decided to break a promise but be part of the decision-making process. Such consultations are not always possible, but the emphasis Ross gives to the promisor's intuitions for resolving conflicts of duty all but ignores the relationship set up between promisor and promisee and what this relationship requires in the form of open and honest dialogue. It is, I believe, precisely at those times when a promisor decides to break a promise that she must be prepared to confront a promisee who has very different intuitions about the promisor's conflicting duties. If we assume that neither promisor nor promisee has the inside edge on moral intuitions, then such a conflict can be resolved only by a dialogue between the two parties or by consulting a third or more parties. Such a dialogue may come to no discernible conclusion, or it may force them to reshape their intuitions, but this is precisely what such dialogues are meant to do. We cannot rely too much on our moral intuitions alone. In fact, all real moral conflicts force us out of ourselves and to distrust our intuitions. The intuitional approach, then, has us going in the wrong direction when confronting a moral conflict. It has us retreating into ourselves when we should be making our views known to the person(s) most affected by these views; and it has us listening to ourselves when we should be consulting others.

Finally, this approach to promise suggests that the duty to keep a promise is defeated only when it is trumped by an equal or greater duty; but there are other types of promissory exceptions that are not also duties. It is doubtful, for example, that I have a duty to hear Kenny Baron play the piano when he unexpectedly comes to town, though my going to hear him might count as an exception to a promise made earlier in the week. Louise does not have a duty to spend a weekend in Vermont with her spouse, though there might be good reason for her to do so. Not every important moment in our life is also a duty to be performed. Not all promises are such serious affairs that they can be broken only by serious and robust conflicts of duty. The intuitional approach to promise construes the moral life as living one's life in accordance with an intuitive ranking of duties, but even if we take Ross's account to be saying that there are indeed occasional legitimate exceptions to a promise, we still need to have some understanding of how we ought to proceed in particular cases. Our philosophical efforts should be spent demonstrating not only why the keeping of promises is obligatory but also why and when some promises cease to be obligatory. Most of us would share the intuition that promising is an important part of—perhaps even a necessary condition for—the kind of life we are living. But surely we do not believe that all promises ought to be kept unconditionally or only when they do not clash with other duties. If we do not believe this, then we need to say a great deal more about promising than simply that it is intuitively clear that promises create obligations where none existed before. Promise theorists, intuitionists included, should concentrate some of their efforts on unpacking the shared and more complex intuition that some promises are not obligatory.

Insufficient Evidence

P. S. Atiyah argues that promises merely evidence previously existing obligations and that such obligations are grounded in the promisor's benefit and the promisee's detrimental reliance. Mutual executory promises and unilateral gratuitous promises create little or no obligation on the part of the promisor. Some authors question whether a contractual account of promise is particularly useful in the moral realm. R. S. Downie, for example, argues that the jurisprudential view—as he calls it—is not radically in error but rather "is based on a specialized range and cannot be generalised to cover all cases, especially those which lie within the sphere of ethics."[1] Similarly, Stanley Cavell claims that the contractual view of promise sees all human relationships as contractual rather than personal.[2] Cavell believes that promising is more akin to commitment and urges us to reject this contractual picture of our moral form of life. It is not apparent that construing promise along strict contractual lines would give us either a theoretically correct picture of promise or one that would be best suited to our form of life. Just as we should preserve both the contractual and committal forms of relationships, so too we should preserve the contractual and committal forms of promise. Atiyah has given us an excellent account of the contractual form of promise but errs in selling it as the only form.

Although Atiyah is to be commended for his use of legal examples in informing his account of promise, the use of legal examples is unnecessarily restrictive. The law is a formal mechanism for dealing with obligations of various sorts, but it is a mistake to construe every example of a promise as founded on a legalistic interpretation of obligation. Atiyah refers to judicial decisions to support his account, but judges represent only a small portion of the population. It would be a mistake to conclude that a decision by a judge or judges represents the view of the social group. Further, a judge is not deciding her own case but a case brought to her. Indeed, it is imperative that she be neither promisor nor promisee in the case she is judging. Hence what she decides is not necessarily what she would decide if she were the promisor or the promisee. In addition, a judge is often constrained by legal precedent. A judicial decision, then, is hardly evidence representative of the social group or of how the common person would judge in individual cases. The law covers only certain types of obligations; others it leaves to various nonlegal realms. If we use as evidence for the evidentiary approach to promise only those cases lawyers take and judges hear, we are likely to get a narrow interpretation of promise. Indeed, none of the examples from Chapter One would qualify as a full-fledged promise according to the evidentiary approach. If we are interested in a theory of promise that can capture the wide range of promises available to us, we need to go well beyond the law for our examples and our analysis.

Further, Atiyah's use of the external point of view, wherein only behavior and its outcome count, creates unnecessary confusion in those instances where promises misfire and one's intentions and behaviors—or perceived intentions and behaviors—do not match up. This brings us back again to the relational aspects of promise. I suggested in Chapter Two that someone might intend and promise to meet a friend for lunch and believe that he has created in his friend a detrimental reliance. It is a weak and nearly unintelligible response on the part of the friend who does not show up for lunch to say that no promise was made because he never relied on the promise in such a way that its not being kept would be detrimental to him. A similar situation could arise where a person causes another to rely in a detrimental way on an intention he never formed. Clark's banker comes to mind here: he surely never intended for Clark to rely on his promise to get the paperwork finished by a certain date. But Clark did rely on it, and he had good reason to do so. Clark sees an intention where there isn't any and relies on it to his detriment.

Imagine another example where Daryll, through various nonexplicit verbal remarks and nonverbal cues, leads Tim to believe that he intends to spend a week with him in Cape Cod in an exclusive, intimate manner. Tim relies upon his verbal and nonverbal gestures and makes irrevocable plans. Daryll benefits from his perceived expression of intention. They go to Cape Cod, and on the second night Daryll tells Tim that he has met another man with whom he would like to spend the night. Tim is angry and tells Daryll that he has an obligation to treat this relationship and this trip to the Cape in an exclusive manner. Tim would never have agreed to the trip if Daryll had not made his intentions of exclusivity known. Tim believes Daryll to be so obligated because Tim has detrimentally relied upon his intention, and Daryll has already benefited from it. For his part, Daryll tells Tim that, in all honesty, he never intended the trip to be exclusive and would have told Tim had he so asked. It is true that Daryll has benefited from Tim's false assumption and that Tim has detrimentally relied on a nonexistent intention, but Daryll never intended to treat their relationship or the trip in an exclusive manner. No amount of argument is likely to persuade Daryll that he is obligated when he feels quite justified in claiming that he is not obligated. He might admit that he can see how Tim could construe his actions as creating an obligation and even feel bad about Tim's reliance without thereby admitting that he has an obligation. Admittedly, it is a hard case to decide, but what seems clear is that Tim's perceptions of the situation ought to count for something.

Atiyah might respond that the law often requires us to be explicit and to use exact language when expressing intentions. The law will often hold us responsible for misspeaking or unintentionally leading another person on, for example. But here, again, the law is not always helpful. There are many occasions where explicitness is undesirable or simply not possible. A great deal of human communication is nonverbal or implicit. To be explicit is often to be lacking in sensitivity or acting in bad taste. One of the reasons people are thought to promise when they do not and not thought to promise when they do is that human communication often takes place at the nonverbal level. It would be undesirable to force the explicitness of legal language onto the wide range of human communication and human relationships where it is unwelcome and unworkable.

Another response of the law when dealing with situations like that of Daryll and Tim is for a judge to consider the evidence and to decide whether the defendant is liable for the damages incurred by the plaintiff. Despite Atiyah's suggestion that the sphere of morality could work in this way, it is not a course of action that would work well outside of the law. First, there is nothing like a body of law on which a moral judge could rely; nor is there any procedure in deciding moral cases. Second, legal judges are thought to possess some expertise regarding the law. However, it is doubtful that such experts could be provided to decide moral cases. Third, having a third party render judgments—as opposed to offering advice or moral insight—would interfere in the relational character of promise. If a person mistakes my words for a promise, then we should work it out together. He expresses his anger, and I either defend my actions or apologize and try to compensate for his loss. A great deal of our everyday lives takes place at the interpersonal level. It would seem both unnecessary and undesirable to do away with this characteristic of our form of life in favor of the law, where an impartial third party renders final judgments. Fourth, and most important, a moral judge could intrude upon the life of autonomous individuals by taking away their ability to make decisions, no matter how wrong they appear to be. A crucial characteristic of our form of life is the ability of individuals to make autonomous decisions and to live with these decisions. Third-party judgments would effectively destroy this feature. This is not to say that we should not consult third parties who can help us see more clearly the details of the situation. But third parties should be like Aristotle's person of practical wisdom and not like a judge in a court of law.

Atiyah wants to see the social context as somehow expressing the will of the people, such that its judgments are the judgments desired by the social group as a whole. But when he looks at what these judgments are, he looks at legal judgments. The social group expresses itself in ways other than legal judgments. Atiyah says also that obligations can just be created, because the social group is in charge of the rules of the group. But even if we can accept the view that there are laws governing certain aspects of the social group, we can still maintain that such laws and the legislators and judges who make them do not and should not extend to all realms of our life. The social group is much richer than its legalistic aspects. If we take seriously the notion of a social group, then we should make a greater attempt to understand it. Such an attempt would go far beyond what the law tells us. Contrary to what Atiyah asserts, the data of the social group—legal cases aside—tell us that unilateral gratuitous promises create obligations. If this is correct, then a theory of promise ought to be able to tell us why such promises are thought to be obligatory. Atiyah informs us that the law does not recognize such promises, but he is too hasty in concluding that such promises are therefore not obligatory. Social groups speak with many voices. A theory of promise ought to be able to capture this plurality or at least allow these voices to maintain their integrity. The evidentiary approach does neither.

Expect the Unexpected

A pattern is beginning to emerge. In focusing on a single aspect of promise—how promises create obligations—each approach offers a single answer, usually in terms of one feature of promise. I suggest that we focus on the paradox of promise and that we see it as a social practice: as arising for a certain reason, as learned either well or badly, and as fully dependent upon the relational qualities that exist between promisor and promisee. If we set our sights on the larger question of how promise functions in our form of life, then none of the approaches outlined in Chapter Two will be satisfactory.

The expectational approach places the greatest emphasis on the expectations we form when a promise is made to us. Even if our expectations do not lead to detrimental reliance, some harm is done when our expectations are not met, and it is to avoid doing this harm that promises should be kept. One can note at least three points that this approach will have trouble addressing. The first concerns the problem of differentiating between expectations that create promissory obligations and those that do not. H. A. Prichard was quite right when he said that a promissory obligation is not generated each and every time a person's expectations are raised. How, then, does this approach distinguish between those expectations that do and those that do not create promissory obligations? We can see immediately that the answer to this question forces the expectation theorist into a dilemma. If she says, as Henry Sidgwick and Jan Narveson do, that it is important to establish at the outset that one is or is not speaking with the intention of creating an expectation in another or that one does or does not expect the speaker to do as he said he would, then informal promising would appear to drop out of the picture. Clarity about one's intention to create expectations in another is best expressed in formal ways. But if she says instead that a successful promise occurs only when the promisor expresses himself in a formal way, then it is no longer clear that raised expectations in the promisee create the obligation. If clarity of intent is achieved by using a formalized utterance, then promising becomes dependent upon—at least in part— a speech act, and this is something this approach wants to deny.

It does not seem possible for this account to claim both that promises are created by raised expectations and that such promises can occur informally. The problem caused by trying to distinguish between raised expectations for which one is obligated and those for which one is not obligated appears solvable only by doing away with the claim that promises can occur informally or by adopting a speech-act account of promise. If the expectational theorist wants to maintain her position, she will need to say more about how expectations differ and why some create promissory obligations whereas others do not. Despite Narveson's claim that there is nothing more to promising than the creation of expectations, closer examination reveals that perhaps a bit more needs to be said after all.

A second problem with this approach is that it places too great an emphasis on the promisee in determining when a promise is made. It implies that a weakly expressed intention voiced to someone who forms inordinately high expectations creates, at least *prima facie*, a stronger obligation than would a solemn promise expressed to a pessimist who rarely expects anything positive to come his way or to someone who has no interest in the promise. Does the strength and extent of a promise depend solely upon the degree of expectation formed by the promisee? If a person develops unwarrantedly high expectations, do we have a greater obligation to do as we promised? Suppose, by contrast, we have made a solemn promise to someone who is unable or unwilling to form high expectations. Is our degree of obligation diminished? Perhaps these are examples that take us out of the mainstream of promising or rely on "abnormal" people who are either naive about the future or too depressed by it. But we should not ignore that people form expectations in different ways. Even if promising does rely in part on raising expectations in the promisee, we should question an approach that explains promising solely in terms of expectations and, in so doing, gives the decision of determining the existence and strength of a promise to the promisee alone.

Third, though admitting that exceptions may occur that

outweigh the raised expectations of a promisee, neither Sidgwick nor Narveson indicates how conflicts between expectations and exceptions are to be resolved. Even if we allow that
there exist many excusing conditions to a promise, we still
need to know how to identify these conditions and, more important, how to evaluate them against the expectations that
were raised when the promise was made. There is always the
danger that the parties to a promise are unable to see the situation clearly enough to make the correct decision. But even if
they do make a decision, what are we to say if their appraisals
of the situation differ markedly—if, for example, the promisor
believes his exception outweighs the promisee's raised expectations, but the promisee does not? How are such conflicts to
be resolved? Whose appraisal should be used? Does Louise's
exception outweigh Russ's expectations? Has Clark's banker
made a promise because of Clark's high expectations? The
discussion of excusing conditions by Sidgwick and Narveson
goes a long way to dispell the notion of promising as an un-
complicated affair, but the discussion ends rather abruptly
and needs to be filled out in greater detail. Exceptions may
outweigh expectations, but the how and when, as well as a
method for resolving conflicts, need to be discussed. And even
if these problems are resolved, it is not clear that an appeal
to raised expectations alone can adequately explain promise.
Sidgwick and Narveson rightly maintain that promising is a
complex affair, and both chide other philosophers for not taking this complexity into account in discussing it. Though the
expectational approach is an improvement over other approaches in terms of its ability to capture some of this complexity, it is still limited by its focus on expectations alone.
Our understanding of promise is enhanced by the expectational approach, but we do not yet have a workable theory of
promise.

When Promising Is Just a Game

The institutional approach is, in many ways, the most serious contender to serve as a theory of promise. It purports to describe and explain the structure of promise as an institution with origins, rules, and practitioners. It is also the most influential account of promise in the literature, as evidenced by the sheer volume of response it has generated and in terms of its use to enumerate historical treatments of promise, specifically Hume's. It is for these reasons that I devote the bulk of this chapter to the institutional approach to promise and to urging readers to reject it. I argue that the institutional approach to promise fails not only because of problems stemming from its account of constitutive rules but also because it succeeds only by ignoring aspects of promise that appear essential in understanding promise. This approach devotes little attention to the question of exceptions to a promise or how such exceptions are ascertained; nor does it discuss in any detail the promisee's interest in the promise or how the terms of a promise are affected if the promisee's interest wanes. This approach claims that promising gets its force by being a performative speech act, but it ignores the problems caused by promises whose language is not precise or by overanxious promisees who mishear a speech act. Even if a successful speech act does create an obligation for the promisor, this account does not address the problems caused by conflicts of obligation.

This section has two parts. The first part develops in greater detail two arguments sketched in Chapter Two. I first argue that constitutive rules presuppose some understanding of the behavior they define and therefore are not fully constitutive. Second, I argue that the notion of constitutive rules being learned unconsciously is incoherent. I claim that it is a mis-

take for John Searle to assume that some forms of human behavior can be explained only by reference to the ability to
follow rules. The second part focuses on rules. I develop arguments showing how the rules of promise differ from game rules.

The Promising Game

The phrase "the promising game" was first used by R. M.
Hare in an article by the same name.[3] Hare's criticism can be
phrased in the following way: either the promising game presupposes an obligation or commitment to the game itself, and
hence the obligation of a promise is not defined by its constitutive rules alone, or, like any other game, one can choose to
play or quit promise at any time. Put another way, the promising game presupposes an obligation to play the game, and
this obligation can only come from outside the game. Searle
claims that he is not interested in questions external to the
institution, but in important ways the question of commitment to the institution is not an external question. Most
critics urge that the way out of this difficulty is to accept the
view that promising is, in important ways, not like a game.
Mary Midgley carries the argument further by claiming that
there is, at most, a family resemblance between games and
that nothing as simple as the notion of constitutive rules will
capture this resemblance.[4] Games and institutions presuppose
commitments to them that cannot be defined by rules; or,
more generally, games and institutions presuppose a form of
life that makes them both necessary and possible. No set of
rules can create a form of life, and hence constitutive rules
constitute only partially.

John Rawls claims that social institutions are created by
constitutive rules and that it is possible to imagine a hypothetical situation in which rational members of a community
choose their social institutions by applying the principle of

fairness to the constitutive rules of these institutions. Searle argues that it is possible to generate the constitutive rules of any institution by first generating the necessary and sufficient conditions for the institution and then extracting the constitutive rules from these conditions. Searle says further that these constitutive rules will cover such aspects as commitment and fair play. The success of these arguments depends on presupposing the conditions that make these institutions and their rules possible, conditions that both Rawls and Searle think rule-governed institutions create. Such a presupposition, however, is not open to either proponent of the institutional approach. I begin with Rawls.

Rawls admits that not all institutions are created by constitutive rules when he says that it is possible to conceive of some as arising *de novo*. Assuming that he is correct about this, what does it mean to say that some institutions arise afresh or for the first time? And what does the answer to this question tell us about the nature of institutions that are created out of constitutive rules? So as not to beg the question in any way, I use an example of a *de novo* practice that does not resemble either a game like baseball or a practice like promising. I use for my example the *de novo* practice of waving.[5] Waving is an activity one often sees at American sporting events. Describing it is not easy, though on observing it you see immediately why it is called waving. It can be described in the following way. Place the seating section of any large sports arena onto a Cartesian (x,y) coordinate system. The vertical seats are on the x-axis and the horizontal seats are on the y-axis. Assume also that the $(1,1)$ point occurs at the far edge of the seating section (where the section begins or ends). A wave occurs when, nearly simultaneously and usually with the help of a cue of some kind, all those sitting along the x-axis at $(x=1)$ stand and sit rapidly, followed immediately by all those along the x-axis at $(x = 2)$ standing and sitting rapidly, and so on down the seating section (or the x-axis). When done well, this motion creates the visual effect of a human wave flowing across the seating section.

How did this practice arise and why? It is unlikely that anything as cryptic as my description could have been written on fliers and distributed to the spectators who created this practice. No set of rules is likely to create waving *de novo*. What is more feasible is that a small group of people (perhaps a college cheering section) started waving spontaneously or perhaps were encouraged by someone in their midst, who got the idea. But there is still the problem of communicating this idea to the thousands of people in the stands whose cooperation is necessary for the success of a wave. (It is an interesting feature of waving that you cannot see the wave-effect you are helping to create.) How would a person in the middle of a seating section know that some college students have started standing and sitting rapidly, hoping to create a human wave? How do the original wavers get the attention of thousands of fans watching the game, and how do they motivate them to participate in this activity? Simply put, how do the fans learn what to do if there are no rules to define waving or how to participate in one?

Waving is made possible not because there is a set of constitutive rules to define it but because it is causally dependent on certain shared features of its participants; that is, the activity of waving presupposes common features of those who wave. What are some of these features? First, the participants must be capable of participating in group activity. Second, they must possess observation skills, motor skills, and a rudimentary sense of rhythm (you will never get a wave going if too many people are not able to time correctly when they should stand and sit). Third, participants must be able to recognize and share a common goal, and this requires a level of cooperation and trust. Other features might include being impulsive, fun-loving, bored with the game on the field, and a casual fan (an enthusiast of the game is too involved in it to be distracted). Finally, for a wave to be successful, its creation must not go against the values or cultural norms of its participants. If it is the case, for example, that spectators at a bullfight are always careful not to distract the matador and that this sort of behavior is expected of them, then it would be unlikely that a wave would ever get started during a bullfight attended by natives of the culture.

If waving were to become a fixture at sporting events and hence an institution or practice, it would be possible to generate some rules that described it and instructed people how to engage in it. But these rules would not be constitutive rules in the sense implied by Rawls and Searle. These rules would not create a new form of behavior; they would simply describe what initially arose spontaneously and now occurs frequently. Likewise, it would be possible to generate some advisory rules to tell us when we ought or ought not to wave (e.g., "It is bad taste to wave during the playing of the national anthem or while an injured opposing player is taken from the field"). But such rules do not define or create the condition of acting in good or bad taste. If we accept that certain features of human life necessarily precede both *de novo* and constitutively ruled institutions, we can begin to see how these institutions would and could arise. As Hume says, because of certain features of human nature (selfishness, confined generosity, creativity) and the natural conditions of scarcity, certain artificial institutions such as property and promise arise spontaneously and quickly, much like the practice of waving. How the details of these institutions are filled out will depend on local variations, but the institutions themselves are going to arise in one form or another in almost all cultures that share a common form of life.

We begin to see also what it is and is not that those in the original position choose when they choose their institutions, either those defined by constitutive rules or those *de novo* institutions that can be chosen as if they had constitutive rules. The social institutions chosen in Rawls's original position presuppose the basic form of life that creates both the necessity and the possibility for such institutions. One's ability to cooperate with another in arriving at the principles of fairness in the original position is not dependent on a constitutive rule in the same way as my ability to strike out a batter does. That members of a community are gathered together in the original position to debate and choose their common institutions presupposes some ability to cooperate. It would seem unlikely that they could discuss whether to accept the social institution of cooperation in the same way that they might discuss whether a batter should get three or four strikes, and this is because the former discussion already presupposes a level of cooperation. They might create some constitutive rules that define what does and does not count as cooperation during their meetings in the original position, but these rules would not and could not define or create cooperation. Cooperation could not be defined by rules, because the creation, promulgation, and acceptance of constitutive rules depend upon cooperation.

Constitutive rules might create games or moves in a game that did not exist prior to the rules, but they could never create the context in which the purpose of the game could be understood. Likewise, what constitutes an institution is the form of life underlying it, not the rules defining it. The structure of our form of life might change because of evolutionary changes or dramatic changes in climate or social conditions, but we cannot rearrange it in any conscious way. To paraphrase Hume, changing the structure of our form of life or creating one anew is as difficult as rearranging the stars in the sky. Hence rule-governed institutions chosen in the original position are not different from *de novo* institutions. Both share and presuppose basic features of our form of life that cannot be defined or created by rules. Those in the original position do not choose the constitutive rules that create their social institutions. To the contrary, many of these social institutions preexist the original position and make it possible for members of the original position to come together in the first place.

What is left for those in the original position to do is to debate and choose variations or formalized versions of these institutions and to use constitutive rules to create these variations and versions. Hence the institution of punishment would presuppose a form of life that included the concepts punishment, justice, and fairness, but a particular community could decide the specific parameters of its institution of punishment, including the creation of rules or laws outlining the types of offenses that would be punished, how the conviction process would work, and the nature and duration of the punishment. But the success of these rules in regulating behavior and defining types of punishment presupposes the community's understanding of the concepts of punishment, justice, and fairness. The case is similar for promising. The form of life that makes possible the activity of promising would preexist, exist alongside, and exist long after any rule-constituted institution of promising. Rules do have a function in shaping social institutions, but this function does not come at the beginning. Constitutive rules do define certain actions within social institutions, but they do not define the form of life presupposed by these institutions. Constitutive rules, then, have a limited function in defining and regulating social institutions.

We turn now to arguments against Searle's method of extracting constitutive rules from necessary and sufficient conditions and his claim that constitutive rules can be known unconsciously. Searle claims that what we do in generating the rules of promising is what someone does who has learned to play the game of chess without ever having the rules formulated and who now wants to formulate these rules. Like the chess player, we extract the necessary and sufficient conditions and then formulate the rules that follow from these conditions. I argue that such a chess player could not exist (or could not play chess) and that the rules of chess could not ever be formulated in the way Searle describes unless certain features of the game existed prior to the rules.

For Searle, game rules define not only the pieces of the game (knight, rook, etc.) and the moves of the game (castling, checkmate, etc.) but also the motivations one brings to the game (competitiveness, fair play, etc.). We must now ask what it means to say that a person can play chess without ever having any of these rules formulated. By "formulated" I take it that Searle means that this person is playing chess without ever having someone tell her or without yet having told herself, "This is a rook and it can only move in such and such a way," or, "Checkmate occurs when a player is unable to move his king safely," or, "Chess is a competitive game and one plays it by trying to checkmate one's opponent." Searle's chess player has never seen a game of chess played and knows nothing about it. She would have to learn all of the aspects of the game by observing the game of chess. She could not learn by playing, since all beginners are told the rules along the way and ask questions while playing, the answers to which are formulated in terms of the rules of the game.

Let us assume that our chess player is a careful observer of the game: she listens to what the players say, and she watches how they move the pieces. But because constitutive rules define so much of what is basic to the game, our observer must start at the beginning. She must discover that what she is watching is a *game* called *chess*, that this game is *played* with two people, and that each *player* wants to *beat* the other by *checkmating* her *opponent's king*. She must also observe that while the players are competing with each other, they are also *cooperating* and playing *fairly*. She may also observe signs of *nervousness*, such as sweating or hair pulling, and signs of *confidence*, such as a smile or exaggerated physical movement when moving a piece. She must be a very good observer indeed, since she must be able to discern that cooperation, fair play, and competition are necessarily part of the game, whereas hair pulling and smiling are not. She would have to learn all of these concepts even before beginning to learn what the pieces are called, how they are to be moved, and the myriad strategies of the game.

We are apt to ask how this observer could discern that chess is a competitive game unless she already possesses the concepts *game* and *competition*. How would she be able to recognize the importance of cooperation when two people are playing a game, unless she already knows what cooperation is? Even if we assume that our observer figures out how the pieces are moved and how the game is played, would she be able to recognize instances of fair and unfair play, unless she already understood what fair play is? What is our observer doing there in the first place? She is observing the game of chess with the hopes of discerning and formulating its rules. Whether she is a cultural anthropologist or someone who wants to learn the game, her interest in formulating the rules reflects her interest in chess. Since she has an interest in formulating the rules of chess, she must already know something about chess; in fact, she must already know a great deal about it. If our observer does not bring a number of presuppositions to her observation of the game of chess, it is not clear that she will observe much of anything. She will not be able to make sense out of what she sees. She might be able to give a brute description of what she sees, but such a description will tell her nothing interesting about the game; nor will it bring her any closer to discerning the rules of chess. If she is to have any chance of formulating the rules of chess through her observations, she must already know something—a great deal—about the form of life that underlies the game.

Suppose we cheat a bit and allow our observer to ask a question, and she asks, "What is the purpose of chess?" We could tell her that the purpose of chess is to beat the other player, to win, to compete, to checkmate the opponent's king, or to relax. How are we to respond if our observer registers no understanding of the concepts *win, compete, beat,* and so forth? Providing the observer with constitutive rules is unlikely to help her to understand these concepts. The rules will be expressed as tautological definitions, and unless she already understands the meaning of the subject terms and predicate terms, she will be unable to understand the rules.

Fortunately, our observer is not likely to need an explanation of game, cooperation, fair play, or competitiveness because she already has an understanding of these concepts. It is her understanding of these concepts that allows her to express an interest in formulating the rules of chess in the first place. These underlying concepts can be expressed as our common form of life, which we bring to the specific games we play. Searle, then, is blocked from using constitutive rules to define such concepts as fair play and competitiveness. These concepts must be presupposed in any game. They are the concepts we bring to games, not the concepts defined by games. If someone does not already possess them, it is unlikely that she will ever figure out what is going on, no matter how good her observation skills are. Someone who does not share our basic concepts, our enabling practices, our forms of life, will either stare confusedly at a chess game or not see the game going on in front of her. There can be no chess player interested in formulating the rules of chess who does not already know in a formulatable way some of the rules that make both chess and her interest in the game possible. Searle underestimates the complexity of observation necessary to facilitate his conception of constitutive rules as rules extractable from the necessary and sufficient conditions of a game or institution. As my argument demonstrates, when the complexity is reintroduced, this method of generating constitutive rules is shown to be untenable. Searle's objective observer masquerades as an outsider, but she is a longtime member of the community. She pretends to extract rules from observed behavior, but the rules and behavior have long been a part of her life. She is a fraud.

Searle also claims that constitutive rules must be known subconsciously if we are to explain adequately aspects of human behavior. In formulating a rule of phonetics, Searle claims that he has formulated a constitutive rule and not a mere regularity. Further, Searle asserts that although this rule has some exceptions, it is nonetheless a good rule and one that the speaker of a language necessarily follows when speaking phonemically. A speaker of the language is understood by other speakers of the language because he is subconsciously following a constitutive rule of pronunciation. Even though the person is unable to formulate this rather complex rule, it is because he knows the rule subconsciously that he is able to speak correctly and to convey meaning with his speech. I assert that, in his analogy with game rules, it is neither possible nor necessary to know rules unconsciously.

This rule of pronunciation is considered by Searle to be a constitutive rule and similar to the rules of baseball and promising. But we can point out an important difference: though Searle claims that one can speak phonemically without consciously knowing the rules of phonetics, one cannot play a game without consciously knowing its rules or without being able to articulate them. You cannot play baseball unless you know the rules, and you cannot know the rules unless you can articulate them in some way. In learning to play a game you must ask questions, the answers to which form the rules of the game. You then are able to articulate these rules, if only to yourself and imprecisely.

Suppose that we have an exchange student visiting us for the summer who has never seen the game of baseball or anything resembling baseball (cricket, for example). As an experiment in applied philosophy, we tell him to spend some time watching us play baseball. When he thinks he knows how to play, he can join us. Now, even if he is able to figure out what is happening on the playing field in this way and decides to join us, he will still have to formulate what he is going to do on the field in the form of crude rules: for example, "If I manage to hit the round object with my stick I will run toward the white bag to my right, rather than toward the other bags on the field." He will have formulated this rule after having seen that no one has ever run to any other bag after hitting the round thing. But he is not going to internalize this feature of baseball subconsciously; he is not just going to start doing it on his own. He generates for himself a rule, however crude, and is able to articulate it. Only later is he given the actual rules of the game. Whatever he knows about baseball he knows because he has observed games of baseball being played. He is able to play because he has formulated rules for himself, rules of which he is consciously aware though they may be known only to him. It is only after someone becomes an expert at a game—because he knows the rules so well—that following the rules becomes subconscious. It is not possible to play a game for the first or second time without knowing its rule in a conscious way.

Game purists might argue that our foreign friend is not actually playing baseball until he is told the rules of the game. The rules he generates on his own are more like brute descriptions of the activities on the field than like rules per se. He will not be playing baseball until he knows the rules that define "batter," "base," "hit," "strike," and so forth. If this is correct, then the example only shows the difficulty in accepting a view that claims that one can know subconsciously the rules of a game. Even someone who has spent a lifetime observing the game of baseball—but who was unable to ask questions, to refer to its rule book, or to understand the form of life in which the game takes place—will experience difficulty in generating a list of rules that matches the actual list of constitutive rules. Even if his actions are perfectly imitative of the actions of those who play baseball—and this is unlikely—we can still claim that he is not playing baseball, and this is because he cannot articulate why he is doing what he is doing: why he hits the ball, why he runs to the bag, and so forth. You cannot be said to be playing a game unless you can articulate in some detail what it is you are doing and why; and you cannot know what you are doing and why unless you know, in a conscious way, and can articulate the rules of the game.

That we can learn to speak phonemically without knowing consciously the rules of phonetics but cannot learn to play baseball without knowing consciously its rules is because, I

CHAPTER THREE

submit, the phonemic aspect of language is not defined or constituted by rules. We learn to speak phonemically long before we can articulate phonemic rules. This can be seen in two ways. First, there are exceptions to phonemic rules, instances that do not conform to the rules. This means that there will be occasions when speaking phonemically requires that one not follow the rules. (There are seldom any additional rules to cover these special cases.) In learning a new language, one is usually made aware of the exceptions to the rules and told to memorize them. Game rules, however, do not work in this way. Exceptions never stand outside of the rules but are always carefully defined by the rules. Second, young children appear to learn the alphabet, how to read, and how to speak phonemically by repetition and imitation. They do not begin to learn formal phonemic rules until they are in elementary school. In school they learn the parts of speech and how they function; they diagram sentences and learn the rules of pronunciation. Some of this is pretty complicated business, and some do better than others in learning it all. But one thing is certain: even the dullards in English class can give you a tongue-lashing on the playground, create limericks, or curse a creative blue streak. They can do this not because they subconsciously know the rules of phonetics and grammar that others do not but because they are especially creative or because they live with adults who curse or who are verbally abusive. The most diligent teacher will sometimes fail to overcome with the rules of phonetics and grammar a local accent or ungrammatical speech learned and reinforced at home. The patterns of pronunciation learned at home and in daily life often outlive and override the rules of pronunciation learned at school.

I suspect that many young children experience a certain incongruity between those torturous moments diagramming sentences at the chalkboard and the times spent making funny sounds or rhymes, making up jokes, or talking to their parents. Language is a creative instrument in the mouths of children, and it seems incomprehensible that their ability to use language depends on their subconscious knowledge of the rules of phonetics and grammar, which they come to learn only later and in a most incomplete way. Children learn language the way some people pick out tunes: with good ears. When we do correct their mistakes, it is rarely by giving them the rule from which their speech deviated. Instead, we give them the correct pronunciation, the correct noun–verb agreement, or a version, without the slang, of what they just said. They often repeat what we say and then go on with what they are saying. Sometimes the corrections hold and sometimes they do not. My son has got it into his head that the past tense of "bring" is "brang." It is a good guess, but wrong. My wife and I correct him at least ten times a day. We do not give him any rules, nor does he—to my knowledge—formulate any. He says "brang," we say "brought," and that is the end of it. We sometimes make up little games, or he intentionally says it wrong and gets a good laugh from our our reaction. Our hope is that, by brute force of habit, the correct usage will become second nature: from habit to virtue, as Aristotle says. Children grow into adults without having learned a great many rules of grammar and pronunciation and having forgotten some they did learn, though they often manage to write grammatically and speak phonemically.

Phonemic rules, I submit, are most unlike the rules of games. Knowing the rules of a game is crucial in being able to engage in it. At most, phonemic rules pick out the phonetic from the unphonetic, the educated from the uneducated, the resident from the foreigner. These rules do not create or constitute pronunciation; they merely regulate, describe, and ex-

CHAPTER THREE

plain it. The crucial difference is that one cannot play a game without consciously knowing the rules, whereas one can speak phonemically without consciously knowing the rules; and this can be explained by postulating that the rules of formalized games are constitutive, whereas phonemic rules are not.

How, then, do we learn proper pronunciation, if there are no constitutive rules underlying it? I cannot address this question here, but it is plausible to drop Searle's assumption that we can explain some forms of human behavior only by appealing to the notion of constitutive rules known subconsciously. We can begin by observing that it is simply the case that we are able to learn and speak phonemically without having to learn or know any constitutive rules. What needs explaining is how this is possible. This is not to deny that some conception of rules will be necessary to explain how we learn to speak phonemically, but it is not necessary to assume that these rules are constitutive rules. They may be behavioral rules or psychological rules, which govern the operation of the human brain. But such rules do not create meanings or pronunciations. People create words and pronunciations, and they formulate rules to describe what it is they are doing when they speak phonemically. These rules, I submit, are not constitutive in nature but rather are rulelike formulations. They do not create meanings or activities. They do not define the form of life that allows us to speak phonemically. Rather, the features of our form of life are what enable us to speak phonemically, to play games, and to participate in social institutions that lack constitutive rules. We participate in such institutions when we perform the wave at a sporting event for the first time, when we go on a date, when we make tea the way the British do, or—as I argue in Chapters Four and Five—when we make promises.

The institutional approach to promise makes presuppositions that it cannot explain and raises external questions that it cannot answer. Constitutive rules constitute only partially, and the comparison of social institutions with games fails both because of important disanalogies and because both Rawls and Searle underestimate the complexity of games and game rules. In one way Searle is right to want to ignore external questions and certain disanalogies between games and social institutions. Any attempt to address these issues will cause the collapse of the institutional approach, either because the approach will fail to address these issues adequately or because it will be shown to be unnecessary in explaining complex social behavior. These results can be avoided, I submit, only by scrapping the assumption that the only way to understand how people create and participate in social practices is by reference to rule-constituted institutions.

Rules, Rules, Rules

I continue my evaluation of the institutional approach to promising by arguing that constitutive rules, though they may be used to understand how some games function, are not clearly defined, are not clearly demarcated from other sorts of rules, and, most important, will not work when applied to social institutions. It is a mistake to identify the rule(s) of promising with game rules.[6] As I mentioned in Chapter Two, Rawls is unclear whether the practice of promising is governed by a single rule or by rules. I demonstrate that either conception is untenable. I then develop a series of arguments against the view held by both Searle and Rawls that exceptions to a promise can be covered by a rule, albeit an imprecise one. I argue that there are too many disanalogies between a game rule and an exceptions rule; that an exceptions rule could not be a constitutive rule; and that the nature of promissory exceptions is such that no rule could ever capture it.

Rawls speaks both of the rule of promising and of the rules of promising, so we should examine the plausibility of both views. Assume, first, that promising is an institution defined by rules. According to Rawls, two important aspects of institutional rules are that they are constitutive rules and that they are public rules. But he also claims that the rules of promising are not codified the way that game rules or institutional rules are codified and that one's conception of the nature and extent of these rules depends on one's moral training. It is difficult to see how institutional rules could be public rules if they were not codified in some way, because what allows us to participate in games is that, in most cases, the rules are written down or agreed to beforehand. What allows people to play a game is their shared conception of it. If there is a dispute, it can be resolved by referring to the rules. How does the institution of promising function if its rules, though apparently public, are not codified? If there is some commonality among the rules individuals learn regarding the institution of promising, then there is a strong reason to suppose that this commonality depends on some sort of codification and dissemination of the code among the members of the community, perhaps along the lines of religious or legal laws. It would be unlikely that everyone would learn exactly the same rules in the privacy of their homes, if what they are supposedly learning are the constitutive rules of promising. If we share common rules, then they must somehow be public, and this implies some degree of codification.

Second, if we grant that one's conception of the nature and extent of the institutional rules of promising depends upon one's moral training, how then could these rules be constitutive? If constitutive rules define or create behavior, then their wording will be important, since a slightly different rule will produce different behavior. What would happen, for example, if the strikeout rule in baseball were defined roughly as a specifiable number and type of swings, but the actual specification was left open for interpretation among individual members of the baseball-playing community? We could imagine the large number of varying interpretations (and rules) coming out of this open-endedness. One thing would be certain: the diversity of rules that would come out of this allowance for interpretation would cease to make the strikeout rule a constitutive rule under any meaningful interpretation. One of the points of a constitutive rule is to create unambiguous behavior and to close off interpretation. If there is to be interpretation, it, too, should be governed by a constitutive rule or rules.

We can see what would happen to one's conception of the rules of promising if one's upbringing were under the influence of Aristotle, Immanuel Kant, Jeremy Bentham, the Ten Commandments, the teachings of Christ, or an anarchist. It is not at all clear that the rules one receives will be similar in any sufficient detail between any two of these conceptions. What is true, however, is that among the many different conceptions of promising that exist, people of different religious, philosophical, and ideological persuasions still manage to make and keep promises to one another, though not always smoothly. What this suggests is that, in many respects, the moral life is not at all like playing the game of baseball. For one thing, it appears that baseball cannot be played without common, public rules, whereas promising can be "played" quite easily without such rules or without any rules at all. I suggest that Rawls cannot have it both ways. If one learns the rules of promise in one's moral training, then the rules will be neither constitutive nor necessarily public. If the rules of promise are public rules, then they may be constitutive, but they must be codified in such a way that there will be strict uniformity in the moral training of members of a community.

We are no better off if we conceive of the institution of promising as being made up of a single rule. Rawls gives the following version of such a rule: "If one says the words 'I promise to do X' in the appropriate circumstances, one is to do X, unless certain excusing conditions obtain."[7] Such a rule, I maintain, is too sparse to function as a rule we could teach to someone engaged in moral training. It does not tell the person what is meant by "promise," "excusing conditions," "appropriate circumstances," or even "rule." Even if we did tell her what these concepts mean, we have still taught her little. We have told her that she should keep a promise unless circumstances arise such that she does not have to keep it. She would rightly ask us, "And what sorts of circumstances are these, and what rules am I to use?" Our answer ("Well, that all depends") would indicate just how little we have taught her about promising by citing this rule and just how little this rule tells anyone about the institution of promise. It would make a mockery of the claim that we could teach a newcomer about promising by teaching her a single rule. The rule that Rawls provides tells us almost nothing except—if we are paying close attention—that social institutions are not governed by solitary rules. His conception of the rule of promising is actually akin to a rule about how one should participate in the institution of promising. The rule "keep your promises" is similar to a rule in baseball, such as "always try your best" or "always run your hardest to first base" or "keep your eye on the ball." These are rules that tell us not how to play baseball but how to play the game well. Likewise, Rawls's rule of promising tells us how to be a good promisor but leaves it for the newcomer to figure out how she is supposed to do this. If this rule tells us how to excel in the institution of promise, then it is not a constitutive rule. But then, no single rule alone is likely to be constitutive of any game or institution.

We find further problems when we turn to the rule governing exceptions to a promise. Although Rawls claims in *A Theory of Justice* that both the circumstances giving rise to a promise and the excusing conditions must be defined, he nowhere tries to define the excusing conditions. Searle, by contrast, inserts *ceteris paribus* clauses and claims that the boundaries of promising are necessarily loose. But in *Speech Acts*, Searle does away with the clauses altogether. Both Rawls and Searle, then, have claimed that there is a rule of promising (or a set of necessary and sufficient conditions) covering promissory exceptions, though neither attempts to generate such a rule or the conditions.

If we were to generate such a rule in the institution of promising, we would see that it would be different from the rules governing exceptions in games and social institutions. It is an important feature of games that exceptions are covered by rules. So, for example, in baseball a pop fly in fair territory is a live ball and must be caught for an out, unless there is a man on first base and the ball is hit in the vicinity of the infield between first and second base. If, at this time, the umpire invokes the "infield fly rule," the batter is automatically out whether the ball is caught or not, and the runner on first base may advance at his own risk. This rule is designed to guard against an infielder intentionally dropping the ball and getting two outs instead of one. Similar defeating conditions are listed in some legal documents as well. Purchase agreements can have a clause listing the contingencies that, if they arise, render the contract null and void; the seller and buyer can each list their own contingencies. But there is nothing even remotely like this in the case of promising. There are no rules governing the defeating conditions of promising, other than the rule stating that such conditions exist. There is not even a rule to the effect that "such conditions will be determined by the promisor and promisee prior to the promise." There is simply the rule, if it is a rule at all, stating that there are defeating conditions to a promise and that these conditions are complicated, a bit loose, and so forth. Of course, if we say that it is part of the nature of the institution of promising not to have rules that cover all or even some of the defeating conditions to a promise, then we have pointed out how promising is very much unlike games or certain legal institutions.[8]

In *Speech Acts*, Searle avoids the problem of promissory exceptions by constructing an idealized model of promising, in which he claims that the defeasibility conditions of promising are "considerations outside the act of promising" and "irrelevant to our present concern." A problem arises if we try to use Searle's idealized case to teach a newcomer about the institution of promising. What would she be able to learn about promising by referring to Searle's constitutive rules of the institution of promising? She would learn that promising (uttering the words "I promise") predicates some future act that is preferred by the promisee; that a promise is uttered only if it is not obvious that the promisor will do what she has promised to do; that the promisor intends to do what she promised; and that by promising the promisor has undertaken an obligation. This is all vital information, but in learning these rules the newcomer surely is left in the dark about an important aspect of promising: namely, that there may arise conditions subsequent to the promise where the performance of the promise becomes impossible or unnecessary. These conditions may even create a situation where the promisor has an obligation not to perform her promise. This is important information if the newcomer is to have any hope of being successful at promising. Granted, she does not need to know this information to make a promise (and perhaps this is all Searle is trying to show), but she does need this information if she is to be a successful promisor.

What are we to say when the newcomer comes to us and complains that this institution of promising sure is tough going or that someone else told her that she was crazy to have kept that particular promise? We are likely to tell her that, of course, there will be times when a promise will be defeated by certain unspecifiable conditions or when a conflicting obligation will override the obligation of a promise. "But why," she will ask us, "didn't you tell me this when you gave me the rules?" Here Searle's answer that the defeasibility conditions are irrelevant in abstracting the rules of promising will ring hollow. If we tell our angry and confused newcomer that the defeasibility conditions of promising are too complicated to be covered by precise rules, she is likely to criticize our effort to use rules in the first place to teach her and others about an institution that, in obviously important ways, is not fully captured by such rules. In teaching someone about promising, we cannot fail to mention defeating conditions. As a future-referring institution, it is important to make some reference to conditions in the future that will annul a promise or, stronger still, create an obligation on the promisor not to perform her stated promise.

If Searle insists on using an idealized case of promising, devoid of any mention of excusing conditions, then we can insist that he is no longer talking about promising, either in its strict institutional form or in the loose way that ordinary people refer to it. No list of necessary or sufficient conditions or the rules that follow from these conditions will ever be complete if they exclude mention of excusing conditions. This is not to say that an idealized case is a logically impossible conception of promising. It says only that such an idealized picture of promise does not reflect what we do in our form of life when promising.[9]

Even if there existed a rule governing exceptions, it could not be a constitutive rule. This is because the existence of exceptions to a promise is a preexisting feature of the practice of promise and hence presupposed by any constitutive rules. If we assume that the institution of promising is possible only if one presupposes certain features of our form of life that are not defined or created by rules, then the institution of promising as a system of rules was subsequent to a primitive or non-ruled practice of promising and not constitutive of it. If our form of life contains all of the features that make promising a possible institution, then there is no reason to believe that the institution must wait upon rules. Given the right conditions, promising will spring up on its own. A descriptive feature of our form of life and, therefore, of this primitive practice of promise is that there will arise situations when a promise cannot and should not be carried out. One of the reasons people make promises to one another is that they have little idea of the future that lies ahead. It is because we do not know what will befall us as promisor or promisee that promises will sometimes be defeated by conditions outside of our control. This is simply what it is to make a promise in our form of life. It does not seem feasible, then, that any exceptions rule that might function in the institution of promising could function as a constitutive rule. No constitutive rule could define this feature of promise; nor would it be necessary to do so. The fact that promising is an institution characterized by exceptions that defeat individual promises is embedded in our form of life, and this form of life precedes any rules that state this fact. Hence whatever rules regarding exceptions that Rawls and Searle refer to are not constitutive rules.

As a final argument, I maintain that the inadequate treatment of rule-governing exceptions is indicative of the failure of the institutional approach. The problem of exceptions (What counts as one? Who decides? What happens when there is a disagreement between promisor and promisee?) looms large over any theory of promise. To say, as Searle does, that the boundaries of the concept of promising are a bit loose or, as Rawls does, that this issue is complicated is to ignore the very problem needing attention. A more damaging result of remarks of this sort is that they undermine an essential tenet of the institutional approach: if constitutive rules define institutional facts, then how is it possible that exception rules define defeating conditions in the institution in such an imprecise way? Either the rules define the exceptions of a promise, thereby making these conditions precise, or the rules do not define the exceptions. Since neither Rawls nor Searle gives any precise rules, we can conclude tentatively that the rules of promise do not define exceptions. If the rules do not define exceptions to a promise, this is either because they do not *though they could*, as a matter of empirical fact, do so or that they *cannot*, as a matter of empirical fact or logic, do so. If they could define exceptions, it would be possible to generate a list of rules covering the conditions governing the exceptions to a promise. This list would have to be complete to block someone from getting out of a promise by appealing to an exception not covered by the list.

It is likely, however, that no finite list could cover all of the possible, legitimate exceptions to a promise. There are two reasons for this: first, there are too many permutations of these conditions to make such a list workable; and second, and more important, it is ultimately up to the promisee (assuming he is a rational agent) to decide to accept an exception as defeating a promise (though it is not ultimately up to the promisee alone to reject an exception as not defeating a promise). The promisee is under no compulsion to follow a list of rules governing the exceptions to a promise. If he feels that the promisor has a legitimate excuse, the promise is thereby defeated. Even if we stand on the sidelines shouting to him that he is mistaken or that the promisor is lying, it is ultimately up to the promisee to decide to excuse the promisor. He need not give us or himself any reasons for doing what he does; and least of all must his behavior accord with a rule.

The institutional approach does not and cannot provide us with an adequate account of exceptions because it fails to take into consideration the relational aspect of promising. Promising usually occurs between two parties, and it is ultimately up to them to decide on the defeating conditions of any particular promise. No rule is likely to cover these conditions or the relational aspects of promise, because what exceptions are allowed and how they are arrived at are not decided in advance. What is to count as a legitimate exception will depend on the conditions surrounding it, who is making it, the relationship between promisor and promisee, and so forth. The institutional approach fails to address adequately the problem of exceptions to a promise not because its rules are too imprecise or too few but because the problem of exceptions to a promise is not captured by anything as precise as rules, constitutive or otherwise. Promises generally occur between people, and human action and interaction are rarely captured informatively by rules. The moral life is fundamentally open and spontaneous. Any attempt to bring our lives under control with rules fails either because the rules will not work and are run over roughshod or because they work too well and destroy our freedom.[10]

The purpose of this chapter was to demonstrate that there are serious problems with contemporary approaches to promise in terms of their ability to function as a theory of promise. Each approach focuses largely on the question of how promises create obligations and answers the question in terms of one or another single aspect. I have urged a view that sees promising as a social practice within a form of life; a view that is interested in issues other than promissory obligation; and that is capable of accommodating more than a single aspect of this human practice. Because we are after a theory of promise with these characteristics, none of the currently available approaches will do. A theory of promise that satisfies our requirements will need to say something about rules, intentions, expectations, and the like, but it will do so in a way that is comprehensive, not piecemeal. Having examined contemporary approaches to promise and having found them wanting in important ways, I turn now to the more difficult task of making good on my claim to provide an alternative.

CHAPTER FOUR
Outlines of a Theory of Practice

As in the other cases we must set out the appearances, and first of all
go through the puzzles. In this way we must prove the common
beliefs about these ways of being affected—ideally, all the
common beliefs, but if not all, then most of them, and the most
important. For if the objections are solved, and the common beliefs
are left, it will be an adequate proof.
ARISTOTLE, *Nicomachean Ethics*

What has to be accepted, the given, is—so one could say—
forms of life.
LUDWIG WITTGENSTEIN, *Philosophical Investigations*

The institutional approach to promise uses constitutive
rules to create and define actions within institutions.
There is no checkmate without the rules of chess, no
touchdown without the rules of football, and no promissory
obligation without the rules of promise. I argued that although such a view may be able to capture certain aspects of
games and public institutions, it cannot capture promise or a
number of other meaningful activities. Making tea in Britain
(or as the British do), for example, appears to be recognizable
activity in which one participates without there being any
constitutive rules to govern it. So too with dating, bluffing,
joking, booing or performing the wave at ball games, curtain
calls, walking on busy streets, driving, standing in elevators,
ordering in restaurants, and standing in lines. To capture
these activities, one must posit another sort of theoretical explanation, and I do so here.

In this chapter I outline a theory of practice, relying, when appropriate, on examples drawn from the above list. In describing these practices and in outlining a theory of practice, I focus on how practices begin, how they cohere, how they are taught, how they undergo change, and their localization, as well as how evaluation and judgment take place within them.[1] I want to reiterate that this chapter is very much an outline in two respects. It is an outline, first, in terms of the detail and accuracy that any theory of a social practice can achieve. The very nature of the activity we are here describing eludes the kind of accuracy and detail to which modern moral philosophy has accustomed us. As Aristotle says, we can only be as accurate in our theoretical musings as the subject matter allows. But this chapter is also an outline in another sense. It is, as it were, a first run at a theory of practice. I lay out the conceptual features of a theory of practice and suggest in a general way how these concepts can be filled in. I suggested in the previous chapter that none of the contemporary approaches to promise could support the load that a social practice account of promise would put on it. The theory of practice outlined below has potentially the structural capacity to support such a load, and I demonstrate this in Chapter Five, but it is not yet ready to be put to work. Chapters Four and Five are intended to serve as demonstration models of a philosophical method and to encourage further work in this area.

Outline of the Theory

A theory of practice defines a practice as any human activity that is recognized and described (though description is not a necessary condition for recognizability) as a specified conventional pattern of behavior undertaken by two or more persons in a homogeneous community. Practices are to be distinguished from habits. Habits are activities of isolated individuals, whereas practices constitute the common actions of individuals within social groups. Similar habits of members of a community create a practice when they become identified as conventional forms of behavior (and when they fulfill the other conditions of a practice listed below). If, at home, I normally step out of the tub or shower stall before toweling off—thereby dripping water onto the floor or mat—I am engaged in a habit. If, however, I and others with whom I live engage in this activity, and it becomes identified as conventional behavior for this group and is discussed at a floor meeting in the dorm where we live, then we are engaging in a practice (assuming that other conditions are met). In general, the creation of a practice requires that two or more people belonging to a homogeneous community be engaged in conventional behavior. Of course, once practices come into existence, lone individuals can engage in them; though practices, like games and institutions, have an essentially social character.

Practices are not defined by rules. Practice rules—or rulelike formulations occurring in practices—serve a descriptive function. Rulelike formulations help us to talk about practices, to describe practices to others, to assist someone in acquiring a practice role, or to excel in the practice. But acting in accordance with these rulelike formulations is neither a necessary nor a sufficient condition for participating in a practice; nor are practice rules in any way constitutive. Because practices lack constitutive rules, they are not to be seen as arising from human design or out of a hypothetical original position. Practices originate from and are maintained by human action. In discussing this feature of practices, I rely upon the explanatory device of *spontaneous order* employed by Scottish Enlightenment philosophers, notably David Hume and Adam Smith.[2] Both use spontaneous order to explain how practices and institutions begin without original agreements or constitutive rules and how practices are maintained without governmental or central control. The theory of spontaneous order explains both how practices originate and how they undergo change without losing their recognizable features.

Roles, not rules, characterize practices. Practice roles constitute practices, though they do not define them in the precise way that constitutive rules define actions within institutions. By "constitute" I mean that practice roles circumscribe, characterize, give shape to, or help pick out a practice. Describing practice roles as constitutive emphasizes their importance in understanding practices. A practice may have many practice roles the acquisition of which is required to participate in it.

Acquisition of practice roles is achieved by both active and, often, unconscious participation in these roles, and by imitation and imagination. One result of this learning process is that one can become conversant with a practice role through subconscious learning. A second result is that the practice role acquired is not always an exact copy of the role model one is imitating. Since there are no constitutive rules to define behavior, each practitioner can give his or her own interpretation to a practice role. These various interpretations give a practice its characteristic shape. Because the acquisition of practice roles relies on imagination, imitative role-play, and, in general, the active participation of a community at large, the relationships between practitioners become very important. One's success in acquiring a practice role will depend in part on fellow practitioners in one's immediate circle, who impart this practice to you. How important, for example, is the practice to them? How competent in this practice are those whom one imitates? More important, what is the relationship between novice and role model? If the relationship is a poor one, the transfer of some practice roles may be incomplete. In general, relational factors are important in the acquisition and maintenance of practices.

Because practices are characterized by the various interpretations of their practice roles, it follows that there are no definitive or standard practices. The practice roles of dating, for example, vary among generations, communities, and even among members of a homogeneous community. Because the practice roles differ, the practice itself will be seen as different. Practices change; they have histories. To describe a particular practice is to describe it as it is found in eighteenth-century Scotland or nineteenth-century Prussia, among the indigenous peoples of Australia or in a Hasidic community. This is not to say that certain practices do not occur almost everywhere on the planet or that some have not existed for thousands of years. But a practice is influenced by conditions specific to its time and place. Though the behavior taking place within a practice is conventional, the behavior is constrained and shaped by the natural and social conditions of the community in which the practice occurs.

Even though there are no standard or definitive practices and practices are not defined by rules, evaluation and judgment are nevertheless possible in practices. Evaluation measures the competence of one's interpretations of practice roles and is used primarily in the teaching of practice roles. Judgment reflects more than competence within practice roles, however; it reflects one's character as it is expressed in a practice role. For example, a practitioner can be evaluated as competent in the practice of bluffing while being judged negatively because his particular use of bluffing reflects poor character. Evaluators and judges must be conversant with the practices in which they operate, as well as familiar, at least in some respects, with those they are evaluating or judging. Both use criteria abstracted from their own experience within the community of practices. Because of this, both evaluator and judge must be willing to consider excusing conditions, to update their criteria, and, when possible, to engage in a dialogue with the person whose behavior is being evaluated or judged. The quality of their evaluations and judgments will depend on their ability to satisfy these three conditions.

Practices have many purposes, but in particular they facilitate a form of life and, in some cases, assist those within it to flourish. It is not a paradox to say that practices are necessary for the maintenance of a form of life and, at the same time, make this form of life possible. The relationship between practices and the form of life of their practitioners is essentially a cybernetic one. Together they form a system that maintains itself through the interchange of and reaction to information, which each supplies to the other and to the system as a whole. In biological systems this is called symbiosis. We turn now to filling out the details of this outline.

The Theory Delineated

As described in this way, a great number of human activities are not practices. The games of chess and baseball are not practices; nor is buying a house or getting married. Whatever they might have been in the distant past, these activities are now defined by rules and regulations. But though it may be impossible to play baseball or to get married without rules that give meaning to one's actions, people seem perfectly able to make tea the way the British do, go on dates the way Americans do, boo the way soccer fans do, and walk on busy streets the way New Yorkers do without referring to constitutive rules. We can likewise speak with perfect intelligence of the proper way to make tea in Britain, acceptable and unacceptable behavior on a date, predictable booing at the soccer stadium, and techniques for walking in New York. It is to such actions, as well as to many others, that a theory of practice is applied. We begin with an example.

Anthropologists or sociologists might describe dating as a cultural practice designed to bring together compatible mates, to control the sexual urges of adolescents, or to reinforce monogamy in young adults. Dating might then be compared to arranged marriages or the practice of prepubescent promiscuity in some cultures. But social scientists who study the practice of dating do not have available to them a handbook of dating or a rule book that defines this practice in late twentieth-century America. They might initially make use of a book of etiquette, but they would quickly discard it once they realized that it was rarely used—except perhaps by certain social classes—and is generally out of date. (Teenagers rarely refer to such books, though their parents or grandparents might.) Instead, social scientists often depend on informants who are knowledgeable in the practice.

This is also how young adults learn about dating. They do not have recourse to a book of rules to teach them what to do but rather read about dating in romance novels and observe their older siblings on dates. Of course, unlike anthropologists, their education is facilitated by actually going on dates. Because there is no rule book to govern this practice, what characterizes dating is open to interpretation. Even though a teenager's first date is often an abysmal affair and filled with uncertainties, both parties normally recognize that they are on a date. It is not as if they recognize this because they see themselves as satisfying the necessary and sufficient conditions of dating; nor do they claim that because they did not hold hands or kiss each other good night, their actions failed to constitute a date. A wide range of behavior characterizes dating, and yet despite this wide variation across history, across cultures, across age groups, and across personal experiences—and despite the absence of constitutive rules—few would deny that there is a practice called dating. We can make similar remarks about making tea, telling jokes, bluffing in poker, or booing at sporting events. Each of these is a form of conventional behavior, even though none of them has a set of rules defining or creating this behavior. How then does conventional behavior arise and how is it recognized?

Spontaneous Order

One useful feature of constitutive rules is that they give meaning to otherwise meaningless actions. According to the insitutional approach, it is not possible to score a touchdown or hit a home run or make a promise unless there is a rule that defines a touchdown, a home run, or a promise. As John Rawls says, prior to the rules, one's actions lack a sense. One function of constitutive rules, then, is to explain how institutions originated. I argued in Chapter Two that there are serious objections to this explanation. The main point of these objections is that constitutive rules presuppose a large number of dispositions and actions that it is not possible to define with rules. In a theory of practice, both the dispositions and the background conditions necessary for a practice to originate can be explained without reference to constitutive rules; nor is it necessary to appeal to constitutive rules once a practice is in place. Practices originate in human action, not by human design or constitutive rules. According to this view, it is a form of life that originates a practice. When a form of life has a particular configuration, a practice specific to that configuration will arise—in evolutionary terms—spontaneously.

This practice will maintain itself as long as that form of life is in existence and is facilitated by it.

The phrase "spontaneous order" was first used by F. A. Hayek to explain the phenomenon of complex social arrangements without invoking deliberate calculation or design. In his essay "The Results of Human Action but Not of Human Design," Hayek argues that the long-standing distinction between the natural (wholly independent of human action) and the artificial (the product of human design) must have inserted between the two a third category, "comprising all those unintended patterns and regularities which we find to exist in human society and which it is the task of social theory to explain."[3] He cites thinkers of the Scottish Enlightenment as building up a social theory that took the undesigned results of individual action as its primary subject matter. He credits them with engaging in what we now call social anthropology and suggests that we need to continue in this tradition if we are to make sense of the origins and developments of certain social institutions.

Ronald Hamowy details the use of spontaneous order by Scottish Enlightenment philosophers in his monograph *The Scottish Enlightenment and the Theory of Spontaneous Order*. He describes the theory in the following way:

> The theory, simply put, holds that the social arrangements under which we live are of such a high order of complexity that they invariably take their form not from deliberate calculation, but as the unintended consequence of countless individual actions, many of which may be the result of instinct and habit. The theory thus provides an explanation of the origin of complex social structures without the need to posit the existence of a directing intelligence. Rather, such structures come into being as a consequence of the aggregate of numerous discrete individual actions, none of which aims at the formation of coherent

social institutions. Society is not the product of calculation but arises spontaneously, and its institutions are not the result of intentional design but of men's actions which have as their purpose an array of short-term private objectives.[4]

Hamowy cites Hume as using spontaneous order to explain the growth of technical knowledge, the origins of justice, the stability of property and its transference, promising, and the evolution of money and language. Hume claims that individual human beings, sharing the same natural passions and the same natural desires, act on their own and for their own purposes in ways that turn out to be mutually beneficial for all. In addition, Hume says that "mankind is an inventive species; and where an invention is obvious and absolutely necessary, it may as properly be said to be natural as anything that proceeds immediately from original principles, without the intervention of thought or reflexion."[5] In Hume's view, the social and political artifices can be seen as arising spontaneously. Adam Smith, too, uses spontaneous order to explain the general rules of morality. These rules are produced by "countless instances of moral evaluation made by large numbers of individuals over time. . . . From these specific instances, rules of morality evolve and gradually come to be obeyed because, Smith added, men seek the approval of their fellow men or, in the case of rules relating to justice, because they also fear the punishment and the resentment of others that attend certain acts."[6] Hamowy likewise points to Smith's discussion of the four stages of humanity (hunters, shepherds, agriculture, commerce) as evidence that Smith saw the institution of property as changing according to social conditions.

A theory of spontaneous order is a viable alternative to constitutive rules in explaining how various social practices arise. It can be applied to the social practices of dating, booing, or making tea. These practices originate and are maintained by people who share common interests and common dispositions. As Smith used sympathy and Hume used confined generosity, we can speak of the dispositions of desire, competition, cooperation, or propriety. Where Smith describes the four stages of history and Hume speaks of the common scarcity of capacities and resources, we can speak of the influence of our social and historical setting. Without a common background there would be little chance that practices could arise. It is this common yet complex backdrop that I identify as the form of life necessary for any practice to originate, evolve, and be maintained. Our form of life allows us to recognize certain actions as practices, to learn practices without learning rules, to teach practices without teaching rules, and to alter practices without altering rules. It is our form of life that makes the spontaneous order of practices both necessary and possible. Practices help to overcome the constraining conditions in which potential practitioners find themselves (scarcity or limitations in general), and they are made possible by the enabling conditions surrounding and contained within these practitioners (natural and social conditions, creativity, ingenuity, the ability to communicate, etc.).

It is this common form of life, for example, that makes people expect hometown fans to boo the opposing team. The practice of booing is made possible by a form of life that is shared generally by human beings and specifically by spectators at sporting events. Spectators are often excited by the actions on the field and will want to express themselves but are often restricted from doing so. Booing and cheering enable them to express themselves and participate in the game, sometimes with great effect. Given these conditions, it is natural for large numbers of individuals to cheer or boo spontaneously and to continue to engage in this activity in a recognized and ritualized way. Now, not all sports have identical practices of fan participation. Booing and cheering are constrained in golf, tennis, and bowling. It is also interesting to note how the practice of booing has undergone change. Thirty years ago it would have been in bad taste to distract a member of a visiting basketball team while he or she attempted an important free throw. Distractions at this critical time are now commonplace. It is difficult to be specific about the details of this transition, but the transition has occurred. Perhaps in fifty years it will be common practice to distract an athlete while he or she is putting for a tournament-winning birdie or serving for the match. Such change is a feature of practices and occurs spontaneously when the right conditions are present.

Even with a form of life as a backdrop to practices, it is still necessary to show how these practices are able to originate spontaneously. I offer three examples. In Chapter Three, I described briefly the practice of waving at sporting events. The wave is a perfect example of a practice that appears to have arisen spontaneously when a number of conditions were present. Those who participated in this practice for the first time shared some common features. They recognized certain behavior and were able to imitate it by simply watching it. They had a sense of rhythm (otherwise they would not be able to time when to stand and sit). They enjoyed sporting events. They were only partially interested in the game they were attending (serious sports fans do not usually wave). We could go on listing these sorts of conditions, but it is clear that a wave is likely to happen only when certain constraining and enabling conditions are present. Take away enough of these conditions and the practice will disappear. But when these conditions do exist, groups of people will be able to wave even if they cannot name what is happening as a wave and even if this is the very first time it occurs. Practices such as the wave occur when people act in concert, and the practitioners are able to act in concert because they share a similar background and similar interests. Knowing this to be the case, it is possible for a practice such as waving to have had multiple origins. If large numbers of people with similar interests find themselves in similar conditions, a practice such as waving can spring up spontaneously, in this case at a number of sporting arenas.

Another example of common activity springing up spontaneously in different places is the practice of joke telling. Normally a joke will travel a slow and circuitous route from person to person, but there are times when particularly tasteless jokes will arise spontaneously immediately following a national tragedy. It seems unlikely that these jokes, almost always identical in form, could travel around the country in a matter of days. It is more likely that the originators of these jokes share a common background. An example of this phenomenon occurred when the space shuttle Challenger exploded. Within a twenty-four-hour period I heard the same joke—involving a line from a Bud Light beer commercial—from two people who did not know each other and who lived three hundred miles apart. According to a theory of spontaneous order, this phenomenon would be explained by the conjunction of a national disaster with a national beer advertising campaign. To create nearly identical national jokes of this kind spontaneously requires a relatively small number of people around the United States who are good at thinking up jokes, who have seen the Bud Light beer commercials, and who are aware that the Challenger space shuttle exploded.

The final example comes from Julius Kovesi's book *Moral Notions*. The practice he describes is a British one:

> I expect the reader is familiar with those little machines which are used by bus conductors in some places for printing the

tickets. Now suppose that a passenger asked for a fourpenny ticket and for some reason the conductor dialled five, thus producing the wrong ticket. He made another ticket but kept the fivepenny one as he had to account for all the tickets printed. Some time later someone else asked for a fivepenny ticket and was given the one printed earlier. So far so good, but the trouble arose when the inspector boarded the bus, for since the ticket had been printed some time before the passenger got on the bus it had by now expired, and the conductor had to be called on to explain. All this was rather a nuisance as it took up the conductor's time while other passengers were getting on and off; besides, he felt that the inspector must have thought him careless and inefficient. When he came off duty he stayed to have a cup of tea at the canteen where he told the story to a group of other conductors who replied with similar stories. Some had to do their explaining during rush hour or to an inspector who was slow to understand. When I want to suggest that the conductors might eventually coin an expression to refer to these stories I do not of course want to say that they all suddenly decide one day: "Well, let's call it making a misticket." It might take several years of exchanging stories before some conductor coins this word, and perhaps even longer before it becomes general currency. Now if it is only the conductors who talk together over their cups of tea the word will become part only of their vocabulary, but if they share their discussion with the inspectors it will become part of their vocabulary as well. In the first case the word could only function as a "nuisance-word," in the second, it could function as an "excuse-word." What I mean is that in the first case a conductor could not use the new word to the inspector when he wants a short-hand explanation to excuse a passenger and himself; he could only use it among the other conductors when he wants to say that this trouble has come up again. In the second case, however, he can tell the inspector: "There is a misticket in the back," thus achieving what before the existence of this word needed a long explanation. . . . Before the existence of this word the conductors had a point in telling the inspectors what had happened; they wanted to excuse them-

selves and the passenger. But the success of this excuse de-
pended on how articulate the conductor was, how able he was
to master the relevant details and leave out irrelevant ones that
might only annoy the inspector. . . . The existence of the new
word changes all this. A conductor now does not need to rely on
his own personal capacity to formulate and put his case well nor
can the attitude of the inspector so freely influence the success
of the excuse. The efficacy of the excuse is achieved by the conductors and admitted by the inspectors when the word is accepted in their common language. The rules for the proper use
of the word are also rules in the way of life in which it plays a
part.[7]

Kovesi is making a point about the word "misticket" and
the rules for its usage, but his remarks are nonetheless infor-
mative about how a practice such as misticketing might arise.
He says later that the use of this word and the notion of making mistakes are both a part of our form of life. Once we see
what the conductors share in common—the constraining and
enabling conditions—it is easy to understand how this practice arises spontaneously. In this regard, Kovesi points out the
importance of naming a practice. It is not until the individual
habits of the conductors become known, recognized, and
named "misticketing" that misticketing takes on the qualities of a practice. Misticketing becomes identified with a
fairly specific activity. "The new word 'misticket' . . . does
not refer to the experience of an individual conductor but to
that of *any* conductor, and incorporates those features of the
experiences that any of them may have."[8] Just as practices
have unique characteristics, they are also uniquely named. As
Kovesi suggests, naming a practice has advantages over and
above the practice itself.

These three examples suggest that practices can arise spontaneously without having been designed or defined by rules.[9]

Indeed, it would be difficult to explain how some of these practices could arise with constitutive rules. Other examples abound in the literature. The Associated Press reported about a town in Indiana where, for more than twenty-five years, residents have been throwing shoes of various sorts into a forty-foot oak tree, and nobody seems to know why. New York City teenagers have begun a new sport called "surfing" or "hang on," where they stand on the roofs of moving subway trains. In another part of the city, expediters waiting to see an examiner at the Department of Buildings mark their places in line with their briefcases. One expediter gets up at five-thirty in the morning, throws a coat over his pajamas, and rides a taxi to the buildings department. He puts his briefcase in line and returns home to bed. The *New York Times* recently reported a shift in etiquette in the halls of government (January 13, 1992). Formerly well behaved legislators are now insulting one another in public and using strong language. Recently and in front of television cameras, a New Jersey lobbyist referred to the legislature as a bunch of prostitutes, with the governor as their pimp. Practices associated with euthanasia are also on the rise. Despite strict laws in the Netherlands outlawing euthanasia, researchers found that the practice was secretly thriving. And it was the practice that led in 1993 to a new law giving the Netherlands the world's least restrictive euthanasia policy. In each of these cases, the practice arises spontaneously and in response to a particular need or interest. Such practices, I believe, defy explanation by constitutive rules.

Someone might respond, however, that it is possible to know full well what one wants to accomplish ahead of time and intentionally to create a practice for this purpose.[10] Spontaneous order does not rule out the possibility that practices can be created or invented as a specific response to a situation. What is ruled out is that practices can be designed in advance of the situation arising—in advance of the conditions that make the practice both possible and desirable—and that they can be fully captured, designed, taught, and practiced by appealing to constitutive rules. It is perfectly possible to imagine a "practice designer" hired by some organization to design a practice. For example, a corporation seeks to increase employees' satisfaction in their positions and ultimately to increase productivity. A practice designer is hired and she creates the practice of dressing down. Employees can dress down (dress casually) on a particular day of the week or month. The practice is introduced and employees are encouraged to engage in it.

Two points can be made here. First, the rules of this practice cannot be fully constitutive in the manner suggested by the institutional approach to promising. The rules that govern this practice can constitute only partially. Second, the acceptance of this practice in a particular corporate atmosphere and its success in achieving its intended goals will depend primarily on its acceptance by the employees. Their actions may shape this practice in ways that are unintended or unforeseen by its creator. Hence even a designed practice may spontaneously change its shape because of "the unintended consequence of countless individual actions, many of which may be the result of instinct and habit."[11] The first point is a technical argument against a rival position. The second point is a claim about the way practices function.

To review, the origin of a practice depends on the shared traits of the practitioners and their local conditions. Taken together, these traits and conditions constitute a form of life that makes specific practices both necessary and possible. The conventional behavior that is eventually identified as constituting a practice often originates in the similar but separate actions of individuals, but these actions are quickly recognized as having elements in common, and these elements coalesce into those features that give a practice its identifying characteristics. Although the origination of practices is hardly spontaneous, practices do arise quickly. This should not be surprising when we consider the common ground potential practitioners share. Practices have backdrops and histories but they have futures as well, futures that are not predetermined. A theory of spontaneous order commits one to an explanation not only of how practices begin but also of how they develop. In the same way that they originate in spontaneous human action, so, too, practices undergo change.

Practice Rules: Descriptive, Not Constitutive

If someone asks for the rules of bluffing in poker, they will most likely be told instead the purpose of bluffing or have it explained to them how one goes about bluffing. Even if this information is transmitted in rulelike formulations, the rules will be somewhat loose and will vary among card players. There might be certain hard and fast rules (e.g., "Never bluff with new players because they are likely to have strong hands"), but even these rules have exceptions. In general, practice rules serve as rules of thumb. They are descriptive of the practice and function by giving advice or a strategy for excelling in it. But one can certainly engage in a practice without having to ask someone for its rules of thumb. One does not bluff by following rules; one bluffs by engaging in an activity, by actually bluffing. Practice rules are not definitive of a practice; nor do they need to be consciously or subconsciously present in the practitioner. Instead, practice rules are rulelike formulations that serve a descriptive or strategic function.

That practice rules are descriptive, not constitutive can be seen in the following example. Imagine that you have a friend, Brad, who is interested in dating—though he has never done it before—and asks your advice. He comes to you with questions because he perceives you to be an expert. Brad's request is not as straightforward as it seems. It is more than likely that he is a shy fellow who is currently interested in a woman but who is unsure how to ask her out on a date or how to begin and maintain a courtship. But Brad knows what dating is and why he wants to engage in the practice. He shares the background conditions of those who engage in the dating practice. These conditions are what make him want to learn how to date in the first place. Brad might begin by asking how you go about getting dates or how you maintain a romantic relationship. What you tell him is nothing rulelike. You tell him some stories in which you share your experience, and he listens and asks questions. Instead of giving him rules, you give him advice or you describe what you do when dating. You tell him that, as general rules of thumb, you avoid physical intimacy on a first date and do not get too specific with your personal life. But you also tell him that you have broken these rules when it seemed appropriate. You tell him not to think of dating in terms of strict rules. Both you and Brad recognize that his request for advice stems from his desire to be successful at dating, and you know that this success stems in part from not thinking of the practice of dating in terms of rules.

That the practice of dating has no hard and fast or constitutive rules can be seen from the fact that Brad or anyone else can manage to go on a date without having to follow any of the rules you give him or any rules at all. There is no list of necessary and sufficient conditions that Brad must satisfy if he and his date are to recognize their actions as constitutive of dating. Indeed, it might strike Brad's date as exceedingly odd if when she invited him to spend the night he refused, stating as his reason that he had been told of a rule that one is not sexually intimate on a first date. And since Brad wants to consider himself on a date, it is important to follow all of the rules. (Such a remark would not sound odd coming from a newcomer to baseball who was trying to hit the ball, and, in our efforts to be kind, we had offered him four strikes and he responded by saying that in learning to play baseball he wanted to abide by the rules.) Brad need not follow your rules of thumb. As the date comes to an end he might follow the general strategy you suggested for setting up a next date, but he might just as easily dispense with your suggestions altogether. What separates the novice from the expert is that the novice often begins his participation in a practice by appealing to rulelike formulations as if they were constitutive rules. Unsure of himself, the novice avoids spontaneity and acts in strict accordance with rules that are not meant to be followed strictly. After a time, the proficient practitioner no longer interprets practice rules so strictly. He sees that they are unnecessary for—and even an interference with—his success in the practice.

Suppose, instead, that you are with a foreign anthropologist who is studying the practice of dating. The anthropologist and you are at a large public function to observe people dating, and she has asked for your expertise in pointing out people who are on dates. Although you can formulate some general rules for distinguishing a date from other sorts of relationships, the anthropologist will have to recognize that these rules are not constitutive of the practice of dating. These rulelike formulations merely provide guidelines for recognizing this practice and for talking about it. To become a good participant observer requires not that one master rules but that one become an expert at recognizing behavior within cultural contexts. This is why it takes a long time to become an expert in observing practices. It takes an even longer time to become proficient in the practices themselves.

This formulation of practice rules applies to other practices as well. When the British make tea they always first warm the pot with some boiling water. They dump this water out and pour in fresh boiling water over the tea. One could say that for the British, warming the pot is a rule for making tea, but this rule is not a constitutive rule. One could reply with complete confidence to one's British guests that, though you have neglected to warm the pot, you have made tea and not coffee. Your actions have a sense at some level. This rulelike formulation does not define actions that lacked a sense prior to the rule; nor must one know the rule either consciously or subconsciously to participate in the practice. The rulelike formulation that one must warm the pot, I submit, gives the practitioner strategic advice to follow if he desires to excel at making tea the way the British do.

Practice rules are rulelike formulations that function either descriptively or strategically. They do not define practices, and they are not essential in guiding action. Instead, they are used primarily to talk about practices or the actions taking place within them. In this regard we can refer to practice rules as having a metafunction. In their descriptive function, they serve as a way to talk about practices. In their strategic function, these rulelike formulations provide advice on how to perform well within practices.[12]

If practice rules do not function in the creation, maintenance, and continuation of practices, it is necessary to explain these features of practices in another way. Obviously, practices are characterized in ways that identify them as the practices they are. If rules do not give practices their characteristic shape, this feature must be explained some other way. In addition, the longevity of a practice depends on the ability of practitioners to teach it to their children and to new members of the community. How do novices learn to participate in a practice if there exist no rules that could serve to teach it to them?

Practice Roles

I use the term "role" to circumscribe those conformative behaviors that take place within a practice. A practice contains a cluster of roles, and the sum of actions taking place in these roles gives a practice its characteristic shape. To be acting in a practice role is to be engaged in a practice; to be observed in a practice role is to be observed as acting within a practice. Practice roles, then, and not rules are what give practices their unique shape. Individual interpretations give shape to practice roles, and the practice roles give shape to practices. The range of these interpretations and the extent to which practice roles—and the practices themselves—undergo change are constrained by traditional, or standard, interpretations and in other ways discussed below. The ongoing interaction and tension between traditional and modern interpretations are what allow practices to undergo the slow but constant change necessary to keep them viable. Without this change, practices lose their importance or cease to exist altogether.[13]

In learning to make tea the British way, one begins by watching and listening to experts in this practice. In time, one becomes proficient at this practice (here proficiency entails not only technical mastery but also social mastery: e.g., sharing the seriousness of tea drinking, drinking tea at certain times of day, etc). But one's proficiency is tested not by the ability to cite rules or to act in accordance with them but by one's ability to actually make and drink tea the way the British do. One becomes proficient at this practice when one's actions become synonymous—or nearly synonymous—with the actions of longtime practitioners, and this occurs when one has successfully acquired the proper roles. It is not always clear to the novice or to fellow practitioners when novices become proficient, but the transition does occur.

The same can be said of bluffing.[14] After mastering the rules of the game of poker, one may also want to learn how to bluff. Unlike the game itself, there are no rules to ease one's entry into this practice. One can receive some rules of thumb, but the only way one can learn the bluffing practice is to be a role-player in it. To excel in a practice requires a certain proficiency in its roles, but proficiency is not required to begin participating in a practice. This can be seen in the fact that novice bluffers often bluff out of ignorance: for example, when they mistakenly think they have a winning hand. If you are playing with longtime poker players and for money, you will quickly realize the need to become good in this practice—good not only at bluffing other players but at recognizing their bluffs as well. If you are to become proficient at bluffing, you will learn from those around you, as well as from your own successes and blunders. The roles of this practice are characterized for you by those who are already familiar with them, and you take these people as your role models, but the roles are eventually characterized by your own interpretations of them. In time, you may develop an original approach to bluffing. Because of individual interpretations, practice roles undergo constant adaptation and revision. Of course, there is no certainty that role-play in a practice, even with the help of role models, will make one proficient in it. Perhaps you so much dislike being deceived that you choose not to participate in this practice; or perhaps, as hard as you try, you are just a lousy bluffer and always give yourself away or fail to read correctly the faces of your opponents. Engaging in a practice role is no guarantee that one will ever become a proficient practitioner. It takes more than an acquaintance with a form of life to become proficient at practices that take place within it. This is seen clearly in the practice of humor.

We have all had the experience of hearing a joke that we find hilariously funny but then not being able to get anyone to laugh when we tell it. There is an old metajoke about a prison where inmates, having attached numbers to jokes, simply shout out the numbers. When a new inmate tries this technique, nobody laughs. He is told that some people can tell jokes and others cannot. There is more to telling a joke than just reciting words. Besides knowing when to tell a joke, you also need to know how to tell it. Delivery is important; but what does good delivery entail? If we look to our experts, we see that there is a wide range of successful deliveries, from Jack Benny's to Robin Williams's. Just as there are many ways not to be funny, there are also many ways to be funny. Most successful comedians can point to role models, people they thought were funny and whom they tired to imitate. From these role models aspiring comics learn the role(s) of comedian. But young comedians always shape these roles in individualized ways. Judging from the variations among comedians, these roles are individually created and shaped by each and every comedian. Because of this ever-present variation, the practice of humor undergoes change. What is humorous in one generation often ceases to be humorous in another.

I have argued that one becomes a practitioner by participating in a practice, and that this occurs when one acquires its roles. I suggested that newcomers do not acquire practice roles by learning rules, since the rule like formulations of practices are only broadly descriptive. Instead, newcomers learn a practice's roles by imitating role models and by playing the roles themselves. This way of learning a role requires that the newcomer be able to imitate the behavior of others and to imagine himself as playing the role he is trying to learn. Practice roles are acquired primarily through imitation and imagination.

The most obvious place to see this method of role acquisition in action is in young children. Children learn the habits and practices of their elders primarily through imitation. What makes this imitation possible is a shared form of life. A one-year-old child is able to speak certain words because she has the organs and muscle control to do so, because she has heard the words so many times, and because she watches her parents' mouths as they speak the words. Nobody teaches her where to place her tongue or lips when she speaks; she just does it. Nobody teaches her to imitate words; she just imitates them. That she can imitate the sounds we associate with words and that she wants so badly to imitate them are features of her form of life. Human beings learn successfully through imitation because we are repetition-sensitive, and we are repetition-sensitive because we are imitative creatures.

In this way children acquire various habits in the bathroom or at the dinner table, often to the consternation of parents unaware of their own habits. A child learns to brush his teeth by first watching adults brush their teeth and then imitating them, albeit roughly. By the time the child is old enough to take explicit verbal instructions regarding the motion of the brush or the frequency of brushing, he already knows in a general way what brushing one's teeth entails. For example, he has internalized the physical movements of brushing, and he knows the times of day when teeth are brushed. Learning habits this way is not specific to children. Adults learn new habits and new languages by listening to instructors, by watching their movements, and, in general, by imitating them. Adults, like children, often learn best from careful observation and persistent imitation. They are told that the best way to learn a language is to live in the country where it is spoken, because this is the best place to observe and imitate native speakers.

Practices are acquired in a similar way. Children learn the practices of their religious denomination by first observing elder practitioners and then imitating them. Children learn to date, to bluff at cards, to make tea, or to be patriotic by imitating their elder role models. Regardless of the practice, most people are adept at imitating a practice's roles. We can see this imitative behavior in young adults who first come to college. Wanting to fit in, first-year students are slow to act and very observant. In this way they learn what is "in" and what is not "in" and quickly engage in the "in" or acceptable behavior. It has become common practice at the university where I teach for students to call a two-semester great-books course that all first-year students are required to take "GFI." The course number is LS 195, but it came to be called "Great Ideas"; then, presumably, "GI"; and then "GFI" (the "F" does not stand for "fundamental"). It is astonishing how quickly incoming students learn the term "GFI," despite the fact that they traditionally have little contact with sophomores, juniors, or seniors. What they do learn from the older students is that this required course is a hassle, worthless, and a waste of time. One of the "in" roles at this university requires students to denigrate the liberal arts, and one way that they can do this is to refer to this course as "GFI." But the role is more complex than that. It requires that one not do the reading, not participate in class, not like the course, and, in general, be negative about courses outside of one's major. However, even the students who like this course call it "GFI," though they know it is not a term of endearment. They do it, some claim, because everyone else does. Some of my colleagues have even started calling the course "GFI." There are even people who use the term without knowing its origins or its meaning and who make up an explanation for it. Others may imitate the behavior of role models without wanting to or without being conscious of it. Imitative behavior is, after all, often subconscious behavior.[15]

There are, no doubt, many important features that are necessary for a person to acquire practice roles through imitation of a role model(s), but I focus here on one: the imagination. I use the term "imagination" to mean nothing more than the ability to see oneself in a role prior to one's actually being in it or to act the part of the role with seriousness, even in unreal or mock situations. Again, it is easiest to think of children, who play all sorts of "let's pretend" games with the utmost seriousness and who, through such games, have a way of learning the practices reflected in such games in a safe and pressure-free environment. One of the first things that children learn who study the violin or piano using the Suzuki method is how to bow after a performance. They are encouraged to play their instruments with the confidence of a professional musician and to end each performance as if they had just ended a concert. These young music students are encouraged to see themselves as professional musicians and to treat their performances seriously. It is their ability to imagine this, despite the quality of the performance, that allows them to begin to learn the role of a concert musician. The same is true for young children who play domestic or professional games ("house" or "doctor"). By imagining themselves in these practice roles, they are better able to imitate them. It is also one way by which they subconsciously adopt the values of their community.

There are other examples. Young teenagers playing sports or music will pretend that they are their role models as they step up to bat or to the microphone. Children wear the jersey numbers of their favorite football players and have posters of their role models on their bedroom walls. Being able to imagine themselves in the role helps them to concentrate on it and to excel in it. The imagination is at work when adult soldiers fight in mock battles or when graduate students are given mock interviews to prepare them for the job market. These situations are most effective when those involved treat them seriously, imagining themselves to be at war or at a real job interview. The power of the imagination is not lost on sports psychologists, who now work at helping athletes to imagine an entire race or game in which they are victorious. Baseball players attest to having visualized a brilliant catch just prior to—and identical to—a catch they actually made. Of course, no one is going to make a brilliant catch if he is out of shape or out of position. The imagination alone is not going to make one successful at anything. But it can help one to acquire a practice role more quickly and to excel in it. The imagination is a visual aid, if you will, by which one sees oneself within a practice role, though one is not always conscious that one is acquiring a practice role. Children imagine themselves in all sorts of roles, though they do not usually recognize their playtime and games as methods of acquiring practice roles. The imagination is a valuable resource at any age for the purpose of learning a practice role. It greatly facilitates role acquisition.[16]

Assuming that practice roles are acquired, at least in part, through the imitation of role models, how do we know, as novices, that we have become proficient in a practice role, or, as proficient practitioners, that a novice has become a proficient practitioner? These are particularly difficult questions to answer regarding practices, because there are no rules to which one can appeal and because each practitioner interprets practice roles in his or her own way. Ultimately, a practitioner's interpretation of a practice's roles characterizes the practice for her and for those who use her as a role model. But if practices are characterized by such variation, how is proficiency recognized?

I offer a partial answer to this question. First, a person is said to be a proficient practitioner when she no longer needs to look to a role model, when she no longer sees herself as imitating someone else. That is, the proficient practitioner believes she no longer needs role models and is recognized by these role models as no longer needing their assistance. Second, someone proficient in a practice role no longer imagines herself in this role. An initiate becomes proficient when she and a practice role merge in a seamless whole. Her actions become synonymous with the role. The imagined becomes real, and she no longer sees herself as in a role. The person who imagines herself to be a warrior becomes a warrior, in her mind and in the mind of others; the person who imagines herself as a professor becomes a professor, from her own perspective and from the perspective of those who observe her. This is not simply a change that occurs when one finds oneself on the battlefield or when one is lecturing to a class. Whether or not one is on a battlefield or lecturing to a class, a practice role becomes real when one no longer sees oneself in the role of a such-and-such but sees oneself simply as a such-and-such. Imitation and imagination help one to acquire a role, but there comes a time when the role is real and no longer imitated or imagined. Unlike the initiate who thinks about what she does before she does it and who makes a conscious effort to assume a role, the proficient practitioner effortlessly and subconsciously acts the role. In the theater it is the difference between good acting and bad acting. It is what Pierre Bourdieu calls "learned ignorance."[17]

This internal state of proficiency is likewise reflected in the practitioner's actions. To other practitioners she is no longer clumsy, she no longer asks questions, and she no longer must be given correctives. Proficiency occurs when the initiate "becomes one of us." When this occurs, fellow practitioners are just as likely to ask her for advice or guidance as she is to ask them. She is now capable of becoming a role model herself. She is now a full member of the practice.

A final feature of proficiency is that the practitioner is held responsible for her actions in the practice. We generally forgive children for their awful table manners or for their rambunctiousness during solemn practices, because they are too young to know how they should behave. When they do become old enough to understand what behavior is expected of them—and this is often difficult to know with any accuracy—we hold them responsible. The same is true with foreigners who have—from our point of view—equally horrible dining practices. We may tell them how we act at the dinner table, but we usually forgive them for not knowing any better. A person who is considered proficient at bluffing, however, will not be allowed to excuse his marking of the cards by saying that he thought this was an acceptable form of bluffing; nor will the joke teller be excused for telling ethnic jokes at a dinner when he knew the ethnic group in question was in attendance. Proficiency entails that one knows enough about the practice to be held responsible for one's actions within it.

It is difficult to say when proficiency in a practice role is acquired, especially when both the learning process and teaching process are often subconscious. It is doubtful that English children receive daily lessons in making tea. As for all children, there comes a time when they want to help around the kitchen and when they start to imitate mannerisms and ways of acting. In time, many British children become experts at making and drinking tea (again, this includes the social aspects of this practice as well). Practices are not activities where competence can be easily tested. Most children pass unnoticed from novice to expert and become proficient in practice roles without remembering when or how they became proficient in them.

We turn now to the issue of interpreting practice roles. Despite the fact that individual practitioners interpret practice roles for themselves and, in effect, characterize these roles and the practice itself—both for themselves and for others—their interpretations are nevertheless constrained. Despite the many, varied interpretations of a practice role, each practitioner sees himself as participating in an identifiable practice. It is as if the practice itself, by its very ability to be recognized, limits the range of interpretation of its roles. In addition, the form of life that allows each practitioner to interpret practice roles also limits the range of these interpretations. Certain interpretations are just not open to practitioners, either because of the practitioners' sheer inability to conceive of them or because of some other constraining conditions: for example, social, economic, or historical conditions. Practitioners can be creative with their interpretations, but the range of this creativity is sometimes dependent on conditions over which the practitioners have no control. Interpretations of practice roles must sometimes wait on specific social and historical conditions for them to be realized. There was little chance for upper-class teenagers in the Victorian period, for example, to sleep together on the first date. This is not to say that teenagers of that period did not have sex or did not want to have sex on first dates; rather, sex within the practice of courtship, at least in the upper classes (as portrayed in Victorian novels), was simply not possible during that period. First dates were usually public affairs and well supervised. More important, if the question "Did you have intercourse on the first date?" were asked to a character in a George Eliot or Anthony Trollope novel, the constraints of the courtship practice in this period would have made the question and affirmative answer impossible. Intercourse on a first date would not be a role interpretation open to a person engaged in this practice in that period of time. In the late twentieth century, on the other hand, sexual intimacy on a first date has, at least, become a possible interpretation of a dating role. Though a practice role may have a wide range of interpretations, some interpretations cannot be created or even imagined prior to specific conditions.

The range of possible role interpretations is also limited by the fact that people who participate in practices want to become recognized as excelling in them. In many cases, then, the intention of a novice is to show other practitioners that she has become competent in a practice. This requires that her actions fall within an identifiable range. Whether one's learning of a practice role is conscious or not, it follows from the way that one learns it that there will be an overlap of roles. The process of imitation requires a copying of at least a significant core of the original. Without accurate copying, a person would never be recognized as achieving proficiency. It is no coincidence that young children want very much to be recognized as having achieved proficiency in their role imitations. The nature of learning a practice role requires that the learner reflect back to the teacher either a correct copy of the role or an acceptable interpretation of it. Though all copies contain some variation, this method of learning limits the variation.

Finally, considering that most practices exist prior to their newest members, what counts as an acceptable or deviant interpretation will be measured against the baseline of the practice as it is presently conceived. One is free to interpret a practice role in any way one chooses, but one's interpretation will be evaluated against the background of already existing interpretations. The role one creates is constrained by the interpretations that precede it. If a novice insists on an interpretation that is outside of the variations accepted by fellow practitioners within the community, he will be seen as a rebel within the practice and will be either tolerated or excluded from participation in the practice. There is a fine line between variations and violations of practice roles. Having sex on a first date was a clear violation of the courtship practice among the upper classes in nineteenth-century Europe; in America, it is now considered a sometimes acceptable variation. Date rape, by contrast, is a clear violation of the dating practice and is unlikely ever to be recognized as an acceptable variation, though it is still a far too frequent occurrence on American college campuses. The practice of waving at American sporting events is acceptable during certain parts of the game but not during the playing of the national anthem or when a seriously injured player is being removed from the field. The use of tea bags is considered by some a violation of the British practice of making tea. There was a time in baseball when a player who hit a home run would run quickly around the bases and take a seat in the dugout, despite the crowd's demand for a curtain call. It was considered both dangerous and in bad taste to show up the pitcher with displays of bravado. If you did show them up, some pitchers would, as a matter of course, hit you with a pitch the next time you came to bat. Even Ted Williams, who hit a home run his last time at bat—and who did not have to worry about the next pitch—did not take a curtain call. However, it is now commonplace for hitters to dance around the bases and take curtain calls after every home run. They are now expected to step out of the dugout and wave to the cheering hometown fans. It is not surprising that this practice coincides with stricter rules governing the use of "purpose" pitches by pitchers.

Because practice roles do undergo constant change, it is difficult to make specific, ironclad judgments about a person's behavior within a practice role. Behavior that is expected in one generation of practitioners is unrecognized, intolerable behavior in another. How, then, is it possible for consistent and coherent evaluation and judgment of practitioners to take place?

Evaluation and Judgment

A discussion of evaluation and judgment is important for a number of reasons. First, it needs to be demonstrated that both can occur within a practice despite the absence of constitutive rules. Because practice rules (or rulelike formulations) generally serve a descriptive or strategic function, they would have little use in guiding an evaluator or judge. Second, if practices are of the nature described in this study, it would seem difficult to understand how evaluation is possible at all. If practitioners jointly characterize a practice by their separate interpretations of its roles, then how can there be anything like an objective or definitive evaluation? If our actions within a practice role are being evaluated by those who interpret the role differently than we do, how should we take their remarks? More important, how do we even begin to pass on the practice to a new generation if our evaluation criteria are based on an outdated interpretation of its roles? The same can be said of judgment. How can I justifiably render a negative judgment on a person who violates my conception of good character if he honestly believes himself to be acting in accordance with a conception of good character? The very nature of practices seems to preclude evaluation and judgment.

Despite these difficulties, it is clear that practices must have the components of evaluation and judgment. Evaluation and judgment make possible standards of excellence. They are part of the process of teaching practice roles to newcomers, and they help us to enforce standards of behavior within practices. Without such standards, novices would not be able to identify proficient role models; nor would they be able to set goals for themselves in the acquisition of practice roles. However practices are conceived, there must be ways of evaluating competence in role acquisition as well as ways of judging the character of practitioners.

Evaluation and judgment are distinguished in the following way: evaluation has to do with one's competence within practice roles. A novice is evaluated by proficient practitioners in terms of how well he masters the roles. Evaluation is used in teaching a practice to others; it aids in correcting their mistakes and, generally, in allowing them to improve their performance in accordance with the criteria used by the evaluator. One might, for example, evaluate a person's manners on a date, how a novice poker player bets in a particular hand or game, or a comedian's delivery of a joke. Evaluation serves the purpose of helping a practitioner to improve his performance within practice roles. Judgment, by contrast, considers already competent practitioners. Judgment is rendered not on individual performances but on the practitioner himself, over a course of time and in a number of separate performances. Whereas we evaluate a person's competence within a practice role, judgments are made about a practitioner's character. If you judge a person whom you are dating to be sincere and honest, your judgment extends beyond the dating practice. If you judge a bluffer to be shrewd, you are likely to consider him to be shrewd in other aspects of his life. Though judgments take place within practices, their outcome extends beyond them. We begin with a discussion of evaluation.

Those most capable of evaluating a practitioner's performance within a practice role are those experienced in the practice. For example, those competent to evaluate the role performance of a novice engaged in making tea the way the British do are generally proficient practitioners in this practice. Evaluators are familiar with a practice's finer points. They have lived in Britain or are familiar with British customs. They are familiar with the techniques for making a pot of tea, the variety of teas, what tea to drink, and when to drink tea. In addition to this proficiency in the practice's roles, an evaluator has taken the time to abstract from her experience evaluation criteria, which can then be used to teach and evaluate novices. These criteria are based on the evaluator's own characterization of the more important aspects of the practice's roles and the best methods by which the novice can acquire them. Because these criteria are based on an evaluator's own interpretation of a practice's roles, such criteria are not without rivals. Other experts in the practice may have evaluation criteria that differ from hers, or the practice might have undergone change in such a way as to render her criteria outdated. An evaluator can never blindly apply her criteria but must be aware of the varieties and vagaries of the practice and be willing to alter her criteria when they no longer appear to fit the practice as it is presently interpreted by its practitioners. In the same way that practitioners characterize practice roles by their interpretations of them, so, too, they characterize evaluation criteria. Like the practice roles themselves, evaluation criteria will always vary across evaluators, localities, and time periods. Good evaluators will recognize variations of practice roles, even if they do not agree with them.

In addition to her familiarity with the details of a practice, an evaluator is familiar with the conditions surrounding the individual practitioner being evaluated. She evaluates a practitioner in terms of his actions within specific situations. What an evaluator says by way of constructive criticism may depend on the age of the practitioner, his level of competence, or the specific situation in which he finds himself. An evaluator's remarks will also depend on other conditions. For example, what are the motives behind the practitioner's actions? Is he acting to change one aspect of a practice with which he is in general agreement? Perhaps he is acting like so many of the people in his generation, and though his actions violate an accepted interpretation of a practice role, they might reflect a subtle shift in the practice. Or perhaps he has simply run out of loose tea, the stores are all closed, and he comes upon some tea bags in the back of the cabinet, and bag tea is better than no tea. As long as there are no fast and easy rules to apply, an evaluator must be keenly aware of the details of the practice, the practitioner being evaluated, the specific situation in which the practitioner finds himself, and the reasons why the practitioner acted as he did.

The requirements for evaluation are not as difficult as they appear. Assuming that most practices are acquired over the course of many years and usually through subconscious learning, most adults are at least competent practitioners and therefore *prima facie* capable of evaluating the actions of others in various practice roles. In addition, an evaluator may be a role model or someone who knows the novice well. Because of this, the evaluator may be in the perfect position to decide how a specific situation affects the practitioner's performance. Because of her relationship with the practitioner, a successful evaluator will know when to deliver critical remarks with kind encouragement or as a stern rebuke. She will be in the best position to decide if the initiate should be held responsible for his actions or forgiven. For any proficient practitioner, the acquisition of the role of evaluator is as natural as the practice roles themselves.

Three important results follow from this understanding of evaluation. First, evaluators need to engage in practical reasoning.[18] Evaluation requires more than a comparison of the rules with a practitioner's performance within a role. The evaluator is required to take into account a large number of details and to weigh the importance of these details against her evaluation criteria. She must be able to discriminate between her interpretation of a practice role and the interpretation of the novice. In addition, neither the evaluator's method of analysis nor her conclusions must stray too far from the details of the practice, from the practitioner himself, or from the practitioner's unique situation.

Second, because of the nature of practices and the level of detail that must be considered in successful evaluation, the weighing of excusing conditions becomes an important part of the evaluative process. Because there are many correct ways to interpret a practice role and because one's behavior within a practice role is often influenced by conditions external to the practice, excusing conditions will need to be considered.[19] In the practice of making tea, such excuses may include lack of experience in the practice (the excuse for failing to warm the pot); local conditions (hot water may be scarce); extraneous or invasive conditions (you forgot, and this was due to some pressing issue); or rebellion (you think it is a waste of time or a waste of energy to warm the pot). Though limited, many types of excuses can be used to justify one's apparently incorrect or inappropriate behavior in a practice role. We do not, for example, consider pushing people to be acceptable behavior in the practice of walking on busy streets, but one should be forgiven if this is done accidentally and perhaps complimented or rewarded if it is done to save someone from a mugger or an out-of-control taxi. An evaluator cannot jump to conclusions when evaluating competence within a practice role. She needs to know not only what the practitioner has done but what the practitioner thinks he has done and his reasons for acting in this way. Not all excuses will be equally effective or appropriate, but this cannot be decided in advance of hearing them. The discussion and evaluation of excusing conditions are an inseparable part of the dialogue between practitioners. The practitioner defends his actions within the practice role, and the evaluator gives her reasons for accepting or rejecting this defense. Dialogues of this type are an important feature of practices.

Third, as there are many interpretations of a practice role, so, too, there will exist many correct or acceptable evaluation criteria. The fundamental disagreement that will exist among various evaluation criteria is an inherent feature of practices. This disagreement forms part of the ongoing dialogue between practitioners and is one of the factors that cause practices to change. As long as there exist more than one interpretation of any practice role, there will also exist more than one evaluation criterion. We might be able to discriminate between two competing evaluations by comparing the experience of both practitioners, as well as their ability to articulate their respective criteria. But if both experts appear to be equally competent within a practice's roles and if they have equally acceptable evaluation criteria, their conflicting evaluations will have to be accepted. However, for the same reasons that interpretations of practice roles are constrained, evaluation criteria cannot diverge too often or by too much.

In sum, evaluation is a process requiring experience in a practice, the ability to abstract criteria from one's experience, practical reasoning, the capacity and willingness to engage in a dialogue with a practitioner whose performance within a practice role conflicts with one's evaluation criteria, and a willingness to correct one's criteria against the practice. These conditions are not as difficult to fulfill as they might sound. Any person who is competent in a practice role is *prima facie* competent to evaluate another's competence in it.

We turn now to judgment. Judgment extends beyond individual performances within practice roles. Judgments entail conclusions—in the sense that they are final—regarding a person's character, based on his performance within practice roles. One's behavior within a practice role is usually indicative of one's character. If, for example, a proficient practitioner of bluffing uses techniques that seem to us to be unfair (perhaps he tries to distract others or tries to get them drunk), one may negatively judge his character within this role, but in most cases one's judgment will go beyond his performance in this particular role. One is unlikely to engage in other practices with someone who displays an undesirable character in the practice of bluffing. The same is true when we make positive judgments of someone's character on the basis of his behavior in a particular practice role: we are likely to engage with him in other practices. Judgments take longer to form than evaluations, but, then, they are also longer lasting than evaluations and extend over a wide range of practices.

We can see this with the practice of dating. You might consider some of the actions of the person you are dating to be a bit forward or out of context. You might indicate by your comments that you do not approve of them. But if you find these actions to be unacceptable and contrary to your values, and you see no indication that she is attempting to alter them, you may judge her character negatively and thereby end the relationship. Though you judge her character within the confines of the dating practice, your judgment applies to her character as it extends into the community of practices. In making a negative judgment, you pronounce an unwillingness to separate her actions within a practice role from her character, to allow excuses, or to otherwise forgive her. You are certainly not likely to participate in other practices with her. You are not judging competence within practice roles but the character of the person who participates in them. Judgment differs from evaluation in this important respect.

To make judgments of character, one must be a member of the community of practices in which one is making judgments, have a familiarity with the criteria employed in this community for making judgments of character, and have an awareness of the details surrounding the practitioners being judged. The first criterion requires that a judge be a member of a community of practices and proficient in the practices in which his judgments take place. One cannot judge a person's character based on what he does in a practice role unless one knows what is required of him in these practice roles and what is expected of him in the community. Likewise, one cannot make judgments of practitioners who are engaged simultaneously in multiple practices unless one is familiar with these practices. A community member who is familiar with the singing of national anthems at sporting events but not with performing the wave will be unable to make sound judgments about people who are engaged in both. A good judge is proficient in all or most of his community's practices, and he understands the interrelationships among them.

The second criterion asserts that one be familiar with a community's standards for judging character. It is not enough to be proficient in the practices and practice roles of a particular community; one must also be aware of the standards of judgment used by this community. In some communities, casual sex before marriage results in banishment or death; in others, it is accepted or perhaps even expected. Familiarity with standards of judgment requires a great degree of participation and commitment within the community. One obvious way to acquire this commitment is to be raised in the community. Like practice roles, community standards of judgment are inculcated during childhood. It is a mark of one's membership in a community to be able to apply its standards of judgment and to have those standards applied to oneself. People not competent to apply these standards (the very young, the mentally impaired, those outside the community) cannot make judgments of character and will not themselves be judged in this way. One would not be considered qualified to make character judgments of practitioners in certain Scottish practices, for example, unless one also belonged to the Scottish community in which these practices take place. In the same way, a newcomer to that community will often not have his character judged until he is competent in applying the community's judgment criteria to himself and others. One's membership in a community makes one at least *prima facie* qualified to make judgments within it.

The third criterion requires that a judge take into consideration the details surrounding the practitioner's circumstances. For example, before one can judge negatively and accurately the characters of those engaged in the practice of waving during the singing of the national anthem, it is necessary to know some details. What did these people intend by their actions? Were they a large group of foreigners, who were unaware that waving is considered inappropriate during the national anthem? Were they paid by the stadium owners (and provided with the appropriate red, white, and blue banners) to imitate a flag waving in the wind? How might we judge a group of baseball enthusiasts who waved during the national anthem in the hope of bringing harsh judgment on their actions and on waving in general, so as to rid the game of so much nonsense? The ability to judge a person's character is impaired if one is unfamiliar with the practitioner's ignorance or intentions in so acting. A good judge of character considers such details.

A judge should also be aware of the practitioner's familiarity with the community standards used to judge his actions. A person cannot be blamed for admiring publicly the beauty of a person's spouse if such behavior is expected in his community. A judge must take into consideration that new community members, though competent in practice roles, may be unaware of the community's standards regarding character. Someone who is competent in a practice role is usually aware of the community's standards for character, though it is possible to be competent in a nonnative practice, perhaps because it is nearly identical to a practice in one's own community, but unaware of the standards of judgment used by this nonnative community.

Like evaluation, judgment requires the use of practical reasoning. The judge must consider the specifics of the situation in which a practitioner is being judged, the interrelationships between practices and practice roles, and the excusing conditions offered by the practitioner. The reasons a practitioner gives for his actions may absolve him from a harsh judgment or may cause the judge to forgive him and hence to rescind a negative judgment. Like an evaluator, a judge should be willing to engage in a dialogue with the practitioner when such a dialogue helps to resolve disagreements between them or uncertainties the judge may have. In such a dialogue, practitioner and judge give their versions of the situation being considered, and each argues for the conclusion he draws from it. Admittedly, such a dialogue is not always possible; nor is it a necessary condition for making judgments. Such a dialogue, however, can improve the quality and accuracy of one's judgments. The dialogue between practitioner and judge can inform the view of the judge and can cause him to revise his assessment of the situation. A good judge of character should consider a number of issues when making a judgment; the more he understands about the situation, the better his judgment will be. The dialogue between practitioner and judge helps to facilitate this understanding.

Judges, like evaluators, must be prepared to update their criteria. Community standards undergo change, and judges must at least take these changes into account. Disagreements between generations about what counts as good character attest to this. There was a time in baseball when it was a sign of character for pitchers to hit batters who crowded the plate. However, the severity of injuries this practice has caused and the various changes in the game have modified somewhat how a pitcher's character is judged today. Baseball is a more civilized game now, and the standards of character assessment that attach to it are, appropriately, more civilized. Orel Herschiser is a pitcher who exudes this modern standard of character. This mild-mannered, devout Christian man—and extremely good pitcher—would never intentionally hit a batter. A good judge uses current criteria. If his criteria are not current, a competent judge is at least able to recognize this and to defend his criteria against the current ones.

All competent practitioners can and do serve as evaluators and judges. They do this when they evaluate or judge their own behavior or the behavior of other practitioners within their community. Within the confines of local communities, however large or small, the young and newcomers to the community are initiated into the community's practices. In doing so, both proficient practitioners and novices engage in evaluation and judgment. Some practitioners develop reputations as experts. They are sought out by those who are interested in learning the finer points of a practice role, or who are faced with a dilemma of character or conflict of role interpretation, or who seek assistance in reaching an evaluative or judgmental conclusion regarding a fellow practitioner. These practitioners are often asked to make definitive evaluations of competence or judgments of character. They are sought out to help resolve the tough cases. Such experts rarely have formal titles or formal robes, and they do not operate from chambers; but they exist in every community and in every circle of friends. As experts, they speak with authority. Such authority may compete with equally authoritative rivals, but newcomers as well as competent practitioners nevertheless seek out this authority and feel a certain comfort when their actions are said to conform with what such and such an expert would have done in this instance or when their characters are judged positively by someone who knows.

The relationship between the evaluator or judge and the one whose competence is being evaluated or whose character is being judged is part of the ongoing dialogue that advances practices. This dialogue is often marked by a tension between traditional interpretations of practice roles or of community standards of character and new interpretations and standards. But this tension keeps practices vital. Because each new generation of practitioners interprets practice roles and community standards of character to fit the conditions in which their practices take place, evaluative and judgment criteria must necessarily be flexible. Onetime experts become historical artifacts or old-fashioned oddities; onetime revolutionaries become sought-out experts. It is the tension between those who pine for the old days and those who demand change. Practices could not function without this dynamic dialogue.[20]

This completes the outline of a theory of practice. Many questions have been left unanswered and many details left out. The very nature of practices excludes the sort of precise responses we have grown accustomed to with institutional or game theories. The details of a theory of practice must wait upon an understanding of the details of a particular practice and its context in time and place. Though only a small sampling of practices has been used, the list of practices is obviously large. Practices are part of our daily lives, from how we greet people in public to the way we drive our cars in crowded cities to how we raise our children. A theory of practice is an attempt to identify these activities, to distinguish them from other sorts of activities, and to attempt to explain how they function. It is a theory offered not to replace institutional or game theories but to cover those areas of life not captured well by these alternatives. A theory of practice takes its place alongside game and institutional theories and broadens the range of human activity describable and explainable in theoretical terms. It is seen as an addition to, rather than a replacement for, these theoretical approaches. We turn now to the important question of whether promise can be captured by a theory of practice.

CHAPTER FIVE

Promise as Practice

Not only rules, but also examples are needed for establishing a practice.
Our rules leave loop-holes open, and the practice has to speak for itself.
LUDWIG WITTGENSTEIN, *On Certainty*

The truth in questions about action is judged from what we do and how
we live, since these are what control [the answers to such questions].
Hence we ought to examine what has been said by applying it to what
we do and how we live; and if it harmonizes with what we do, we
should accept it, but if it conflicts we should count it [mere] words.
ARISTOTLE, *Nicomachean Ethics*

All people of broad, strong sense have an instinctive repugnance to
the man of maxims; because such people early discern that the
mysterious complexity of our life is not to be embraced by
maxims, and that to lace ourselves up in formulas of that sort is to
repress all the divine promptings and inspirations that spring from
growing insight and sympathy. And the man of maxims is the
popular representative of the minds that are guided in their moral
judgment solely by general rules, thinking that these will lead
them to justice by a ready-made patent method, without the
trouble of exerting patience, discrimination, impartiality—without
any care to assure themselves whether they have the insight that
comes from a hardly-earned estimate of temptation, or from a life
vivid and intense enough to have created a wide
fellow-feeling with all that is human.
GEORGE ELIOT, *The Mill on the Floss*

Characteristics of a Practice

Having outlined a theory of practice, it is time to address the questions of whether promise is describable as a practice and whether the practice approach to promise is superior to the alternatives canvassed in earlier chapters. I begin by showing how promise fits into a practice framework and then argue that this approach avoids the many criticisms leveled at alternative approaches. In short, I claim that a practice approach of promise is not only possible but preferable to these other alternatives.

Recognized Conventional Behavior

A practice was described as, among other things, recognized, conventional behavior that takes place between two or more people. It is, I believe, uncontroversial to say that promising is a recognized, conventional human behavior engaged in by large numbers of people. Most people are aware of when they are promising to others and when others are promising to them. Promising is a practice we use to commit ourselves to a future act and the practice on which we rely to have our future actions coincide with another's. The most obvious cue that one is engaged in this practice is the speech act "I promise." When said in the proper contexts, this speech act commits the speaker to a future act. But any number of other communication acts are equally successful. A promisor might use no words at all, implying by her silence or a nod of the head or a wave of the hand that she is promising. A promisee can accept a promise in similar ways. Steve's promise to Moya and her acceptance of it was probably done in this way. Indeed, a number of the promises described in Chapter One would qualify as informal promises. My students claim that such phrases as "no doubt," "definitely," and "no problem" function, in the appropriate circumstances, as informal promises. In each case, a proficient practitioner interprets words or nonverbal signs to indicate that a promise has been made.

Though promising is recognized as a practice, its identifiable cues are subject to interpretation. For some, the practice is recognized by what someone does not say or by body language; for others, promising occurs only in those situations where the speech act "I promise" is used. There are long-term and short-term promises, solemn and lighthearted promises, unilateral gratuitous promises, mutual executory promises, promises between individuals, and promises between groups. Some promises are formalized in written contracts; others occur without words. New words or gestures can become identified with promising while old words and gestures lose their meaning. Like any practice, promise is a variable one.[1]

Spontaneous Order

A practice arises spontaneously when there occur together in a form of life constraining conditions that a practice is capable of overcoming and enabling conditions or dispositions that make the practice possible. The constraining conditions are those that surround the practitioners and against which the practice is a response. The enabling conditions are those that allow the practitioners to respond in the way they do. Promise is a practice arising from a specific conjunction of constraining and enabling conditions. We begin with the constraining conditions.

First, as David Hume makes clear, human beings find themselves in a harsh world. The necessities of life are scarce and are difficult to gather or utilize. Humans are limited by their size and strength. The constraints of our environment and our physical condition make human interaction necessary. Despite the abundance of nature, lone individuals find it difficult to reap nature's harvests and must rely on others for assistance. In general, human beings seek out companions and often come to delight in one another's company, though the need for this interaction is itself a kind of constraint on individual choices and actions. A second constraining condition is our relative blindness to the future. Although humans are able to intend a future and to imagine themselves in that future, we are less able to see this future with any clarity. We are the kind of creature we are because of our ability to form and act upon our intentions, but our inability always to act in this manner is due, at least in part, to our inability to know about such conditions in advance. This liability also makes us an excuse-making animal. We must often account for why we have not acted as we had intended. It is not enough to have the future interrupted by conditions that we could not or did not foresee. We must also be able to take account of this interruption and present it in such a light as to relieve ourselves of the responsibility for forming this intention and not acting on it.

Constraining conditions such as these make promising a potential practice. Without them, there would be little need to make promises and hence little chance for the practice to arise. But these conditions alone do not cause this practice to spring into existence. Certain enabling conditions must also be present. For one thing, human beings have a concept of future time and are able to project themselves into it. We are able to have thoughts such as "Tomorrow I shall rise early" and "Next week I shall visit my friend David." Forming intentions requires the ability to negate: to say to oneself that in choosing to visit a friend, one is also negating any number of other choices that might just as easily be put in its place but which are now no longer options.

Included in the ability to form intentions is the capacity for memory. Without a good memory, we would not be able to remember the intentions we formed and probably would not be able to have any intentions at all. Because there is always a time gap between an intention and its execution, a person must be able to remember what he intended when the time comes for its execution. Memory is like gravity: it keeps us secure in life's patterns, and it keeps us moving forward. You look at the clock in your office and know that you intend to go to a luncheon in twenty minutes, but you only know this because you remember that you intended to go to a luncheon. The clock is the fulcrum of the present on which you swing between past and future, memory and intention.

Memory and a concept of the future allow one to form expectations as well. The ability to form expectations is important because it allows one to plan for the future, giving the future a semblance of security and certainty. The future is precarious, but the forming of reasonable expectations is an attempt to make it less so. People expect the future to turn out the way they are led to believe it will. For example, you look forward to a picnic on Saturday and are especially happy when the weather forecaster predicts sunshine. On Saturday it rains, and the picnic is canceled. You are likely to be more upset about the turn of events because of your raised expectation of sunshine. Expectations have a tendency to intensify one's reactions: the greater one's expectations, the more intense the response when they are not met. It is difficult for us not to form expectations, so great is our need to make the uncertain future certain.[2] Another enabling condition is creativity. Humans are capable of inventing an array of artifices that facilitate our interests. This is seen in the games that children and adults play, as well as in the development of social and political structures. As Hume says, we are a creative species, and though what we create is artificial, the act of creation is natural. Faced with novel problems, we find creative solutions. Finally, human beings are able to express themselves to one another. This communication takes many forms, spoken and unspoken. With it, we are able to express, among other things, our intentions and expectations to one another. Human communication in all of its forms makes promising possible.

Even with this admittedly brief sketch of our constraining and enabling conditions, it is not difficult to see how promising could originate spontaneously as a practice.[3] Indeed, it is far more difficult to imagine how, given these conditions, promising could not arise. Having both the need and the capacity to make promises, human beings naturally do so. If the practice did not exist, it would arise anew with individuals who share these conditions or others like them. The mere interaction of humans who share these conditions would cause the promising practice to originate spontaneously.

I offer three examples to show how the promising practice originates in the actions of human beings who share a form of life. Imagine a state of nature where promise is not yet a recognized practice. As a member of this state of nature, you recognize another person as your neighbor (social, interdependent) and you recognize tomorrow at noon (concept of future). You communicate to your neighbor in some form of language (not necessarily verbal) that you intend at noon tomorrow to help him with a project (recognition of interdependence, cooperative spirit). He understands what you say and appears to form an expectation about it. Tomorrow at noon you arrive (memory), he smiles (memory), and both of you work. Even though neither of you knows anything about the word "promise" or the concept of promise, you are both participating in an activity you both recognize. If your educated brother-in-law arrives from the city and tells you that what you and your neighbor are doing is called promising and that you are not committed to help your neighbor, because you have not explicitly promised to do so or because you have received no consideration from him, you are likely to ignore his remarks. These details have no relevance to your relationship with your neighbor. It does not matter that what you are doing has a name and is interpreted somewhat differently in the city. As far as you are concerned, you told your neighbor that you would help him and you did. You would tell your brother-in-law that out here in the country (state of nature), you do not need fancy words, and that a person's word (however he chooses to express it) is his bond. It does not matter that your neighbor did not offer to help you, though you fully expect his help in similar circumstances.

Both you and your neighbor likewise recognize that there are conditions that make your intention to help impossible to carry out, but it is not necessary to formalize these conditions. A blinding windstorm may make travel impossible; you may injure yourself in an accident; your child may become ill; you may oversleep; or you may just change your mind. In each case, when you do not arrive at noon, your neighbor is not pleased and may be harmed by your absence. Even without a formalized practice, you would recognize the need to tell him why you did not arrive to help and to offer him an apology or your services on another day. He would expect this kind of response from you. All of this is part of being neighborly.

On another occasion, you are in need of money and you ask your brother-in-law to lend you some. Not being as cooperative as your neighbor is, he makes you write words to the effect that you borrowed money from him and that you will pay him back with interest within the year. He also makes you sign your name and give him something of value, which he will keep as collateral in case you are unable to pay. Although such a transaction might be governed by rules, it is quite possible for something like it to arise spontaneously. In desperate need you might offer something as collateral, though you do not use the word "collateral." Your brother-in-law might want you to sign a piece of paper, though he might not call it a contract. Exceptions also have a role to play here. Your death might cancel the "contract," or you may be granted an extension because of circumstances beyond your control, or your brother-in-law might cancel the contract as an expression of goodwill. Over the course of time such local practices might become better known and be utilized by other members of the community. Such practices might even become formalized in local customs or laws.

On a third occasion, you have fallen in love with the doctor's son. In a moment of bliss you tell him that you will never love anyone else but him. Have you promised fidelity to him? Whatever the outcome, your expression of intention has altered your relationship. Your words allow both of you to form expectations about your separate futures (if he does not say something similar to you, then you can be fairly certain that you will have no future together). Here the expression of fidelity results not so much from necessity as from the desire for friendship or companionship. Such a promise springs from the heart in whatever language it can find. It is not necessary to have learned about the practice before making such a promise; one need only to have a form of life that allows one to feel love and to act on it. Even passionate promises have exceptions: people change, you were momentarily weakened by passion or drink, or you were mistaken. Maggie's promise to Philip to kiss him whenever they met was a childhood promise, and neither of them expected it to be carried out when, years later, they met again. Maggie's expression of love to Philip in the Reds Deep was construed by her to be an expression of engagement, though it is not clear that anyone else, including Philip, believed that they were so engaged.

As these examples make clear, promising can be seen as arising spontaneously. Knowing what we do about the conditions in which humans find themselves and the capacities that we have to survive and to thrive under these conditions, the spontaneous creation of the practice of promise by the actions of individual human beings is more than a distinct possibility. It is an obvious, necessary, and predictable outcome.

Rules

In Chapter Three it was argued that the rules of promise could not be constitutive because constitutive rules presuppose a great deal of what they are purportedly defining; nor could the rules of promise likely succeed as educational rules. First, these rules are not public. Second, there are not enough of them to assist the newcomer in the practice. Third, it is not clear how you could use rules to teach someone to make promises. The rule "promises are obligatory" appears to assume that one already knows how to make promises. In Chapter Four, I claimed that practice rules—or rulelike formulations—serve a descriptive or strategic function.

It is accurate, I believe, to label some—if not all—of what John Rawls and John Searle call the institutional, constitutive rules of promise as the rulelike formulations of the practice. When one uses such a formulation to tell a practitioner that he ought to keep his promises, one is not telling him anything definitive about the practice. Even if he accepts this formulation, he is not likely to become automatically proficient in the practice. In addition, though many promises are obligatory, many of them are not, so a formulation of this kind gives, at best, a general description of the practice. When you tell someone that promises are obligatory, you give him a description of the practice. In effect, you are saying, "In our practice of promising you are expected to keep your promises," or, "If you want to succeed in this practice, keep your promises." If a person knows nothing about this practice, then these remarks will not allow him to participate in it. If he is already familiar with the practice, then these remarks add nothing to his understanding of it. Such rulelike formulations serve only a limited function, albeit an important one.

That these rulelike formulations are descriptive and not constitutive can be seen in another way. I argued in Chapter Four that when someone asks about the practice of dating and how to engage in it, he is given rules of thumb or rulelike formulations that are abstracted from a practitioner's experience. But these are not rules he must follow if he is to participate in the practice of dating. The same can be said of promising. If your friend Brad approaches you with a problem he has about keeping his promises and asks for your advice, you will give him some general rules of thumb: "Make sure that the promisee and you both agree on the conditions of the promise"; "Do not make promises you think you cannot keep"; "Think carefully about your future plans before making a promise"; and so forth. It is clear, however, that Brad already knows how to make promises. What he wants to know is how he should act in a particular instance or, generally, how to be more successful in this practice. The rulelike formulations he receives are abstracted from your experience in this practice. But Brad could just as easily generate a set of formulations from his own experience, and they could be quite different: "It is better to break promises with friends than with colleagues"; or "Keeping promises has instrumental value but not intrinsic value." He could, on the other hand, go to someone else for advice and receive entirely different formulations. As with other practices, these formulations are likely to vary among practitioners. Such variation is an indication that rulelike formulations are descriptive of this practice, not definitive of it.

A person could just as easily engage in the promising practice without having to follow or to know any of these formulations. In the state of nature example above, there was a promise to help a neighbor even though there was no conception of any rules of promise. If an anthropologist asks what one did in committing to help a neighbor, one is likely to reply by giving her a description. But this description comes after one's actions, and hence any formulations are abstractions of the actions, rather than rules that precede them. These formulations describe what one did, though they may describe equally well what others do when they engage in this practice. Rulelike formulations allow practitioners to describe a particular practice, to refer to it, or to better improve their performances in its roles, but they are of little use in helping one to participate in promise for the first time or to define it for others.

Roles

As with other practices, one learns to engage in promising by learning its roles. Practitioners give their own interpretations to these roles, and these interpretations jointly characterize the practice. The ability to acquire these roles requires the possession of the constraining and enabling conditions discussed above. Prospective practitioners do not learn to have intentions or to form expectations about the future; nor do they learn to have a need to make promises. For most healthy human beings, these aspects of promising come with the biological and social package. But having the need to make promises and the ability to do so does not mean that one is born a practitioner. To acquire the roles of this practice requires a period of learning.

Children acquire the roles of this practice by imitating role models. Even before children learn the word "promise," they learn about promising. They learn first to be promisees. When you tell your toddler that it is time to brush her teeth, she excitedly runs to the bathroom door. If you hesitate or remember to do something else instead, she becomes impatient. Likewise, if you say something about getting ready for bed, even if you are not addressing her directly, she runs to her bedroom. Again, if you fail to recognize what it is you are supposed to be doing, she yells, leads you by the hand, or becomes frustrated and cries. I do not maintain that you are making promises to a toddler when you say these things, but, from her point of view, your words express intentions that she understands and that cause her to form expectations that she wants met. If you do not carry out your intentions, you appear to let her down and cause her harm in some way. I would suggest that a child's experience of a role model's successes and failures in acting on expectation-creating intentions goes a long way in teaching her about the practice of promising. What she learns at this age may affect her behavior as a promisor when older, despite what her elders say to her about keeping promises. This early subconscious acquisition of promise roles should not be underestimated. When she is older, the child learns how to go about making and keeping promises. She learns that certain words used in certain contexts create commitments to do as she said, though this lesson may take years to learn. Through trial and error she becomes aware of the many ways to promise, the reasons for keeping or breaking promises, and the difficulty of excelling in this practice. She learns that some promises are hard to keep because of conflicts that arise, whereas others are relatively easy to keep.

A child learns that promises create obligations in the same general way that she learns to avoid touching a hot stove or to refrain from climbing on the furniture. In each instance she learns from experience that certain behavior is expected, certain behavior is rewarded, and certain behavior is punished. The child who is punished for climbing on the furniture has a memory of this and learns to expect similar responses from her parents for similar behavior. Based on this memory, the child is able to imagine an outcome that awaits her for similar behavior. The child learns that promises are obligatory in a similar way. When she is old enough to be held responsible for engaging in this practice, she is told that promisees expect promises to be kept. Here the novice promisor has two types of experiences available to her. First, she has the memory of times when her own expectations were let down. From this memory she is able to imagine how promisees feel, in general, when their expectations are not met. Second, she is told that the promisee and other members of the community expect her to keep her promises and that she can expect punishments of varying degrees should she fail to keep them without good reason. The child remembers her experiences of past punishments when she misbehaved and imagines similar outcomes if she does not keep her promises without good reasons. When the child couples her memories of expectations and punishments with her imagination of future expectations and punishments, along with the community's continuous reinforcement of the view that keeping promises is important, she arrives at the conclusion that, in general, promises are obligatory. The novice associates the obligation of a promise with these various experiences. Once proficient in the practice, the child forgets the roots of promissory obligation and concludes only that promises are obligatory. Such forgetfulness—or learned ignorance—actually facilitates the acquisition of the roles of promise.

There are various ways to acquire the roles of this practice. Children learn these roles by unconsciously observing and imitating the behavior of their role models. Children also learn by playing games that deal implicitly with the roles of promising. In the game of "hide and seek," there are implicit promises both on the part of the person blindfolded—to try to find those who are hiding—and on the part of those hiding—to be capable of being found. There are similar implicit promises in a game such as "truth or dare" and in many board games. Any game requiring cooperative behavior, the expression of intentions, and the raising of expectations helps children to learn the roles of promising.

Another way to learn these roles is to imagine oneself in them. This occurs when a child attempts to engage in these roles at the adult level. He does this when he gets his older siblings or parents to make promises, and when he makes promises to them. At a certain age children become infatuated with promising and seem to make every expression of intention into a formal promise, vaguely aware that this changes the situation in some way; or they use promising as a way of emphasizing their sincere attempt to act a certain way: "Can I have the toy, Daddy? I'll be a good boy, I promise." The imagination is also used in making solemn promises within games. In the same way that a four-year-old Suzuki method violinist bows as if she were a concertmaster, children make solemn promises within the games they play. They are playing, but the play is real. These make-believe games of promising help to prepare them for the real world of promising.

The novice has many role models from whom to choose and will often need to reconcile the conflicts he finds among these models. Children will observe some of their role models breaking their promises at the slightest whim, whereas other role models will make great sacrifices to keep promises. How these conflicts are reconciled will depend on a number of factors, but in time the novice will choose his or her own interpretation of the roles in the practice of promise. As with other practices, there is a range of acceptable role interpretations.

The roles of promise are complex. They require the novice to interpret subtle body cues, to interpret various forms of speech (e.g., irony), and to handle conflicts of interest and obligation. A novice must learn the many possible ways to make promises. He must learn that there are exceptions to promises and that some exceptions will nullify a promise whereas others will not. He must learn the varying degrees of seriousness attached to promising and how personal relationships affect the strength of promises. In acquiring these roles, the novice is helped along by the shared experiences of other practitioners, as well as by the stories he reads and television shows he watches. He also learns from his own successes and failures. These roles are not mastered in a short time. Becoming proficient in them is one of the ways he becomes a full-fledged member of a community.

A novice is considered proficient in a promise role when he no longer sees it as a role to be played at. Viewed externally, proficiency occurs when other members of the practice no longer detect any role-play on the part of the novice. When this occurs, other practitioners treat the novice as a full-fledged member of the practice. They assume that when he makes a promise, he knows what is expected of him. Proficiency occurs when a practitioner is held responsible for his actions or when he is praised or blamed for his behavior within a practice role. The excuse of ignorance is no longer available to him.

The roles of this practice are open for each practitioner to interpret for himself or herself. The practitioners' interpretations characterize these roles—and the practice itself—for themselves and for those around them. The interpretations of proficient practitioners are used in teaching novices this practice, though novices will eventually give these roles their own interpretations. Some interpretations represent variations, whereas others represent violations. Both variations and violations represent arguments for change within a practice. Those who make such arguments with their choice of interpretations must be prepared to defend them and to face the consequences that result when these sorts of arguments are played out in their communities.

Despite this range of interpretations, there is a common thread that connects them. This thread is perhaps nothing more than the pressure one generation puts on another to embrace the traditional roles of this practice. Such pressure rarely meets with total success. This is evident in the practice of promising. This practice has undergone change perhaps not fathomable by people living a century ago. The way promises are made and the lack of seriousness that attaches to many of them in the present day reflect a variation in this practice. People still make promises, but how they make them and how well they keep them have changed. Such change is often cyclical, and practitioners may see a time when the practice recaptures some of its lost solemnity.

Evaluation and Judgment

It was argued in Chapter Four that an evaluator must know the specifics of the practice in which her evaluations take place. In the practice of promise, a competent evaluator would be aware of how promises are generally conveyed. Is it only through specific words, or are there a variety of ways to promise? How are promises received? Must the promisee make a verbal recognition or acceptance of the promise, or can she simply nod? Is there a distinction between bilateral and unilateral promises? What sorts of excusing conditions are allowed? Any proficient practitioner will be able to answer these and similar questions. The evaluator's answers to these questions make up her evaluation criteria. Having had a number of experiences within this practice and having acquired a competence in it, the evaluator is able to abstract rulelike formulations from her experience. She will use these formulations to evaluate other practitioners and, in so doing, help them to acquire competence in the roles of promise. As with other practices, there exist many acceptable evaluation criteria. Occasionally these criteria conflict. Because there is no absolute standard to which evaluators with conflicting criteria can refer, evaluators must be willing to engage in a dialogue. They must be capable of defending their criteria and be willing to update them if they are shown to be indefensible or if they no longer fit the practice as conceived by the community at large.

In addition, the evaluator is aware of the practitioner's competence in the practice and the specifics surrounding the situation in which the practitioner is being evaluated. Is the person being evaluated a novice, just learning how to promise, or is he proficient? Was he coerced into making a promise? Was the promise garbled in communication or misinterpreted by the promisee? Was the promise made in the heat of passion or over one too many drinks? What is the relationship between the parties to this promise? In resolving questions like these, an evaluator considers reasons, excuses, and defenses provided by the practitioner. Evaluations of competence are reached through the careful consideration of specifics such as these, not through an appeal to abstract principles.

Evaluation of practice-role competence is used not only to assist newcomers in acquiring the practice but also by proficient practitioners serving as evaluators of each other and by third parties who serve as arbiters between parties of a promise who disagree over an interpretation of a practice role. In each of these cases, evaluation serves both to teach and to enforce a particular interpretation of a role. An evaluator reveals her interpretation of this role when she evaluates a practitioner. When an evaluator, for example, tells a promisor that she should have been more explicit in her expression of a promissory intention, the evaluator is giving an interpretation of the role of promisor. When an evaluator tells a promisee that he incurs some commitment when he accepts a unilateral promise, she is encouraging him to consider a change in how he interprets the role of promisee. The different interpretations of roles and how these differences are expressed in evaluation criteria is an example of the dialogue that takes place within practices. It is through such dialogues that members of the practice share their interpretations of its roles.

A judgment, by contrast, is an assertion about a practitioner's character. If a judge believes that a promisor blatantly disregards his promises, he may consider this behavior as negatively indicative of the promisor's character. Accurate judgment within the practice of promising requires many of the same skills needed for evaluation. A judge of practitioners is familiar with the practice of promising, as well as the conditions surrounding the practitioner in question. When possible, he considers excuses and defenses brought forth by the practitioner and engages in a dialogue with those he judges. He is willing to defend his assessment of the situation.

Like an evaluator, a judge makes use of criteria against which he judges the practitioner's character. These criteria, however, are not as variable as evaluative criteria. Though there are many successful strategies for becoming competent in the roles of promise, the judgment criteria are more uniformly accepted by the community in which the judgment takes place. This is not to say that there are no variations among judgment criteria, only that there are fewer variations. Because standards of judgment regarding character are one of the ways in which a community defines itself, a homogeneous community will not have more than minor variations in its criteria for assessing character. These standards are possessed by most members of the community and so are available to those making judgments of fellow practitioners.[4]

When a promisor is judged negatively against these standards of character, it is not merely his competence in a practice role that is lacking. It is not that he has trouble keeping promises because of conflicts of duty or because he is forgetful or because he uses language imprecisely. He has trouble keeping promises because he is a liar, a cheat, or interested only in himself. His willful disregard of standards of character as they apply to the roles of promising is indicative of his weakness or lack of character. This lack of character is likely to be expressed in other practices as well. Because of the scope of judgments, a person acting in the capacity of a judge must be certain that a promisor is not failing in his roles because of reasons that do not reflect on his character. It is important, for example, that a judge be familiar with the other practices or institutions in which a practitioner engages. A volunteer firefighter might have a hard time keeping promises because the fire horn is always going off; a musician might always be canceling plans because of a last-minute gig; a person with an elderly grandparent might break his promises whenever they conflict with his grandparent's needs or wishes. These people are engaged in many practice and institutional roles. A competent judge considers the interrelationships between the many roles of the person being judged. The essential question a judge must answer is not whether the practitioner knows how to engage in the roles of promising but whether in keeping or not keeping promises a practitioner can be judged as having a good character. Therefore, judgments of character are best made over time. The ambiguities of human behavior in its many contexts should give a judge pause before rendering a quick or unthinking decision. He should be sure that he is not misjudging or prejudging a person's character.

Although judgments have an air of finality to them, they, too, can be overturned. Judgments have the effect of disowning the practitioner from the judge, but people can change. A false promisor can change his ways, and a judge can come to forgive past transgressions. All judgments are open to revision and reconsideration. Unlike judgments at the level of institutions or games, judgments within practices often possess an interpersonal quality.

Though evaluation and judgment can be analyzed as separate activities, they usually occur simultaneously. As a promisee, you tell a promisor that he should have made a greater effort in trying to reach you before breaking his promise (evaluation), as well as that you think badly of him for it (judgment). Despite the list of requirements necessary to be a competent judge or evaluator, any average practitioner of promise will be competent at both. Most evaluation and judgment is done on a daily basis by average practitioners. As with any activity, community members are not equally competent to evaluate or to judge, and difficult questions may be reserved for those who have made a name for themselves as evaluators and judges. We all partake in these roles daily, but few of us become experts.

Evaluation and judgment are important for the vitality and longevity of the practice of promising. They allow practitioners to teach their children and other newcomers how to become proficient in the roles of promising and how to develop good character. They provide a platform for the dialogue between practitioners. The conflict between those who view promises as solemn and those who interpret them less seriously, for example, is played out at the level of evaluation and judgment. Their disagreements force both sides into a dialogue, and the choices made by the majority of practitioners reflect the outcome of this ongoing dialogue. The practice of promising thrives because it is able to undergo such change without self-destructing in the process.

Precursors to the Practice Approach

Aspects of the practice approach to promise are found in the approaches canvassed in earlier chapters, as well as in the writings of other promise theorists. The institutional approach attempts to explain the origins of promising, to provide a list of necessary and sufficient conditions, and to explain how promises create obligations. Although the answers to these and other questions provided by the practice approach are quite different, both approaches attempt to capture many features of promise. The practice approach also incorporates features of the expectational approach. The ability to form expectations holds a central place in explaining the origins of the promising practice. If people could not form expectations, the practice could not get started. Expectations also play a role in explaining how promises create obligations. Both approaches likewise assert that promising occurs at both the formal and the informal level and that certain conditions may arise that defeat a promise.

The practice and evidentiary approaches to promise consider the historical aspects of promising. Atiyah's work challenges promise theorists to take seriously the empirical evidence of promising. The practice approach takes up this challenge. Both accounts maintain that there is a defeasible or revocable nature to promising, and both provide a mechanism for how defeating conditions are to be evaluated and how disagreements over these conditions are to be resolved. Both accounts maintain that such disagreements should be resolved in a social context. Atiyah suggests that just as there are legal legislators and judges, so, too, there ought to be moral legislators and judges who decide upon the details of the practice of promising, as well as whether particular promises are morally binding. Atiyah gives us no indication of how the conflicts over these details are to be resolved, though in the practice approach, conflicts are resolved within a framework of evaluation and judgment.

There are similarities between the practice approach and the intuitionist approach as well. The practice approach recognizes the intuitive clarity of promissory obligation, a clearness that defies further explanation. Practitioners come to see and feel promises as obligatory long before they are able to articulate why or how promises create obligations. Having forgotten the origins of how one comes to see promises as obligatory, such articulation will fail to capture the reasons. It is doubtful that the intuitionists who were discussed in Chapter Two would agree with the explanation given for the intuitive clarity of promissory obligation, but both approaches nevertheless share a common view about this clarity. Both approaches similarly agree that conflicts of obligation arise and that there must be a way of handling these conflicts. Finally, both approaches consider the views of everyday practitioners.

There are likewise some similarities between the practice approach and the intentional approach. The practice approach considers the promisor's intentions to be an important aspect of understanding the practice. Further, Robins's willingness to use the results of the natural and psychological sciences is in the spirit of the practice approach. A theory of practice draws from all of the fields relevant to promising. Both accounts likewise use form-of-life arguments; both recognize that promising is a peculiarly human practice. Despite these similarities, we must keep in mind the reasons given in earlier chapters for rejecting these alternative approaches to promise. I argue below that the numerous criticisms leveled against these approaches can be effectively handled by the practice approach.

Aspects of the practice approach can also be found in some of the literature not covered in earlier chapters. In his article "On Promising," A. I. Melden criticizes promise theorists for analyzing the concept of promising in abstraction. He argues that theorists should resist the temptation to explain promising or to analyze it in a nontemporal fashion. Citing Ludwig Wittgenstein, Melden claims that we should examine the concept of promise as we would an engine: while it is doing work and not when it is idling. We learn how to promise, says Melden, not by learning rules but by "learning how to think and do like moral agents do."[5] We learn by training. "Knowing what a promise is, like knowing what a joke is, is not a matter of having information, . . . but knowing how to think and feel in the way this is done by promisors who speak in good faith and then go on to do as they promise to do."[6] We learn also that promises cannot always be kept and that rectification is in order when a promisor has made an honest mistake. According to Melden's account, people are able to promise because they share a common form of life.

In a later article, Melden emphasizes the moral relationship set up between promisor and promisee and describes it as a moral relation "in all of its rich conceptual complexity."[7] These moral relations take place within a moral community. He describes how children learn to promise. It is not, he says, by learning a formula or recipe:

Rather, the child comes to understand, first, that there are certain central or nuclear sorts of cases to which a rich array of concepts may be applied. Second, it comes to appreciate the fact that certain other cases deviate from these nuclear cases in one or another of a variety of respects. And, third, it learns how the various sorts of differences that exist between such deviant cases and those central or nuclear cases—to which the fully enriched array of concepts apply unproblematically, without truncation or diminished degree—are importantly relevant, and how it is that this array of concepts must receive, in varied ways, limited or qualified application when in various respects the cases under consideration diverge from central or nuclear cases.[8]

The practice approach shares many of the features discussed by Melden. It recognizes that promising is a bitemporal phenomenon and that it cannot be easily abstracted. It offers an analysis that considers the contexts and relationships of promisors and promisees and gives an account of how children come to acquire practice roles. The practice approach examines promising while it is doing work.

John Finnis's work on promising also parallels a practice approach. Finnis argues in his methodological remarks that philosophers should consider the whole range of data affecting their subject matter. "The undertaking [of a theory of natural law] cannot proceed securely without a knowledge of the whole range of human possibilities and opportunities, inclinations and capacities, a knowledge that requires the assistance of descriptive and analytical social science."[9] Finnis takes as his data base the moral community, where by "community" he means "an ongoing state of affairs, a sharing of life or of action or of interest, an associating or coming together. Community in this sense is a matter of relationship and interaction."[10]

Finnis refers to promising as a complex human practice that

takes place in a community. He sees promising as an informal human practice and not simply as the law of contract. A person can have an obligation to keep a promise only in those communities that recognize this practice. Finnis also believes that there can be many forms of the promising practice in any given community, "some wider, some narrower, some more relaxed, others more stringent."[11] He likewise believes that all promises have defeating conditions and that within the practice of promising there will exist a good amount of disagreement about the obligation of particular promises and of promissory obligation in general. "This feedback of various forms and requirements of practical reasonableness lends the extra-legal practice a flexibility without which it doubtless could not survive, but also an elusive variability or unreliability, of a sort that legal thought strives to exclude from legally regulated transactions."[12] What Finnis says conforms to the basic outline of a theory of practice.

In earlier chapters I identified philosophers who are viewed as historical precursors to the five approaches evaluated there. I believe that the practice approach has a historical precursor as well: David Hume.[13] Hume recognizes promising as a uniquely human practice that arises spontaneously because of our human nature and our presence on a planet with limited resources. It is because we are a creative species that we are able to invent the artifice of promising. Promissory obligation for Hume is of two types: the natural obligation to participate in the practice of promising (this obligation arises out of natural necessity); and the artificial or feigned obligation to keep individual promises (this obligation arises when one imagines oneself to be under such an obligation and is encouraged by other members of the community to treat this obligation as real). The most persuasive technique in getting a promisor to believe that this obligation is real is to threaten him with something real: never being trusted again. Like the practice approach, Hume's account of promise is generally descriptive of the practice. Hume has been identified by some scholars with the institutional approach to promising, but though there are some surface similarities between Hume's account of promise and this approach, I believe this reading of Hume to be largely misguided.[14]

I turn now to a discussion of the criticisms leveled against the various approaches evaluated in earlier chapters. I demonstrate below how the practice approach is either immune to these criticisms or can answer them.

Earlier Criticisms Considered

Promise as Intention

Like each of the approaches evaluated in Chapter Three, the intentional approach fails because of its limited scope. First, though any theory of promise needs as part of its explanatory devices an account of intentions, Robins is mistaken to conclude that an intentional theory is all that is needed to capture promise. Second, Robins does not consider sociological and anthropological data that might confirm or deny his account of intentions or that might limit his conclusions to a particular culture or time period. Third, Robins is silent about the defeating conditions of a promise. His theory recognizes that promising has a double-tensed indexical temporal reference, but he says only that a promise takes away from the promisor the freedom to change his mind. The only defeating condition he considers is the promisee's freedom to waive the promisor's obligation. Fourth, the intentional approach gives disproportional weight to the promisee's wishes. In this approach, it is the promisee's right to waive a promissory obligation at any time. The intentional approach gives the promisee too much power and freedom and the promisor not enough.

According to the practice approach to promise, intentions are just one slice of a complex form of life that makes the practice of promising both possible and necessary. Further, this approach recognizes that the promising practice is shaped by its historical and social contexts. As part of this practice, the ability to form intentions would likewise be shaped by these contexts. An account of intentions in this approach would rely on the same types of empirical data used to inform the overall account of the practice. Reliance on these data might reveal that some cultures do not promise at all or have a weaker concept of obligation, because they have not yet developed the capacity to form intentions or because this capacity is underdeveloped or unnecessary in their social arrangement. In addition, because promising is a double-tensed indexical practice, it must contain defeating conditions. The former condition entails the latter. Finally, the practice approach construes promising as a relational practice. In some cases the promisee has an implicit obligation to allow the conditions of the promise to be met. Some people make promises as signs of love or friendship and would be hurt if the promisee had no interest in seeing the promise carried out. Just as the promisee forms expectations, so, too, does the promisor. Even the mere acceptance of a unilateral promise by the promisee may entail some sort of commitment on his part to allow the promisor to carry out his promise. Relational features are also present in determining the exceptions to a promise. Both promisor and promisee are expected to explain themselves when a promise misfires. Relational commitments are part of the practice of promising.

Promise as Intuition

The intuitional approach was criticized for the following reasons: (1) it conceives of promising entirely as a static, homogeneous practice; (2) except for the notion of *prima facie* duties, it generally ignores the issues surrounding excusing conditions; (3) it fails to recognize that intuitions may differ regarding the ordering of duties, as well as what the duties of promisor and promisee entail; and (4) it provides an unworkable method for resolving conflicts of intuition.

The practice approach first recognizes that the practice of promise is not characterized apart from how it is characterized by practitioners living in a particular community in a particular social setting and time period. The practice of promise may have been a homogeneous practice at one point in a community's history and it may become so again, but homogeneity is not a necessary condition of the practice. The practice approach replaces a homogeneous and static concept of promise with a dynamic, historically situated practice. Second, this approach also recognizes defeating conditions as a necessary aspect of the practice and seeks to explain how conflicts over these conditions are resolved. Rather than focusing exclusively on how promises create obligations, it considers the conditions that make this practice possible, how the practice is taught to new generations, how it undergoes change and variation while remaining an identifiable practice, and how promissory obligations are created and defeated. Promise as practice attempts to be comprehensive in its treatment of promise.

Third, this alternative approach predicts that practitioner intuitions will differ within a homogeneous community. Although practitioners share common practices, how they learn and interpret practice roles will vary. A practitioner may acquire the intuition that the duty of one practice role out-weighs the duty of another practice role. Another practitioner may acquire the opposite intuition or acquire no intuition at all. In one person's home, promises may be treated solemnly; in another's, loosely. One practitioner learns that there are many ways to promise; another, that there is only one way. Although practitioners of a homogeneous community may agree that, in general, promises ought to be kept, they will disagree over the details of the practice. A theory of practice explains why this variation exists, how it is dealt with, and how the practice of promise is maintained in spite of—indeed, because of—this variation. Finally, the practice approach provides a detailed method for resolving clashes of intuitions. When promising is seen as a relational practice, it is clear that an appeal to one's private intuitions as a method for ordering duties or considering excusing conditions will not succeed in resolving these sorts of disagreements between practitioners. The practice approach posits a method for conflict resolution that is clearly relational in nature.

Promise as Evidence

There were three problems discussed with the evidentiary approach. First, it construes the whole of the practice of promising from its more narrow legalistic perspective. Second, though Atiyah makes use of empirical evidence to inform his theory, this evidence is limited almost entirely to the law. Third, in focusing on the external conditions of a promise (explicit wording, detrimental reliance, consideration), this approach generally ignores the intentions of the promisor. According to the evidentiary approach, a promise is created when certain conditions are met, whether or not the promisor intended to create these conditions.

The practice approach casts a wide net. The practice of

promise occurs in many guises. Among friends, promises may not require specific words. Strangers may demand the precise language of a written contract, however. All contracts are promises, but not all promises are contracts. The practice approach recognizes both formal and informal promises. Likewise, it does not limit its empirical findings to the opinions of judges and the laws of legislators. A practice account of promise considers all of the relevant evidence. It is premature for Atiyah to conclude that unilateral promises, because they are not recognized presently in the courts, create little or no obligation. What do sociological studies say about unilateral promises? What do religious precepts hold about such promises? The data base of the practice of promise is much larger than the one considered by Atiyah. Finally, promise as practice does not focus exclusively on the external features of a promise. It claims that a successful promise does not depend solely on whether the promisee detrimentally relies on it or the promisor benefits from it. It denies that the promisee always has the correct position, even if he does detrimentally rely on a promise. He might be unable to form reasonable expectations or to read nonverbal communication. A promisor should not always be held to a promise he did not make or intend to make simply because the promisee misinterpreted his remarks and relied on them. In the practice approach, a successful promise is one in which the perceptions of its external conditions, as perceived by the practitioners in question, roughly correspond to their internal states. Such perceptions are rarely without ambiguity, and clarification and explicitness are not always possible or desirable. When these ambiguities do occur, they are best resolved within the relational contexts of this practice. In such conflicts, the determination of whether a promise has been made often depends upon the outcome of a dialogue between its parties.

Promise as Raised Expectations

The expectational approach fails to differentiate between raised expectations that do create promissory commitments and those that do not, and it does not provide a mechanism for conflict resolution regarding excusing conditions. The practice approach recognizes the forming of expectations as an enabling condition for the practice of promise, but it recognizes that this condition cannot serve as the only explanatory mechanism of the practice. As a relational practice, promising depends for its success not only on the ability of the promisee to form expectations but on the ability of the promisor to form intentions and to communicate them successfully. In addition, the promisee must be capable of forming reasonable expectations. What counts as reasonable will depend on community standards, but I would define "reasonable expectations" as those that are tempered with the understanding that the future is uncertain and may not always turn out the way one has planned or has been told it would. By this definition, those who expect either that everything will turn out as planned or that nothing will turn out as planned are unreasonable about their expectations. Forming reasonable expectations is one of the requirements for proficiency in this practice's roles.

The promisee must also communicate to the promisor, when possible, her level of expectation. This helps the promisor to decide whether or not he made a promise to begin with and how he should interpret the strength of his commitment to the promisee. If the promisee makes it clear that she has reasonably low expectations about the promise, the promisor might resolve a conflict of interest or duty differently than if a promisee expressed reasonably high expectations. Reference to a promisee's low expectation level is not an uncommon excuse given by promisors who break their promises. But even when reasonable expectations are raised, the strength of the commitment they produce is not everywhere equal. The strength of the commitment is influenced by the combined interpretations of the practitioners. Expectations do play a role in promising, but the nature of this role is both more limited and more complex than the expectational approach recognizes. In addition, the practice approach places a greater responsibility on the promisee than simply forming expectations. She must be able to form reasonable expectations and to engage in a dialogue with the promisor when they do not agree on the conditions of a promise or on its excusing conditions.

Although the expectational approach does recognize the existence of excusing conditions, it does not indicate how one is to recognize such conditions or how to resolve instances when practitioners do not agree. In the practice approach, the promisor decides to keep or break a promise by assessing the following: (1) the shared understanding of the conditions of the promise; (2) the strength of its commitment; (3) the reasonable expectations of the promisee; (4) the strength of the excusing conditions; (5) the strength of the arguments he could put forth in defense of his excuse; and (6) the possible outcomes of keeping or breaking the promise. In making his assessment, the promisor considers both his role as promisor and the other roles that might be causing the conflict. The decision he makes is not always easily arrived at; nor does it simply consider the expectations of the promisee. If his decision conflicts with the promisee's assessment of the situation, they engage in dialogue or appeal to a third party, if necessary.

Promise as Institution

Much of the criticism of the institutional approach focused on its inability to explain with constitutive rules how members of institutions become participants in them. Put simply, this approach must either presuppose the form of life that makes promising possible (and hence appeal to something other than constitutive rules) or try to define a form of life with rules. The practice approach avoids these problems because it takes a form of life as the basic condition for the existence of the practice. One need only observe the constraining and enabling conditions of our form of life to conclude that promising emerges as a practice. Just as constitutive rules cannot define our competitive spirit or our love of game playing, so, too, they are unable to define our ability to form intentions or expectations. We teach our children the rules of specific games, but we do not teach them to be game players or to love such games. In a similar way, we teach our children about the different types of promises that exist and the conditions that defeat promises, but we do not teach them how to promise. They already know how to do that, at least at a primitive level. The practice approach, then, does not presuppose this form of life but takes it as basic to the existence of the practice. It better explains how the practice of promising could arise *de novo*. The promising practice arises spontaneously when certain conditions are present. It is not designed or defined in response to these conditions. The practice of promising is self-functioning and self-regulating; it originates, undergoes change, and is taught to new members by the collective actions of human beings sharing a form of life and living in homogeneous communities.

Promise as practice explains how someone can become a practitioner without knowing any rules. A prospective practitioner comes to a practice already possessing the dispositions to create or acquire the practice. What he learns in a particular community is how this practice's roles are interpreted and how one goes about excelling in them. These roles are learned primarily through the imitation of role models. By consciously and subconsciously observing and imitating role-model behavior, novice practitioners slowly acquire the roles of this practice. In this way they are practitioners long before they can articulate the aspects of practices or practice roles in words or rulelike formulations.

It might be argued that there is little difference between John Searle's claim that constitutive rules are acquired through subconscious learning and the claim that practice roles are acquired through subconscious learning. But there are differences, and they are easy to see. First, humans are imitative creatures, and we use imitation to learn many things. We learn facial expressions, slang, and accents by watching and listening to those around us. Children are taught to swing a bat, throw a ball, dance, or swim by having adults initially move their bodies for them so that they can get the feel of these activities. Children likewise observe adults engaged in these actions and, perhaps, subconsciously observe their physical movements. It is, I believe, more natural for a child to imitate adult behavior than to learn subconsciously some rule that is constitutive of this behavior. Learning a promise role is just another bit of imitative behavior that observant humans master along with learning how to swing a bat, ride a bike, and lose.[15] Second, because of the range of practice-role interpretations, it is not essential that new practitioners learn these roles in a precise manner. For constitutive rules to function, they must be learned exactly by those who learn them. This feature of constitutive rules makes the explanation of subconscious learning difficult to accept. Acquisition of practice roles through imitation and imagination need not be so exact, thus making the explanation of subconscious acquisition easier to accept.

The institutional approach is also unable to explain how the institution of promise could be governed by one or, at most, a few rules; how these rules could be public in spite of there being variations among them; and how such rules could delimit the exceptions to a promise. The practice approach explains the relatively short list of rules provided by Rawls and Searle as rulelike formulations that describe the practice or provide strategic information. Rawls maintains that institutional rules are public rules and hence are learned in common by participants in that institution. The public nature of these rules helps institutions to maintain their definitive shape. It was argued in Chapter Three that to be public rules, the constitutive rules of promising must be learned identically by all of the members of the institution. Even Rawls admits that variations exist among the rules of the institution's members, though he diminishes this problem for his approach.

In the practice approach there are only rulelike formulations, and these formulations are largely unnecessary in the maintenance of the practice of promise. First, practices are characterized by roles, and roles are characterized by the interpretations of these roles by individual practitioners. But these interpretations are constrained in a number of ways. Certain interpretations are not possible given certain social conditions. Second, practitioners normally want to succeed in acquiring practice roles, and this requires copying many of the details of these roles from their role models. Third, practitioners belong to homogeneous communities where certain role interpretations are reinforced in a number of ways. Practitioners belong to the same organizations, read the same books and newspapers, watch the same TV programs, and so forth. These common experiences help to maintain the consistency of role interpretations. Role models are not just family members and friends but also TV characters, public figures, teachers, ministers, and newspaper columnists. Through all of these influences there are distilled common values and standard interpretations of practice roles. The end result is that the practice of promise is flexible enough to allow a range of acceptable interpretations while being able to maintain its recognizable form.

Constitutive rules are similarly unnecessary when dealing with exceptions to promises. According to the practice approach, exceptions are a necessary feature of the practice of promising in our form of life. Because humans are creatures with a limited vision of the future and because, as members of a community, we take on many roles, our promises are often interfered with. Situations occur that practitioners do not foresee or that they foresee but do not intend. Promising is a practice that reduces the uncertainty of the future, but because it is a double-tensed indexical practice, practitioners cannot escape this uncertainty. A practitioner recognizes that when he makes a promise he should do his best to keep it, but he also recognizes that situations will arise that will make keeping this promise either impossible or undesirable. No rule could define this feature of the practice, but then no such rule is necessary to define it.

On another point, it was argued that no list of constitutive rules is likely to define or list the exceptions to a promise, because what counts as an exception to a promise depends upon the specifics of the situation and the relationship between promisor and promisee. What counts as an exception must wait upon the situation in which it occurs. Practitioners learn about the defeasible nature of this practice and about the types of exceptions generally acceptable in it through their training. This training consists primarily in observing and imitating the behavior of their role models. Within these roles, practitioners experience the conflicts of interest and commitment that a promise can create and the harm that a broken promise can cause. They learn what types of excuses are acceptable by listening to their role models' excuses. Children learn—sometimes the hard way—that parents and adults generally have many different roles to play and that this causes them to break their promises frequently. If children have good role models, this experience will not make them cynical but instead will teach them that conflicts of interest and duty do arise and that these conflicts make the keeping of promises a difficult endeavor. They are further educated when chastised or disciplined for failing to provide adequate justification for their broken promises. Overall, there is a great deal of trial and error in this training. At best, one emerges from it with a sensibility, a kind of practical wisdom, about the defeasible nature of the promising practice.[16]

The practice approach also outlines a method for determining the value of excusing conditions. It recognizes that what is to count as an exception to a promise will depend upon the circumstances surrounding the practitioners in question. Further, this approach characterizes promising as a relational practice. What is to count as an exception is often determined by the nature of the relationship between promisor and promisee. If the relationship is a formal one, few exceptions may be accepted. If the relationship is between close friends, the range of exceptions may be much wider. In situations where there is disagreement, practitioners should engage in a dialogue. The promisor tries to convince the promisee that she has a legitimate excuse for breaking (having broken) her promise, while the promisee argues the contrary position. If there is no clear outcome, such conflicts can be resolved by presenting the evidence to a third practitioner who will offer his assessment. Because it is usually the promisee who is harmed by a broken promise—I say "usually" so as not to forget instances where a promisee breaks his implicit promise to the promisor—the final evaluation and judgment is left for him to make, as long as third-party assessments are inconclusive. If, however, third-party evaluations or judgments consistently side with the promisor and the promisee refuses to change his views, the promisor is nevertheless excused. Such obstinacy by the promisee in the face of such consensus will make him appear unreasonable. His evaluations or judgments will be viewed as violations of standard community criteria. To remain obstinate in one's violation of community criteria is to place oneself temporarily outside the community of practitioners. Resolving such conflicts is a complex affair, but no more complex than the relationships between practitioners.

Two issues remain. The first concerns Searle's idealized case of promising; the second, how one commits oneself to the practice of promising if there is no rule stating that one must. It was argued in Chapter Three that Searle's idealized case ignores whatever empirical data might be used to inform it. Further, it was shown that such an idealized case would be utterly useless in teaching someone how to engage in the practice and that the question of how practices are taught to newcomers cannot be ignored. The practice approach obviously rejects an idealized conception of promise. The accuracy of this approach to promise depends on the data collected from the community in which the practice takes place. If the data change, so, too, must a practice theorist's account of the practice change. There can be no paradigm case of promising in the practice approach. The variations in this practice range across time and localities. In the same way that an unchanging, rigid practice of promise would not survive in a community of practices (at least, in our form of life), Searle's idealized case does not survive the range of data refuting it. The practice approach also better explains how the practice of promise is transmitted to new generations.

Finally, the institutional approach was unable to explain how one becomes committed to the institution of promising. The rules of this institution tell its members what to do only after they decide to engage in it. In the practice approach, promising is not an institution in which one chooses whether or not to play. On the contrary, promising is an enabling practice. It enables us to achieve certain goals and to gain certain goods that are important to the human condition. Human beings have a need to make promises and to accept promises. Commitment to the practice is part of what it means to live a human life. There is difficulty in imagining what life would be like without this practice, though it is likely to be devoid of all relationships. To the degree that such a life is impossible to live, life without the practice of promising is also impossible. The commitment to the practice, then, is a natural commitment; it comes with the territory. This is what Hume meant when he spoke of the natural obligation to promising: it is not possible—or natural—for humans not to feel obligated to the practice of promising. This obligation is a natural feature of being human.[17]

Criticisms of the Practice Approach

The practice approach is not without problems of its own, and I highlight some of them here. First, the general claims about how practices begin, operate, undergo change, and maintain their shape need to be tested against the data still outstanding and the counterarguments of critics. It is possible that the explanations given in Chapter Four fail to describe what actually happens in the formation of practices. The approach, then, is still largely unconfirmed. Second, although the theory provides a general or comprehensive framework for practices, the conclusions it draws about specific practices are constrained by the social and historical conditions in which these practices occur. Not only must practice theorists be accurate in their initial theoretical descriptions of a local practice of promising, but they must also be prepared to update their findings. This outcome will no doubt be resisted by those who seek theories that make general or universal claims about promising.

Third, implicit in the practice approach to promise is a moral relativism that some may find disturbing. A full treatment of this issue would take us too far afield. Suffice it to say here that if a change in terminology is to be preferred, the practice approach is more accurately called pluralistic. It recognizes that there are many practices and many variations of the same practice. These variations assist practitioners in achieving the goods specific to their form of life. Relativism claims that there is no paradigm practice. Pluralism claims that there are many successful forms of the same practice. Further, if relativism or pluralism reflects our present historical setting, then so be it. As a descriptive theory, the practice approach can only report and organize the data it collects.

A fourth drawback is the sheer quantity of data to be collected and explained. The practice approach recognizes that an explanation of any social practice is a much larger and more detailed project than thought previously by most promise theorists. Much of the data concerning this practice are still outstanding. Hence, the results of this approach, though more accurate, may be longer in coming.

Finally, the practice approach is a descriptive theory. It tells us how promising operates as a practice, but it tells us nothing about its normative aspects. It has been an essential assumption of this study that a proper treatment of promise requires that we first see it as a social practice. Only then can we consider its identifying features as a moral practice.

Though such a division of labor may at first be thought to be a drawback to this approach, I believe that the accurate description of a social practice such as promise requires full-time work by practice theorists.

I do not attempt here to defend the practice approach against these criticisms. Some of them are stylistic (critical of the method of philosophizing in this approach), whereas others depend on data still outstanding. One cannot meaningfully argue either about what is still outstanding or style.

I now examine the examples we started with in Chapter One in terms of a practice approach to promise. To begin with, despite the absence of specific words and of satisfaction of necessary and sufficient conditions, each of the examples in Chapter One functions as a promise. Steve's promise to Moya was probably unspoken; Clark's banker and Louise likely used informal language; and Maggie used words that, in her mind, bound her to Philip in important ways. Only Tom's oath on the Bible and the promise he extracts from Maggie are traditional speech-act sorts of promises. In each of the examples, a moral moment occurs wherein one person feels obligated toward another. Two lives become intertwined, and the lives of both promisor and promisee take on an interdependent significance that was lacking before the promise was made. In each case, what occurred between two people was recognized—or was recognizable—as conventional behavior.

How these promises are interpreted will depend greatly on how the people involved understand the spoken words, the expressed intentions, the raised expectations, and the exceptions that arise. Would Moya have understood Helen's difficulties in handling Johnny? Does Clark really think his banker has made him a solemn promise, or was it simply an expression of unfounded optimism? A promise depends also on the relationship between its parties. Knowing the personalities of Tom Tulliver and his father, one can fully expect that Tom would promise revenge on his father's adversary and that his father would ask for such a promise to be witnessed on the family Bible. We know also that Maggie is somewhat impulsive and forgetful. When she was a young girl, she promised to feed Tom's rabbits while he was away at school and then promptly forgot, causing them to starve to death. Perhaps Russ and Louise have the kind of sibling relationship where sudden changes of plans are acceptable. Maggie knows that Philip is deeply in love with her and that her expressions of her love for him—though not fully or deeply romantic—nevertheless create in him high hopes, if not expectations, of an engagement. Maggie then falls deeply in love with Steven but cannot bring herself to harm Philip. It would be a methodological mistake to attempt to extricate these promises from the relationships in which they were made. We need to know much more about each of these examples before we can confidently make evaluations and judgments about the parties involved. I resist, then, a judgment on each of the examples. Such judgments would imply that there are necessary and sufficient conditions against which to compare them or universal moral principles that any of us could apply. Promise as practice suggests that each of us, insofar as we are practitioners of promise, is capable of engaging in evaluation and judgment.

In terms of what these examples tell us, I would say that Steve is not a cad if he tries to save his marriage by sending Johnny away. It is not because of any technical maneuver that he escapes his promise to his sister but rather because he feels a slightly stronger commitment to his wife and child and believes that in sending Johnny to his brother's home he will not lose him entirely. I would think that his sister Moya might understand and accept his decision, considering the circumstances. It is not as clear how Louise should proceed. Depending on the particulars of the personalities involved and other conditions, she might be justified in breaking her promise to her brother, Russ, not because of a conflict with an equally strong moral obligation but simply because she and her husband need a weekend escape from the city. Such a broken promise should be accompanied by a dialogue between brother and sister and an attempt on her part to make it up to Russ. Clark's banker was fully aware of the financial pressure Clark was in and, in my view, was irresponsible in assuring him a closing date and then leaving before all the paperwork could be completed.

As for Maggie and Tom, Maggie's promise of a kiss was made when she was young and not a full participant in the practice, and neither she nor Philip expected the promise to be kept. Her expression of love to Philip, though clearly raising his hopes, was not, in my view, a promise of engagement. She pitied Philip more than she loved him. On the other hand, Tom's promise to his father, though severe, is a commitment—however misplaced—to seek revenge on his father's enemy. One suspects that Tom would seek this revenge whether or not he had made a promise to do so, and in this respect it would not be incorrect to say that his promise evidenced a previous commitment. Finally, Maggie's promise to Tom was clearly coerced and was made by Maggie simply to get Tom to leave her alone. Given the social conditions of the time, such a promise is probably considered acceptable and binding, but it would not likely bind a modern woman to her older brother.

The analysis here is brief, incomplete, and not likely to please. It is meant only to demonstrate the sorts of issues that are important to consider in a social practice account of promise. It suggests, too, that a theory of practice is not designed as a tool of judgment. Questions of evaluation and judgment fall not to philosophers, who engage in long-winded moral analyses and who often make moral judgments when and where they are not invited, but to the practitioners themselves and to other members of the community to which they belong. Our evaluations and judgments are more accurate and more valuable when we are the parties to a promise or when we know the parties involved. Promise as practice resists the urge to make universal pronouncements. It relies on the embeddedness of practitioners within their communities and of practices within forms of life. In this respect it leaves everything as it is.

Postscript

This study has urged a broader view of promise than has been taken by numerous contemporary approaches. If promise is seen as a complex social practice, then theoretical approaches must likewise be conceptually rich and reflect the social nature of this practice. This requires a willingness on the part of philosophers to go beyond the confines of contemporary philosophical theorizing. It demands that philosophical theories concerned with social practices be informed by the empirical findings of those who study these practices and by the experiences of practitioners. It is, after all, no small point if the central case employed by a philosophical theory is inaccurately described. Implicit in my criticisms of contemporary approaches to promise is the claim that if philosophers who use promise as a principal case in their various theoretical pursuits fail to describe promise accurately in these pursuits, they may likewise stumble in their larger pursuits. If these approaches underdescribe promise and ignore or fail to account for the data, it is prima facie plausible that the larger theories in which promise is embedded will fail. The results of this book encourage a reevaluation of the use and accuracy of promise as a principal case in philosophical theorizing, be they theories of language, jurisprudence, ethics, or mind.

This study is likewise highly critical of the methodologies used in contemporary approaches to promise. The range in these approaches is narrow, the analysis is linguistic or conceptual, and the approaches focus on individuals, either as speakers of a language or as focuses of actions and duties. These methodologies are ill suited for the treatment of promise. A theoretical account of promise requires a wide range; an analysis of what people do, not only what they say or think; and a focus on social, interconnected individuals: members of families, communities, and cultures. There is a price to pay for these shifts, but they are necessary if we are concerned with providing an accurate and powerful theory of promise.

Such shifts in methodology require a broadening of the tools of philosophy. Recognizing the limits of narrow theoretical explanations and of linguistic and conceptual analysis, promise theorists should be inspired by this study to explore the confines of other disciplines and to borrow concepts and data not available to philosophers working alone. If, as philosophers, we take our theories of institutions and practices seriously—and if they are to be taken seriously by other disciplines—we must not be shy about our forays into these disciplines. I interpret the recent turn to applied philosophy in the widest possible way to mean that we apply the tools of philosophy to the world around us and that philosophical theories should be applicable to the data they purport to explain. The practice approach requires us to look at a larger picture than do other theories of promise. We should not deny ourselves the views that other disciplines provide.

I have tried to make good my claim that the practice approach is superior in its treatment of promise to any of the five alternatives evaluated in Chapters Two and Three. The thrust of my criticism in those earlier chapters was that the alternatives failed because they underdescribed promise, lacked coherency, and did not conform to the data. In positing a theory of practice, I have sought to provide an approach to promise that is conceptually rich and that can do justice to the details in practice. The value of the practice approach is that it can be used to explain a great number of human activities that were otherwise unexplainable as institutions or games. More specifically, I have argued that promising is one of these activities. Whatever its faults, this approach does not underdescribe promise.

A theory of practice is beholden to the data of promise. Unlike the approaches of Searle and Atiyah, who appear to construct a theoretical model of promising then reject data that do not fit the model, the theory of practice constructs its model from the data. If the data change, the model changes. In the practice approach, the conceptual description of promising is only as good as its ability to describe, explain, and predict the actual data gathered from a homogeneous community in which the practice takes place. Promising is not what any theorist says it is. A practice theorist's job is not to define a promise or the practice itself but to describe it.

Despite its possible drawbacks, I believe that the practice-theoretical approach to promise is superior in explanatory power and descriptive adequacy to any of the approaches here considered. It is ironic that many theorists have used the importance of the practice of promising in everyday life as an argument for its obligatoriness without also appreciating how the various social aspects of this practice undermine their views about promise. If we understand promise as a social practice, then we must consider it in all of its social complexity. A theory of practice is an attempt to see promising as an inherently social phenomenon. Subsuming promise under a theory of practice is a large undertaking, one that I have only outlined here. I have argued throughout this study simply that such an undertaking is worthwhile and extremely valuable, if we are concerned with the accuracy of our treatment of promise.

Notes

Chapter One

1. For those interested in searching them out, there are important differences between oaths, contracts, and the more mundane promises of everyday life. This study casts a wide net and seeks a theoretical explanation that unites rather than divides.

2. I offer here the first of many examples that are woven into this chapter and that function as data, as examples of what people do when they make promises. They reappear throughout the book and serve to test theoretical positions. Some examples are from common life and others from literature. Unlike made-up examples that too often are abstract and emaciated and crafted exclusively to illustrate a theory—when instead a theory should be put in service of explaining an existing example from common life—they are intended to serve as fleshy examples of actual promises in everyday life. See my "Converging Theory and Practice: Example Selection in Moral Philosophy," *Journal of Applied Philosophy* 9 (1992):171–82. In response to Steve's request for advice, I must add that it is at moments such as this that I feel most inadequate as a philosopher. Like Job's friends, I was silent.

3. The anthropological case for this paradox—the simultaneous creation of promise and promisor—is made forcefully by Peter Wilson in *Man, the Promising Primate: The Conditions of Human Evolution* (New Haven: Yale University Press, 1983), pp. 45–110. See also the conclusion of James Wallace's fine book *Virtues and Vices* (Ithaca, N.Y.: Cornell University Press, 1978). I use the phrase "self-in-community" as a way to resist the dichotomous choice between individualism and communitarianism. There are no individuals without communities and no communities without individuals.

4. Hobbes is a customary starting point for the modern period of moral philosophy, though strong cases can be made for giving this distinction to other, lesser known philosophers.

5. See G.E.M. Anscombe, "Modern Moral Philosophy," *Philosophy* (1958):1–19; Stuart Hampshire, "Fallacies in Moral Philosophy,"

Mind (October 1949):466–82; Stephen Toulmin, "The Tyranny of Principles," *Hastings Center Report* 11 (December 1981):31–39; and Alasdair MacIntyre, "What Morality Is Not," in MacIntyre's *Against the Self-Images of the Age: Essays on Ideology and Philosophy* (London: Duckworth, 1971), pp. 96–108.

6. One of the best refutations of this view is found in David Hume's essay "On the Original Contract," in *Essays: Moral, Political, and Literary* (Indianapolis: Liberty Classics, 1985), pp. 465–87.

7. There is a problem with terminology here. Although John Rawls uses the term "practice" in "Two Concepts of Rules" (in *Theories of Ethics*, ed. Philippa Foot [Oxford: Oxford University Press, 1979], pp. 144–70), his use of the term parallels closely what Searle and others refer to as "institution." Despite the fact that Rawls's work precedes Searle's, I nevertheless use "institution" to describe both their views and any view that sees promising as a game, practice, or institution arising from constitutive rules. Rawls uses "institution" in *A Theory of Justice* (Cambridge: Harvard University Press, 1971). As Christopher Cherry remarks in "Two Views of Moral Practices" (*Analysis* 33 [March 1973]:118–23), "The terms 'game', 'practice', and 'institution' feature prominently but untidily in a good deal of current moral philosophy" (p. 118). "Practice" is far more descriptive of the approach I am presenting than are any of the possible alternatives.

8. Contemporary philosophers are not alone in their failure to posit a theory of promise; it is difficult to find an extended discussion of promise anywhere in the literature. David Hume's account of promise in bk. 3 of *A Treatise of Human Nature* (Oxford: Clarendon, 1983) comes closest to qualifying as a full-bodied theory of promise.

9. This is George Eliot's phrase, found in her *The Mill on the Floss*, ed. Gordon S. Haight (Oxford: Oxford University Press, 1986), p. 498.

10. One wonders about the question itself. Asking people if promises are obligatory is like asking them if parents should dress their children warmly in the winter. "Other things being equal"—a favorite gambit of the analytic philosopher—the answer to both questions is an obvious yes. But the moral philosopher's task begins at pre-

cisely the moment when other things are not equal, when parents must choose between health insurance and mortgage payments, between healthful food and warm clothes.

11. It is no accident that philosophers are rarely found advising presidents, governors, and senators; nor are they found on the staffs of Fortune 500 companies or environmental organizations. Many philosophers are now working as ethicists in hospitals, however, and this, it is hoped, is a sign of things to come.

12. I also count Ludwig Wittgenstein as an influence to the extent that he seeks in his later work to describe forms of life.

13. These remarks should not be interpreted as implying anything more than a similarity in methodological style between Aristotle and Hume, or as implying that Hume and Aristotle are the only philosophers who make use of this style.

14. See esp. Martha Nussbaum "The Discernment of Perception: An Aristotelian Conception of Private and Public Rationality," in *Love's Knowledge: Essays on Philosophy and Literature* (New York: Oxford University Press, 1990), pp. 54–105; and her "Saving Aristotle's Appearances," chap. 8 of *The Fragility of Goodness: Luck and Ethics in Greek Tragedy and Philosophy* (Cambridge: Cambridge University Press, 1986), pp. 240–63.

15. Friedrich Nietzsche, *On the Genealogy of Morals*, in *Basic Writings of Nietzsche*, trans. and ed. Walter Kaufmann (New York: Modern Library, 1968).

16. P. S. Atiyah, *The Rise and Fall of Freedom of Contract* (Oxford: Clarendon, 1979).

17. Henry Sidgwick, *The Methods of Ethics* (1874; reprint, Indianapolis: Hackett, 1981).

18. W. D. Ross, *The Right and the Good* (Oxford: Clarendon, 1930).

19. Jan Narveson, "Promising, Expecting, and Utility," *Canadian Journal of Philosophy* 1 (December 1971):207–33.

20. C. K. Grant, "Promises" *Mind* 58 (July 1949):359–66.

21. Marcus Tullius Cicero, *On Duties*, in *Selected Works* (Middlesex: Penguin Books, 1960), pp. 195–97.

22. Thomas Hobbes, *De Cive*, ed. Sterling P. Lamprecht (New York: Appelton-Century-Crofts, 1949), chap. 2, p. 38.

23. Hume, *Treatise of Human Nature*, p. 522.

24. Immanuel Kant, *Groundwork of the Metaphysic of Morals*, trans. H. J. Paton (New York: Harper & Row, 1964), pp. 89–90.

25. Eliot, *The Mill on the Floss*, pp. 497–98. For other novels that have promising as one of their themes, see George Meredith, *The Egoist* (New York: Norton, 1979); Graham Greene, *The Power and the Glory* (New York: Penguin, 1977); and Iris Murdoch, *The Book and the Brotherhood* (New York: Viking, 1988).

26. Alasdair MacIntyre, *Whose Justice? Which Rationality?* (Notre Dame, Ind: University of Notre Dame Press, 1988). In conversation with me, MacIntyre claimed that he would not consider promising a practice. His reasons for this appear to be the following. First, promising is not an activity that is necessary for the achievement of any specific internal good. He gave the example of the Tongas who, it is to be presumed, do not make promises; the Tongas are quite able to achieve various internal goods without the need to promise. I would argue that the Tongas have a different conception of intentionality and, hence, a different conception of promising. Second, MacIntyre claims that promising is not an activity in the way fishing is, for example. Whereas one can say that one has gone fishing for the day, one is not likely to say that one has spent the day promising. The practice of fishing allows one to cultivate certain internal goods, whereas promising does not. In Chapters Four and Five, I take issue with this view.

27. Pierre Bourdieu, *Outline of a Theory of Practice*, trans. Richard Nice (Cambridge: Cambridge University Press, 1986).

28. It is at least logically possible for a person to promise to herself, but, practically speaking, it is difficult to imagine such a promise working without clearly demarcating the person into both promisor and promisee. Does her promisee side argue with her promisor side when it weakens its resolve? Notice, we cannot even meaningfully use the personal pronoun here. We can imagine a promise to oneself in the same way that we can imagine infinity or a twelve-sided figure: only vaguely and somewhat abstractly. I assume in this study that promising is best characterized as a relational, social activity.

29. This example is borrowed and adapted from Tom Scanlon,

"Promises and Practices," *Philosophy and Public Affairs* 19:3 (Summer 1990):199–226.

30. All page references to quotations are from the 1986 Oxford University Press edition of *The Mill on the Floss*. Despite the strong arguments of those who advocate the use of examples from literature, there are dangers. First, Eliot's book may not be known to readers; it is not a well-established part of the canon. To this I say only what many of my teachers said about books they required their students to buy: "It's a good book and you should read it." Second, not all works of literature function equally well. Martha Nussbaum, an inspirational proponent of converging literature and philosophy, refers to Henry James's attack on the "omniscient posture of George Eliot's narrator as a falsification of our human position" ("Form and Content, Philosophy and Literature," in *Love's Knowledge*, p. 45). I offer no philosophical defense of my use of Eliot. It is, I assert, a matter of taste and philosophical disposition. *The Mill on the Floss* is, in any case, one of the best examples of Victorian literature that treats promise as one of its central themes. See also Randall Craig's "Promising Marriage: *The Egoist*, Don Juan, and the Problem of Language." *English Literary History* 56 (Winter 1989):897–921.

31. For a list of necessary and sufficient conditions, see Georg Henrik von Wright, "On Promises," *Theoria* 28 (1962):277–97. We encounter John Searle's list in Chapters Two and Three.

32. In this respect I differ, for example, from James D. Wallace's view, wherein moral considerations are distinguished from matters of etiquette because of their importance (*Moral Relevance and Moral Conflict* [Ithaca, N.Y.: Cornell University Press, 1988], p. 61). In my view, one cannot tell in advance whether an activity, practice, or personal choice will have moral importance; hence such a distinction is not very helpful.

33. One thinks of Kant's categorical imperative or of Hume's "never being trusted again in case of failure." Adam Smith, in discussing a broken promise made to a highway robber, says that "whenever such promises are violated, though for the most necessary reasons, it is always with some degree of dishonour for the person who made them. . . . A brave man ought to die, rather than make

a promise which he can neither keep without folly, nor violate without ignominy" (*The Theory of Moral Sentiments*, ed. D. D. Raphael and A. L. Macfie [Oxford: Clarendon, 1979], pt. 7, sec. 4, pars. 7–13). And I think *my* father has a strict view of promising.

34. See the discussion of Don Juan in Shoshana Felman, *The Literary Speech Act* (Ithaca, N.Y.: Cornell University Press, 1983).

35. David Hume, *A Treatise of Human Nature*, p. xix, and Aristotle, *Nicomachean Ethics*, 1094b12, 1104a3–5.

36. Joseph Raz and David Widerker, "National Self-determination," *Journal of Philosophy* 87 (September 1990):448. See also Wallace, *Moral Relevance and Moral Conflict*, pp. 93–95.

Chapter Two

1. John Rawls, "Two Concepts of Rules," in *Theories of Ethics*, ed. Philippa Foot (Oxford: Oxford University Press, 1979), 168, 163.

2. See John Austin, *How to Do Things with Words* (1962; reprint, Cambridge: Harvard University Press, 1975); and H.L.A. Hart, *The Concept of Law* (Oxford: Clarendon, 1961).

3. Rawls, "Two Concepts," p. 144. See also John Rawls, *A Theory of Justice* (Cambridge: Harvard University Press, 1971), p. 55, for a slightly modified definition of "institution."

4. Rawls, "Two Concepts," p. 164.

5. Ibid., p. 165.

6. *Official Baseball Rules* (Sporting News, 1985), p. 91, rule 10.17.

7. Rawls, "Two Concepts," p. 161.

8. Ibid., p. 163; see also Rawls, *A Theory of Justice*, p. 55.

9. Rawls, *A Theory of Justice*, p. 56.

10. Rawls, "Two Concepts," p. 151.

11. Rawls, *A Theory of Justice*, pp. 55–56.

12. Rawls, "Two Concepts," p. 147.

13. John Rawls, "Justice as Fairness," *Philosophical Review* 67 (1958): 169–79.

14. Rawls, "Justice as Fairness," p. 171, 177.

15. Rawls, "Two Concepts," p. 162–163.

16. Ibid., p. 168; see also Rawls, *A Theory of Justice*, p. 345.

17. Rawls, "Two Concepts," p. 156.

18. Rawls, *A Theory of Justice*, p. 345.

19. Ibid.

20. Rawls, "Two Concepts," p. 170.

21. Rawls, "Justice as Fairness," p. 168.

22. Rawls, *A Theory of Justice*, pp. 342–43.

23. John Searle, *Speech Acts: An Essay in the Philosophy of Language* (Cambridge: Cambridge University Press, 1969), p. 34.

24. John Searle, "How to Derive 'Ought' from 'Is'," in *Theories of Ethics*, ed. Philippa Foot (Oxford University Press, 1979), p. 112.

25. Searle, *Speech Acts*, pp. 35–36.

26. Ibid., p. 34.

27. Ibid.

28. Ibid., p. 36.

29. Ibid., pp. 41–42.

30. Ibid., pp. 54–55.

31. Searle, "'Ought' from 'Is'", p. 54. I argue in the next chapter that the features are stark only because Searle has acted like a sculptor in chiseling the practice of promise to his own vision.

32. Searle, *Speech Acts*, p. 56.

33. Ibid., p. 55.

34. Ibid., pp. 57–61.

35. Ibid., p. 63.

36. Searle, "'Ought' from 'Is'", pp. 102–3.

37. Searle, *Speech Acts*, p. 63.

38. For example, this approach is expressed in the writings of William Paley. See *The Works of William Paley* (Edinburgh: Peter Brown and Thomas Nelson, 1827), bk. 2, chaps. 1–3.

39. George Eliot, *The Mill on the Floss*, ed. Gordon S. Haight (Oxford: Oxford University Press, 1986), p. 449.

40. As I have done with the institutional approach, I generally ignore the affiliation these positions have to larger philosophical enterprises and theories. Though Sidgwick and Narveson, for example, are both considered act utilitarians, the expectational approach is not unique to utilitarians. Paley was no utilitarian; nor is A. I. Meldon,

another proponent of this approach to promise. To reiterate a point made in Chapter One, my interest is in approaches to promise.

41. Henry Sidgwick, *The Methods of Ethics* (1874; reprint, Indianapolis: Hackett, 1981).

42. Ibid., p. 304.

43. Ibid., pp. 306–7.

44. Ibid., p. 307.

45. Ibid., p. 309.

46. Jan Narveson, *Morality and Utility* (Baltimore: Johns Hopkins University Press, 1967), p. 194.

47. Jan Narveson, "Promising, Expecting, and Utility," *Canadian Journal of Philosophy* 1 (December 1971): 211.

48. Ibid., p. 213.

49. Ibid., p. 214.

50. Ibid., p. 215.

51. For a critique of the utilitarian aspects of this approach, see D. H. Hodgson, *Consequences of Utilitarianism* (Oxford: Clarendon, 1967). For responses to Hodgson, see Narveson, "Promising, Expecting, and Utility"; Peter Singer, "Is Act-Utilitarianism Self-defeating?" *Philosophical Review* 81 (1972):94–104; and J. L. Mackie, "The Disutility of Act-Utilitarianism," *Philosophical Quarterly* 23 (October 1973):289–300.

52. P. S. Atiyah, *Promises, Morals, and the Law* (Oxford: Clarendon, 1981), p. 137.

53. Ibid., p. 124.

54. Ibid.

55. Ibid., p. 179.

56. Ibid., pp. 183–84.

57. Ibid., p. 206.

58. Ibid., p. 212.

59. Historical examples of the intuitional approach include: Thomas Reid, *Essays on the Active Powers of the Mind* (Cambridge: MIT Press, 1969); and Immanuel Kant, *Groundwork of the Metaphysic of Morals*, trans. H. J. Paton (New York: Harper & Row, 1964). Contemporary approaches include Georg Henrik von Wright, "On Promises," *Theoria* 28 (1962):277–97; Geoffrey R. Grice, *The*

Grounds of Moral Judgement (Cambridge: Cambridge University Press, 1967); and Joseph Raz, "Promises and Obligations," in *Law, Morality and Society: Essays in Honour of H.L.A. Hart*, ed. P.M.S. Hacker and Joseph Raz (Oxford: Oxford University Press, 1977), pp. 210–28.

60. H. A. Prichard, *Moral Obligation and Duty and Interest: Essays and Lectures* (Oxford: Oxford University Press, 1949), pp. 15–16.

61. W. D. Ross, *The Right and the Good* (1930; reprint, Oxford: Clarendon, 1965), p. 18.

62. Ibid., p. 19.

63. Ibid., p. 20.

64. Ibid., p. 19.

65. Ibid., pp. 20–21, n.1.

66. Ibid., p. 35.

67. This was the answer a Native American woman gave to William James when he asked her to explain her tribe's creation of the world. She told him that the Earth rests on the back of a turtle. James wanted to know what the turtle rested on.

68. See David Hume, *A Treatise of Human Nature* (Oxford: Clarendon, 1983), bk. 3, pt. 2, sec. 5.

69. Michael H. Robins, *Promising, Intending, and Moral Autonomy* (Cambridge: Cambridge University Press, 1984), p. 1.

70. Ibid., p. 2.

71. Ibid., p. 60.

72. Ibid., p. 93.

73. Ibid., p. 100.

74. Ibid., p. 103.

75. Ibid., p. 146.

Chapter Three

1. R. S. Downie, "Three Accounts of Promising," *Philosophical Quarterly* 35 (July 1985):263.

2. Stanley Cavell, *The Claim of Reason: Wittgenstein, Skepticism, Morality, and Tragedy*, (Oxford: Oxford University Press,

1979), chaps. 5, 9, 11. For an extended analysis of P. S. Atiyah's views, see J.P.W. Cartwright, "An Evidentiary Theory of Promises," *Mind* 93 (1984):230–48.

3. R. M. Hare, "The Promising Game," in *Theories of Ethics*, ed. Philippa Foot (Oxford: Oxford University Press, 1967), pp. 115–27.

4. The critical literature addressing this issue is voluminous. For a representative sampling, see Hare, "Promising Game"; Antony Flew, "On Not Deriving 'Ought' from 'Is'," *Analysis* 25 (1964–65):25–37; Eddy Zemach, "Ought, Is, and a Game Called 'Promise'," *Philosophical Quarterly* 21 (January 1971):61–63; Peter Winch, "Nature and Convention," *Proceedings of the Aristotelian Society* 60 (1959–60):231–52; and Mary Midgley, "The Game Game," *Philosophy* 49 (July 1974):231–53. Numerous additional citations can be found in the bibliography. For Searle's reply, see John Searle, "Reply to 'The Promising Game,'" in *Readings in Contemporary Ethical Theory*, ed. Kenneth Pahel and Marvin Schiller (Englewood Cliffs, N.J.: Prentice-Hall, 1970), pp. 180–82. Briefly, Searle denies that he is giving or needs to give reasons for why we ought to keep our promises. Commitment for Searle is not an external commitment to the institution but a commitment to the logical properties of a word.

5. I choose waving for demonstration purposes because it is a relatively simple practice and easy to describe. It is also a relatively recent activity, more recent than the games of chess or baseball, for example, and invites intelligent guessing about how it came about. Some readers may find disturbing the comparison later in the book between promising and waving; promising is serious, after all, and waving is frivolous. I reiterate here that we should resist finding fault with this comparison, for the simple reason that promising is not always serious and waving is not always so frivolous. See Chapter One.

6. The citations are numerous here as well. For a representative sampling, see J. E. McClellan and B. P. Komisar, "On Deriving 'Ought' from 'Is'," *Analysis* 25 (1964–65):32–37 (reprinted in *The Is–Ought Question: A Collection of Papers on the Central Problem in Moral Philosophy*, ed. W. D. Hudson [New York: St. Martin's, 1969], pp. 157–62); Christopher Cherry, "Regulative Rules and Constitu-

tive Rules," *Philosophical Quarterly* (1973):301–15; Hubert Schwyzer, "Rules and Practices," *Philosophical Review* (October 1969): 451–67; and Cavell, *Claim of Reason*, pp. 292–312. Other citations are listed in the bibliography.

7. John Rawls, *A Theory of Justice* (Cambridge: Harvard University Press, 1971), p. 345.

8. For a general critique of applying rules to morality in general and promising in particular, see G. J. Warnock, *The Object of Morality* (London: Methuen, 1971); and Julius Kovesi, *Moral Notions* (London: Routledge & Kegan Paul, 1967), chaps. 2–3.

9. For arguments along similar lines see, Thomas D. Perry, "A Refutation of Searle's Amended 'Is-Ought' Argument," *Analysis* 34 (1973–74):133–39; and Donald R. Barker, "Hypothetical Promising and John R. Searle," *Southwestern Journal of Philosophy* 3 (1972): 21–34.

10. There is a body of literature that argues that one can promise without an institution of promising. See Cavell, *Claim of Reason*, p. 298; Neil MacCormick and Joseph Raz, "Voluntary Obligations and Normative Powers," *Proceedings of the Aristotelian Society* 46 (1972):59–102; Oswald Hanfling, "Promises, Games and Institutions," *Proceedings of the Aristotelian Society* 75 (1974–75):13–31; and Thomas Scanlon, "Promises and Practices," *Philosophy and Public Affairs* 19:3 (Summer 1990):199–226. This is not the place to respond to Scanlon's views in detail, though some response is necessary since his conclusions impact my account of promise in later chapters. Scanlon and I agree that promising does not need to rely on an institution of constitutive rules. But I argue in later chapters that although we do not need a social practice to make promises or feel obliged to keep them, such a practice follows naturally from our need to make promises and from the preconventional behavior that arises as a response to this need. The feelings of having raised expectations and of owing other people what we told them to expect do not exist outside of a community of shared practices. Whatever else the general moral principles are to which Scanlon refers, they are part of a fabric. We can explain these principles apart from the practices that motivate and circumscribe them, but we cannot imagine that these principles exist apart from these practices.

247

Scanlon says, "When I say 'I promise to help you if you help me,' the reason I suggest to you that I will have for helping is just my awareness of the fact that not to return your help would, under the circumstances, be wrong: not just forbidden by some social practice, but morally wrong" (p. 211). I believe that not to return help in this case is morally wrong, for reasons having to do with our natural conditions—the very same conditions that lead to social practices. Both the moral wrongs and the social practices stem from the same contingent natural and social conditions in which we find ourselves.

Finally, Hume is not the culprit Scanlon and others claim he is when they credit him as the father of the institutional approach to promise. Hume says that promising will not occur to us given certain natural and social conditions. But when the simultaneous conditions of necessity and infirmity arise in us, we have to create a practice that makes promising possible. Hume is right to this extent: in a land of plenty I do not have to make promises to my neighbor; nor is my neighbor likely to be harmed by a broken promise. The solitary brute—Homer's Cyclops, for example—does not make promises and has no need to, even though he does form expectations, as evidenced in his disappointment that the Odysseus-laden ram exits the cave last. My point here is that given certain social and natural conditions, Scanlon's general moral principles are not going to arise either. But Hume shows clearly how our natural conditions lead us to form intentions and expectations; to engage in preconventional behavior; and, finally, to form the conventions of property and promise. The social practice does little of the work, but it does embody the work, making it possible and useful. I detail my reading of Hume in an unpublished paper titled "Have We Kept Hume's Promise?"

I agree wholeheartedly with Scanlon's intention to wrest promissory obligation from an institutional account, but I disagree with his reading of Hume and his claim—if it is his claim—that moral principles can somehow exist outside of the social and natural conditions in which human beings find themselves.

NOTES

Chapter Four

1. Others who use the term *practice* or who articulate a theory of practice include D. Z. Phillips and H. O. Mounce, *Moral Practices* (London: Routledge & Kegan Paul, 1969); Annette Baier, "Theory and Reflective Practices," "Doing without Moral Theory?" and "Civilizing Practices," all collected in *Postures of the Mind: Essays on Mind and Morals* (Minneapolis: University of Minnesota Press, 1985); Alasdair MacIntyre, *After Virtue* (Notre Dame, Ind.: University of Notre Dame Press, 1981); Alasdair MacIntyre, *Whose Justice? Which Rationality?* (Notre Dame, Ind.: University of Notre Dame Press, 1988); Pierre Bourdieu, *Outline of a Theory of Practice*, trans. Richard Nice (Cambridge: Cambridge University Press, 1977); Michael Oakeshott *On Human Conduct* (Oxford: Clarendon, 1975), pp. 55–81; and Peter Winch, *The Idea of a Social Science and Its Relation to Philosophy* (Atlantic Highlands, N.J.: Humanities Press, 1959), chap. 2. Places in the treatment by Phillips and Mounce, Oakeshott, and Winch parallel an institutional approach. Baier uses the term "practice," though she does not attempt to characterize her use of it. MacIntyre gives the most detail in his use of the term, though even he does not claim to be providing a theory of practice. The most complete discussion of a theory of practice is provided by the anthropologist Bourdieu. Though the outline I have provided is sometimes in agreement and sometimes not in agreement with the points made by these authors, I do not intend my use of the term to be seen as embracing or rejecting their uses of the term.

2. The phrase "spontaneous order" was first used by F. A. Hayek, *The Constitution of Liberty* (Chicago: University of Chicago Press, 1960), 160–61.

3. F. A. Hayek, "The Results of Human Action but Not of Human Design," in idem., *Studies in Philosophy, Politics and Economics* (Chicago: University of Chicago Press, 1967), p. 97.

4. Ronald Hamowy, *The Scottish Enlightenment and the Theory of Spontaneous Order* (Carbondale and Edwardsville: Southern Illinois University Press, 1987), p. 3. For a similar discussion see Milan Zeleny, "Spontaneous Social Orders," in *The Science and Praxis of*

249

Complexity (Tokyo: The United Nations University, 1985), pp. 312–28.

5. David Hume, *A Treatise of Human Nature* (Oxford: Clarendon, 1983), p. 484.

6. Hamowy, *Scottish Enlightenment*, p. 14.

7. Julius Kovesi, *Moral Notions* (London: Routledge & Kegan Paul, 1967), pp. 46–48.

8. Ibid., p. 49.

9. I have not tried to explain the origins of the conditions that make possible the spontaneous ordering of social practices; nor will I try.

10. I thank an anonymous reviewer for pointing out this possibility.

11. Hamowy, *Scottish Enlightenment*, p. 3.

12. For other conceptions of rules, see F. A. Hayek, "Notes on the Evolution of Systems of Rules of Conduct" and "Rules, Perceptions and Intelligibility," in idem., *Studies in Philosophy, Politics and Economics* (Chicago: University of Chicago Press, 1967); D. S. Shwayder, *The Stratification of Behavior: A System of Definitions Propounded and Defended* (London: Routledge & Kegan Paul, 1965); and David K. Lewis, *Convention: A Philosophical Study* (Cambridge: Harvard University Press, 1969). Lewis makes frequent reference to Shwayder's work. A discussion of these alternative conceptions would take us too far afield. Suffice it to say that I do not think that these conceptions are any more coherent than constitutive rules, though for different reasons. For an interpretation of rules as recipes, see C. H. Whiteley, "Rules of Language," *Analysis* 34 (1973–74):33–39. Though Whiteley is concerned with rules of meaning, what he says is not contrary to what I have argued regarding the rule formulations of practices.

13. I cannot begin here to address the empirical questions of how practices undergo change in this way. There is obviously a range of behavior encompassing most practices, so that one's behavior can be recognized as conforming to, a variation on, or a violation of a practice role. It is perfectly possible that practices undergo change when violations become accepted as variations. It is unfortunate that phi-

losophers are no further along in understanding practices than were those of the Scottish Enlightenment, who first suggested this type of approach.

14. I assume that bluffing is a practice used in many aspects of life. As an approximate characterization, bluffing is a form of acceptable deception. Those who engage in this practice include cardplayers (and game players generally) and those engaged in buying and selling.

15. For a detailed discussion of these types of interactions, see Erving Goffman, *Relations in Public: Microstudies of the Public Order* (New York: Basic Books, 1971). See also Peter L. Berger and Thomas Luckmann, *The Social Construction of Reality* (N.Y.: Doubleday, 1967).

16. There is a detailed social science literature on role acquisition, but I shall not refer to it here, as it will take us too far afield. For a philosophical discussion of roles, see Dorothy Emmet, *Rules, Roles and Relations* (New York: St. Martin's, 1966).

17. Bourdieu, *Theory of Practice*, p. 19.

18. By "practical reasoning" I mean reasoning that leads to action, considers actions (either one's own or the actions of others), or considers the circumstances surrounding action. I contrast practical reasoning with abstract or theoretical reasoning.

19. See J. L. Austin, "A Plea for Excuses," *Proceedings of the Aristotelian Society* 57 (1956–57):1–30, for a general discussion of excusing conditions.

20. For similar views about judgment and evaluation, see Robert Brandom, "Freedom and Constraint by Norms," in *Hermeneutics and Praxis*, ed. Robert Hollinger (Notre Dame, Ind.: University of Notre Dame Press, 1985), 173–91.

Chapter Five

1. I am casting the net widely in talking about the variations of the practice of promising. I am claiming that there are many types of promises (besides those that are attended with solemn obligation) and many ways of promising (besides the speech act "I promise").

What argument there is for this position will be seen below, but the argument itself takes place within a practice theoretical framework. That is, the decision to cast the net of promising in this way is based on an intuition about how people conceive of the practice. But this intuition is also a testable hypothesis: namely, that the practitioners of the practice of promising, at least some number of them, interpret the practice in these ways.

2. I am suggesting only that the ability to form expectations makes promising possible. Expectations almost certainly have a role to play in creating in the promisor the sense of obligation he feels in making a promise, though it is not the primary role that act-utilitarians suggest. In some cases the promisor does do wrong by creating expectations in the promisee and then failing to act in such a way that these expectations are fulfilled. But there is more to the story than that.

3. I have left a great deal out of this discussion. For promising to be possible, one would need a concept of self; to be able to recognize in others the relationship of friend, enemy, and so forth; to have a shared, objective time reference to which one could refer; and so on. The list of enabling and constraining conditions of the practice of promise is, no doubt, longer than the one I have given. My intention, however, was to discuss only those conditions that seem most relevant to the practice.

4. Though practices are specific to homogeneous communities, this does not mean that there cannot be promises made across heterogeneous communities. It is possible for an Inuit and a Japanese to promise to meet for lunch even if neither person knows much about the other's culture or practice of promising. My point is that even if each person has a practice of promising in his or her respective community, the practice will be shaped by the community. There is ample sociological data to indicate the difficulties that occur when representatives of different cultures attempt to participate in overlapping practices. Even if every culture has a practice of promising, we ought not to think that all these practices are identical or even remotely similar. I thank an anonymous reviewer for alerting me to this issue.

5. A. I. Melden, "On Promising," *Mind* 65 (1956):63.

NOTES

6. Ibid., pp. 65–66.
7. A. I. Melden, "The Obligation of Promises," *Rights and Persons* (Berkeley: University of California Press, 1980) p. 53.
8. Ibid., p. 42.
9. John Finnis, *Natural Law and Natural Rights* (Oxford: Clarendon, 1980), p. 18.
10. Ibid., p. 135.
11. Ibid., p. 300.
12. Ibid., p. 309.
13. David Hume, *A Treatise of Human Nature* (Oxford: Clarendon, 1983), bk. 3, sec. 5. See also William Vitek, "The Humean Promise: Whence Comes Its Obligation?" *Hume Studies* 12 (November 1986):160–74.
14. I make this argument in my unpublished paper titled "Have We Kept Hume's Promise?"
15. It might be argued that swinging a bat is a physical activity and, in this way, is different from learning a practice role. I maintain that learning the roles of promising, like learning to swing a bat, requires the ability to discern as well as to execute various physical motions. Promising, like any other human interaction, includes a variety of nonverbal cues. Knowing how to wink or to speak ironically (and knowing what winking and speaking ironically mean) is no less important to the promisor than knowing what specific words are used to make a promise. There are many such cues in everyday interaction, and knowing what they mean and how to perform them are very important in communication, of which promising is a part. And we learn such cues and what they mean by watching and imitating.
16. This process probably occurs in developmental stages. I leave the details of these stages for later work.
17. It has been suggested, in Fred Korn and Shulamit R. Decklor Korn, "Where People Don't Promise," *Ethics* 93 (April 1983):445–50, that present-day Tongas do not engage in the practice of promising. Although this is possible and predictable, when using a practice model of promise I believe that a close examination of the Tongas would reveal a variation in the practice, perhaps even a variation that Westerners or Americans would not recognize.

253

Bibliography

Alexander, Richard D. *The Biology of Moral Systems*. New York: Aldine de Gruyter, 1987.

Anscombe, G.E.M. "Intention." *Proceedings of the Aristotelian Society* 57 (1956–57):321–32.

———. "Modern Moral Philosophy." *Philosophy* (1958):1–19.

———. "Rules, Rights, and Promises." In *Midwest Studies in Philosophy*, Vol. 3, Studies in Ethical Theory, edited by Peter A. French, Theodore E. Uehling, Jr., and Howard K. Wettstein, pp. 318–23. Minneapolis: University of Minnesota Press, 1980.

———. "Authority in Morals." In *Ethics, Religion and Politics*, idem., pp. 43–50. Minneapolis: University of Minnesota Press, 1981.

———. "On Promising and Its Justice, and Whether It Need Be Respected *in Foro Interno*." In *Ethics, Religion and Politics*, idem., pp. 10–21. Minneapolis: University of Minnesota Press, 1981.

Ardal, Pall S. "Promises and Reliance." *Dialogue* 15 (1976):54–61.

Aristotle. *Nicomachean Ethics*. Translated by Terence Irwin. Indianapolis: Hackett, 1985.

Atiyah, P. S. "Promises and the Law of Contract." *Mind* 87 (July 1979):410–18.

———. *The Rise and Fall of Freedom of Contract*. Oxford: Clarendon, 1979.

———. *Promises, Morals, and Law*. Oxford: Clarendon, 1981.

Austin, J. L. "Other Minds." *Proceedings of the Aristotelian Society*, Supplementary Vol. 20 (1946):148–87.

———. "A Plea for Excuses." *Proceedings of the Aristotelian Society* 57 (1956–57):1–30.

———. *How to Do Things with Words*. 1962. Reprint, Cambridge: Harvard University Press, 1975.

Baier, Annette. *Postures of the Mind: Essays on Mind and Morals*. Minneapolis: University of Minnesota Press, 1985.

Barker, Donald R. "Hypothetical Promising and John R. Searle." *Southwestern Journal of Philosophy* 3 (1972):21–34.

Berger, Peter L., and Thomas Luckmann. *The Social Construction of Reality*. New York: Doubleday, 1967.

Berlin, Isaiah. "Equality." *Proceedings of the Aristotelian Society* 56 (1955–56):301–26.

Black, Max. "Austin on Performatives." *Philosophy* 38 (1963):217–26.

Boer, Steven E. "Speech Acts and Constitutive Rules." *Journal of Philosophy* 71 (1974):169–74.

Bourdieu, Pierre. *Outline of a Theory of Practice*. Translated by Richard Nice. Cambridge: Cambridge University Press, 1977.

Brandom, Robert. "Freedom and Constraint by Norms." In *Hermeneutics and Praxis*, edited by Robert Hollinger, pp. 173–91. Notre Dame, Ind.: University of Notre Dame Press, 1985.

Brandt, Richard B. *A Theory of the Good and the Right*. Oxford: Clarendon, 1979.

Cameron, J. R. "Sentence-Meaning and Speech Acts." *Philosophical Quarterly* 20 (April 1970):97–117.

———. "'Ought' and Institutional Obligation." *Philosophy* 45 (1971):309–23.

———. "The Nature of Institutional Obligation." *Philosophical Quarterly* (1972):318–32.

Cartwright, J.P.W. "An Evidentiary Theory of Promises." *Mind* (1984):230–48.

Casey, John. *Pagan Virtue: An Essay in Ethics*. Oxford: Clarendon, 1990.

Cavell, Stanley. *The Claim of Reason: Wittgenstein, Skepticism, Morality, and Tragedy*. Oxford: Oxford University Press, 1979.

Charlesworth, Max, Lyndsay Farrall, Terry Stokes, and David Turnbull. *Life among the Scientists: An Anthropological Study of an Australian Scientific Community*. Oxford and Melbourne: Oxford University Press, 1989.

Cherry, Christopher. "Regulative Rules and Constitutive Rules." *Philosophical Quarterly* (1973):301–15.

———. "Two Views of Moral Practices." *Analysis* 33 (March 1973):118–23.

Cicero, Marcus Tullius. *On Duties*. In *Selected Works*. Middlesex: Penguin Books, 1960.

Clark, Stephen R. L. "Abstract Morality, Concrete Cases." In *Moral Philosophy and Contemporary Problems*, edited by J.D.G. Evans, pp. 35–53. Cambridge: Cambridge University Press, 1987.

Copper, Neil. "Two Concepts of Morality." *Philosophy* 41 (1966): 19–33.

Craig, Randall. "Promising Marriage: *The Egoist*, Don Juan, and the Problem of Language." *English Literary History* 56 (Winter 1989): 897–921.

Dent, N.J.H. *The Moral Psychology of the Virtues*. Cambridge: Cambridge University Press, 1984.

Diggs, B. J. "Rules and Utilitarianism." In *Readings in Contemporary Ethical Theory*, edited by Kenneth Pahel and Marvin Schiller, pp. 260–82. Englewood Cliffs, N.J.: Prentice-Hall, 1970.

Downie, R. S. "Three Accounts of Promising." *Philosophical Quarterly* 35 (July 1985):259–71.

Duncan-Jones, Austin. "Performance and Promise." *Philosophical Quarterly* 14 (April 1964):97–117.

Dyche, Roy. "Is Promise-Keeping a Moral Matter?" *Philosophical Studies* 24 (1973):128–32.

Edel, May, and Abraham Edel. *Anthropology and Ethics*. Springfield, Ill.: Thomas, 1959.

———. "Ethical Theory and Moral Practice: On the Terms of Their Relation." In *New Directions in Ethics: The Challenge of Applied Ethics*, edited by Joseph P. DeMarco and Richard M. Fox, pp. 317–35. New York and London: Routledge & Kegan Paul, 1986.

Eliot, George. *The Mill on the Floss*. Edited by Gordon S. Haight. Oxford: Oxford University Press, 1986.

Emmet, Dorothy. *Rules, Roles and Relations*. New York: St. Martin's, 1966.

Farnsworth, Allan E. "The Past of Promise: An Historical Introduction to Contract." *Columbia Law Review* 69 (1969):576–607.

Felman, Shoshana. *The Literary Speech Act*. Ithaca, N.Y.: Cornell University Press, 1983.

Finnis, John. *Natural Law and Natural Rights*. Oxford: Clarendon Press, 1980.

Flew, Antony. "On Not Deriving 'Ought' from 'Is'." *Analysis* 25 (1964–65):25–37.

Foot, Philippa. *Virtues and Vices and Other Essays in Moral Philosophy.* Berkeley: University of California Press, 1978.

Fried, Charles. *Contract as Promise.* Cambridge: Harvard University Press, 1981.

Goffman, Erving. *Relations in Public: Microstudies of the Public Order.* New York: Basic Books, 1971.

Grant, C. K. "Promises." *Mind* 58 (July 1949):359–66.

Grice, Geoffrey R. *The Grounds of Moral Judgement.* Cambridge: Cambridge University Press, 1967.

Hamowy, Ronald. *The Scottish Enlightenment and the Theory of Spontaneous Order.* Carbondale and Edwardsville: Southern Illinois University Press, 1987.

Hampshire, Stuart. "Fallacies in Moral Philosophy." *Mind* (October 1949):466–82.

———. "Morality and Convention." In *Utilitarianism and Beyond,* edited by Amartya Sen and Bernard Williams, pp. 145–57. Cambridge: Cambridge University Press, 1982.

Hanfling, Oswald. "Promises, Games and Institutions." *Proceedings of the Aristotelian Society* 75 (1974–75):13–31.

Hare, R. M. "Meaning and Speech Acts." *Philosophical Review* 79 (1970):3–24.

———. "The Promising Game." In *Theories of Ethics,* edited by Philippa Foot, pp. 115–27. Oxford: Oxford University Press, 1979.

Hart, H.L.A. "Definition and Theory in Jurisprudence." *Law Quarterly Review* 70 (1952):37–60.

———. "Are There Any Natural Rights?" *Philosophical Review* 64 (1955):175–91.

———. "Legal and Moral Obligation." In *Essays in Moral Philosophy,* edited by A. I. Melden, pp. 82–107. Seattle: University of Washington Press, 1958.

———. *The Concept of Law.* Oxford: Clarendon, 1961.

Hayek, F. A. *Studies in Philosophy, Politics and Economics.* Chicago: University of Chicago Press, 1967.

Hepburn, R. W. "Vision and Choice in Morality." In *Christian Ethics and Contemporary Philosophy,* edited by Ian T. Ramsey, pp. 181–218. New York: Macmillan, 1966.

Hobbes, Thomas. *De Cive.* Edited by Sterling P. Lamprecht. New York: Appleton-Century-Crofts, 1949.

———. *Leviathan.* Edited by Michael Oakeshott. New York: Collier Books, 1962.

Hodgson, D. H. *Consequences of Utilitarianism.* Oxford: Clarendon, 1967.

Holborow, L. C. "Promising, Prescribing and Playing-Along." *Philosophy* 44 (April 1969):149–52.

Hume, David. *Enquiries concerning Human Understanding and concerning the Principles of Morals.* Oxford: Clarendon, 1983.

———. *A Treatise of Human Nature.* Oxford: Clarendon, 1983.

———. *Essays Moral, Political, and Literary.* Indianapolis: Liberty Classics, 1985.

Jack, Henry. "On the Analysis of Promises." *Journal of Philosophy* 55 (July 1958):597–604.

Jones, David H. "Making and Keeping Promises." *Ethics* 76 (July 1966):287–96.

Kading, Daniel. "How Promising Obligates." *Philosophical Studies* 22 (June 1971):57–60.

Kant, Immanuel. *Groundwork of the Metaphysic of Morals.* Translated by H. J. Paton, New York: Harper & Row, 1956.

Kolenda, Konstantin. "Searle's 'Institutional Facts'." *The Personalist* 53 (Spring 1972):188–92.

Korn, Fred, and Shulamit R. Decktor Korn. "Where People Don't Promise." *Ethics* 93 (April 1983):445–50.

Kovesi, Julius. *Moral Notions.* London: Routledge & Kegan Paul, 1967.

Landesman, Charles. "Promises and Practices." *Mind* 75 (1966):239–43.

Lewis, David K. *Convention: A Philosophical Study.* Cambridge: Harvard University Press, 1969.

Locke, Don. "The Object of Morality, and the Obligation to Keep a Promise." *Canadian Journal of Philosophy* 2 (September 1972):135–43.

Lyons, David. *Forms and Limits of Utilitarianism*. Oxford: Oxford University Press, 1965.

Mabbott, J. D. "Moral Rules." In *Readings in Contemporary Ethical Theory*, edited by Kenneth Pahel and Marvin Schiller, pp. 206–24. Englewood Cliffs, N.J.: Prentice-Hall, 1970.

McClellan, J. E., and B. P. Komisar. "On Deriving 'Ought' from 'Is'." In *The Is–Ought Question: A Collection of Papers on the Central Problem in Moral Philosophy*, edited by W. D. Hudson, pp. 157–62. New York: St. Martin's, 1969.

MacCormick, Neil, and Joseph Raz. "Voluntary Obligations and Normative Powers." *Proceedings of the Aristotelian Society* 46 (1972):59–102.

McDermott, John J. "Pragmatic Sensibility: The Morality of Experience." In *New Directions in Ethics: The Challenge of Applied Ethics*, edited by Joseph P. DeMarco and Richard M. Fox, pp. 113–34. New York and London: Routledge & Kegan Paul, 1986.

MacIntyre, Alasdair. *Against the Self-Images of the Age: Essays on Ideology and Philosophy*. London: Duckworth, 1971.

———. *After Virtue*. Notre Dame, Ind.: University of Notre Dame Press, 1981.

———. *Whose Justice? Which Rationality?* Notre Dame, Ind.: University of Notre Dame Press, 1988.

Mackie, J. L. "The Disutility of Act-Utilitarianism." *Philosophical Quarterly* 23 (October 1973):289–300.

McNeilly, F. S. "Promises De-moralized." *Philosophical Review* 81 (1972):63–81.

Margalit, Avishai, and Joseph Raz. "National Self-determination." *Journal of Philosophy* 87 (September 1990):439–61.

Mayo, Bernard. "The Moral Agent." In *The Human Agent*, idem., pp. 47–63. New York: St. Martin's, 1968.

Melden, A. I. "On Promising." *Mind* 65 (1956):49–66.

———. *Rights and Right Conduct*. Oxford: Basil Blackwell, 1970.

———. *Rights and Persons*. Berkeley: University of California Press, 1980.

Midgley, Mary. "The Game Game." *Philosophy* 49 (July 1974):231–53.

Montague, Roger. "'Ought' from 'Is'." *Australasian Journal of Philosophy* 43 (August 1965):144–67.

———. "'Is' to 'Ought'." *Analysis* 26 (1965–66):104–10.

Mounce, H. O. "Mr. Cherry on Moral Practices." *Analysis* 34 (1973–74):29–30.

Murphy, Arthur Edward. *The Theory of Practical Reason.* LaSalle, Ill.: Open Court, 1964.

Narveson, Jan. *Morality and Utility.* Baltimore: Johns Hopkins University Press, 1967.

———. "Promising, Expecting, and Utility." *Canadian Journal of Philosophy* 1 (December 1971):207–33.

Nietzsche, Friedrich. *Basic Writings of Nietzsche.* Translated and edited by Walter Kaufmann. New York: Modern Library, 1968.

Nussbaum, Martha C. *The Fragility of Goodness: Luck and Ethics in Greek Tragedy and Philosophy.* Cambridge: Cambridge University Press, 1986.

———. *Love's Knowledge: Essays on Philosophy and Literature.* New York: Oxford University Press, 1990.

Oakeshott, Michael. *On Human Conduct.* Oxford: Clarendon, 1975.

O'Neill, Onora. "Abstraction, Idealization and Ideology in Ethics." In *Moral Philosophy and Contemporary Problems,* edited by J.D.G. Evans. Cambridge: Cambridge University Press, 1987.

Perry, Thomas D. "A Refutation of Searle's Amended 'Is-Ought' Argument." *Analysis* 34 (1973–74):133–39.

Phillips, D. Z., and H. O. Mounce. "On Morality's Having a Point." In *The Is–Ought Question,* edited by W. D. Hudson, pp. 228–39. New York: Macmillan, 1969.

———. *Moral Practices.* London: Routledge & Kegan Paul, 1969.

Pincoffs, Edmund L. *Quandaries and Virtues: Against Reductivism in Ethics.* Lawrence: University of Kansas Press, 1986.

Prichard, H. A. *Moral Obligation and Duty and Interest: Essays and Lectures.* Oxford and London: Oxford University Press, 1949.

Prior, Arthur N. *Logic and the Basis of Ethics.* Oxford: Clarendon, 1949.

Ralls, Anthony. "The Game of Life." *Philosophy* 44 (April 1969):22–34.

Ransdell, Joseph. "Constitutive Rules and Speech-Act Analysis." *Journal of Philosophy* 68 (July 1971):385–400.

Rawls, John. "Justice as Fairness." *Philosophical Review* 67 (1958): 164–94.

———. *A Theory of Justice.* Cambridge: Harvard University Press, 1971.

———. "Two Concepts of Rules." In *Theories of Ethics*, edited by Philippa Foot, pp. 144–70. Oxford: Oxford University Press, 1979.

Raz, Joseph. "Promises and Obligations." In *Law, Morality and Society: Essays in Honour of H.L.A. Hart*, edited by P.M.S. Hacker and Joseph Raz, pp. 210–28. Oxford: Oxford University Press, 1977.

Robins, Michael H. "Promissory Obligations and Rawls's Contractarianism." *Analysis* 36 (1975–76):190–98.

———. "The Primacy of Promising." *Mind* 85 (July 1976):321–40.

———. *Promising, Intending, and Moral Autonomy.* Cambridge: Cambridge University Press, 1984.

Ross, W. D. *Foundations of Ethics.* Oxford: Clarendon, 1939.

———. *The Right and the Good.* 1930. Reprint, Oxford: Clarendon, 1965.

Ruben, David-Hillel. "Searle on Institutional Obligation." *The Monist* 56 (1972):600–611.

———. "Tacit Promising." *Ethics* 83 (October 1972):71–79.

Rudinow, Joel. "Quitting the Promising Game." *Philosophical Quarterly* 22 (October 1972):355–56.

Sartorius, Rolf E. *Individual Conduct and Social Norms.* Encino, Calif.: Dickenson, 1975.

Scanlon, Thomas. "Promises and Practices." *Philosophy and Public Affairs* 19:3 (Summer 1990):199–226.

Schelling, Thomas C. *The Strategy of Conflict.* Cambridge: Harvard University Press, 1963.

Schneewind, Jerome B. "Virtue, Narrative, and Community: MacIntyre and Morality." *Journal of Philosophy* 79 (November 1982): 653–63.

Schwyzer, Hubert. "Rules and Practices." *Philosophical Review* (October 1969):451–67.

Searle, John R. *Speech Acts: An Essay in the Philosophy of Language.* Cambridge: Cambridge University Press, 1969.

———. "Reply to 'The Promising Game.'" In *Readings in Contemporary Ethical Theory*, edited by Kenneth Pahel and Marvin Schiller, pp. 180–82. Englewood Cliffs, N.J.: Prentice-Hall, 1970.

———. "How to Derive 'Ought' from 'Is'." In *Theories of Ethics*, edited by Philippa Foot, pp. 101–14. Oxford: Oxford University Press, 1979.

Sherman, Nancy. *The Fabric of Character: Aristotle's Theory of Virtue.* Oxford: Clarendon, 1990.

Shwayder, D. S. "Moral Rules and Moral Maxims." *Ethics* 67 (1956–57):269–85.

———. *The Stratification of Behavior: A System of Definitions Propounded and Defended.* London: Routledge & Kegan Paul, 1965.

Sidgwick, Henry. *The Methods of Ethics.* 1874. Reprint, Indianapolis: Hackett, 1981.

Sikora, R. I. "Facts, Promising and Obligation. *Philosophy* 50 (1975): 352–55.

Singer, Marcus G. "Moral Rules and Principles." In *Essays in Moral Philosophy*, edited by A. I. Melden, pp. 160–95. Seattle: University of Washington Press, 1958.

Singer, Peter. "Is Act-Utilitarianism Self-defeating?" *Philosophical Review* 81 (1972):94–104.

Smart, J.J.C. "Extreme and Restricted Utilitarianism." In *Readings in Contemporary Ethical Theory*, edited by Kenneth Pahel and Marvin Schiller, pp. 249–60. Englewood Cliffs, N.J.: Prentice-Hall, 1970.

Smith, Adam. *The Theory of Moral Sentiments.* Edited by D. D. Raphael and A. L. Macfie. Oxford: Clarendon, 1979.

Smith, Holly M. "Robins on Promising." *Nous* 21 (December 1987): 604–8.

Stocker, Michael. "Moral Duties, Institutions, Natural Facts." *The Monist* (October 1970):602–24.

Strawson, P. F. "Social Morality and Individual Ideal." In *The Definition of Morality*, edited by Gerald Wallace and A.D.M. Walker, pp. 98–118. London: Methuen, 1970.

Taylor, Michael. *Community, Anarchy and Liberty*. Cambridge: Cambridge University Press, 1982.

Thomson, James, and Judith Thomson. "How Not to Derive 'Ought' from 'Is'." *Philosophical Review* 73 (1964):512–16.

Tolhurst, William E. "On Hare's 'Promising Game'." *Philosophical Studies* 30 (1976):277–79.

Toulmin, Stephen. "The Tyranny of Principles." *Hastings Center Report* 11 (December 1981): 31–39.

Tuck, Richard. *Natural Rights Theories: Their Origin and Development*. Cambridge: Cambridge University Press, 1979.

Vitek, William. "The Humean Promise: Whence Comes Its Obligation?" *Hume Studies* 12 (November 1986):160–74.

———. "Converging Theory and Practice: Example Selection in Moral Philosophy." *Journal of Applied Philosophy* 9 (1992):171–82.

von Wright, Georg H. "On Promises." *Theoria* 28 (1962):277–97.

Wallace, James D. *Virtues and Vices*. Ithaca, N.Y.: Cornell University Press, 1978.

———. *Moral Relevance and Moral Conflict*. Ithaca, N.Y.: Cornell University Press, 1988.

Warnock, G. J. *The Object of Morality*. London: Methuen, 1971.

Whiteley, C. H. "Rules of Language." *Analysis* 34 (1973–74):33–39.

Will, Frederick L. "The Rational Governance of Practice." *American Philosophical Quarterly* 18 (1981):191–201.

Wilson, Peter J. *Man, the Promising Primate: The Conditions of Human Evolution*. New Haven: Yale University Press, 1983.

Winch, Peter. "Nature and Convention." *Proceedings of the Aristotelian Society* 60 (1959–60):231–52.

———. *The Idea of a Social Science and Its Relation to Philosophy*. London: Routledge & Kegan Paul, 1967.

Wittgenstein, Ludwig. *Philosophical Investigations*. New York: Macmillan, 1968.

———. *On Certainty*. New York: Harper & Row, 1969.

Yeghiayan, Eddie. "Promises, A Bibliography." *Philosophical Research Archives* 7 (1981):1055–92.

Zeleny, Milan. "Spontaneous Social Orders." In *The Science and Praxis of Complexity*. Tokyo: United Nations University, 1985.

Zemach, Eddy M. "Ought, Is, and a Game Called 'Promise'." *Philosophical Quarterly* 21 (January 1971):61–63.

———. "The Right to Quit." *Philosophical Quarterly* 23 (October 1973):346–49.

Zwiebach, Burton. *The Common Life*. Philadelphia: Temple University Press, 1988.

Index

74–75; as grappling hook, 22–28, 92, 99–100; informal, 20, 68, 114–15, 191; judgment of, 19–20, 148–49, 207–10; judicial and legal examples of, 72, 109; and the literature, 3–10; Louise and Russ, as examples of, 18, 102, 107, 116, 231–32; Maggie and Tom, as examples of, 23–26, 69, 99, 197, 230–32; necessary and sufficient conditions for, 52, 54–56, 59–60, 124–33; as obligation, 4, 7, 21–28, 44–45, 70, 73, 80–83, 102–3, 114–16, 238n.10; the paradox of, 1–3, 7, 16–17; as pathfinder, 23–28; pedagogical considerations of, 17; as *prima facie* duty, 80–82, 103–5; relational aspects of, 20, 101–2, 115; Hyacinth Robinson, as example of, 20–21; and role of practical reasoning, 17–19, 180–82, 186–87, 206–9, 251n.18; to self, 240n.28; Steve and Moya, as examples of, 2–3, 77, 99, 106–7, 230–32; theoretical considerations of, 16–29; unilateral gratuitous, 74–75
Promise as evidence of a previous obligation, 9, 70–78, 108–13, 218–29
Promise as institution, 9–10, 36–61, 117–43, 221–28; definition of, 37; as different from other institutions, 42–44; and disanalogies with games, 56; pedagogical features of, 40–41

Promise as intention, 85–103, 211–12, 215–16
Promise as intuitively clear, 8–9, 78–85, 103–8, 211, 217–18
Promise as practice, 97–98, 228–30, 235–36, 251–52n.1; and the concept of future, 193–97; constraining conditions of, 192–93, 252n.3; defeasibility conditions of, 226–27; definition and review of, 29–34; enabling conditions of, 193–95, 252n.3; evaluation of, 205–7, 209–10; examples of, 195–98; and expectations, 194; in homogeneous community, 252n.4; judgment of, 19–20, 148–49, 177–79, 183–88, 207–10; memory and, 193–98; and practical reasoning, 206–9; precursors to, 210–15; and recognized conventional behavior, 191–92; and role acquisition, 200–204, 253n.15; and the role of imagination, 202–4, 223; and the role of imitation, 202–4, 223; and role proficiency, 204–5; roles of, 200–205; rules of, 198–200; spontaneous order and, 192–98
Promise as raised expectations, 61–70, 113–16, 220–21

Rawls, John, 10, 36–48, 117–23, 133–38
Robins, Michael, 85–92; and definition of promise, 90